THE KING OF THE EARTH

THE BOOKSTORE

THE KING
OF THE EARTH

*The Nobility of Man According
to the Bible and Science*

Erich Sauer

THE PATERNOSTER PRESS
CARLISLE, UK

WILLIAM B. EERDMANS PUBLISHING COMPANY
GRAND RAPIDS, MICHIGAN

Copyright © 1962, The Paternoster Press
First Published, 1962
Paperback Edition, 1967
Second Impression, October, 1979

This edition published jointly 1994 by The Paternoster Press,
P.O. Box 300, Carlisle, Cumbria, CA3 0QS, UK,
and Wm. B. Eerdmans Publishing Co.,
255 Jefferson Ave. SE, Grand Rapids, Michigan 49503.

Printed in the United States of America

British Library Cataloguing-in-Publication Data

Sauer, Erich
The King of the earth.
1. Religion and science — 1946-
I. Title
215   BL240.2
ISBN 0-85364-009-2

EERDMANS ISBN 0-8028-1172-8

CONTENTS

PART V. ON THE ORIGIN OF THE EARTH

Comments o the Biblical Creation-Narrative
Introduction

FOREWORD

THE theme of this book is man's call to nobility and to rule as king. Cultural progress and scientific discovery, strength of character and nobility of mind, a refining of the spirit without a denial of the physical, a goal in eternity and a transfiguration of the world, all belong to his vocation as ruler.

His status as king must be seen in its context in the history of the universe. Behind all discord in nature lies a mighty revolution in the spirit-realm. If we are to understand the purpose and goal of man's creation, we must see them from the perspective of eternity before the universe and above all the earth came into being. From this standpoint we shall learn to see him as a kingly instrument in the hand of the Creator for the transfiguration of the world of nature. We shall see him also as a vessel for Divine grace and glory, called to worship, to conformity to God's image, to be a son of God through his creation, and to the vocation of ruler through eternity.

Much here may at first seem strange to the modern reader. For, although mostly unconsciously, we Westerners tend to think of the world outside ours in Greek Platonic ideas which spiritualize it. The influence of the philosophy of Plato (427–347 B.C.) and of other ancient Greek philosophers is greater, and reaches much further into our contemporary Western thinking, than most of us realize. There are those who have perhaps never even heard the name of this great Athenian or of other teachers of classical or Hellenistic philosophy, and who have not concerned themselves at all, or at the best inadequately, with the intellectual roots of our European civilization, who are yet deeply, though indirectly, influenced by their thoughts and ideas, which through the centuries have helped to mould the general outlook of the West. A more realistic concept of the invisible world is quickly dismissed as "theosophic" and "mythological." Yet we must not forget that the Bible itself contains a strongly realistic element in its world-view. We do not seek, therefore, any theosophic or fanciful speculation in this work; we try, in harmony with Scripture as a whole, to place the history of salvation of mankind in the great, cosmic framework of the history of the universe and of eternity, in which it belongs. On this foundation we strive further to comprehend the purpose of man's existence within the prophetic and apostolic world-view of Holy Scripture (chs. 3, 6, 7, 10).

The claims of Biblical truth are often contested on four main grounds:

(1) The untenableness of its ideological foundations.
(2) The weakening and degrading principles of its moral teaching.
(3) The illogical and offensive character of its doctrine of salvation.
(4) The primitive conceptions of its account of creation.
This book endeavours to offer some answers to each of these attacks.
We attempt to show:

(1) That the *ideological foundations* of the Bible are unshakeable, *viz.* the
existence of God, the origin and purpose of creation, the Divine permission of evil, the existence of a personal Devil and belief in revelation
and miracle as justified by natural law (chs. 2, 4, 5, 11, 12).

(2) That the *moral teaching* of the Bible is permeated by strength of
character, true optimism, and the consciousness of the dignity of a royal
race called to Divine nobility. The apparently contradictory Biblical teaching on humility, patience, self-denial, love, grace and repentance are particularly discussed, and its conformity with true nobility of soul and
genuine kingly behaviour demonstrated (chs. 8 and 9).

(3) That the Scriptural *doctrine of salvation*—its proclamation concerning
sin and atonement, God's righteousness in judgment and Christ's sacrifice
of Himself, the impossibility of human self-redemption and the necessity
of a redemptive act by God—stands on a solid and eternal rock-foundation
(ch. 13 and ch. 9, section II).

(4) That a really surprising harmony exists between *the Biblical account of
creation* and modern science, particularly geology and palaeontology, so
far as these have produced really reliable results (ch. 15). For all that, there
still exist, both in the interpretation of the Scriptural narrative and in
natural science, numerous unsolved questions (chs. 14, 16, 17), so that
both sides should show caution and reserve.

We have not given our answers in the form of a systematic apologetic,
but as they arose most appropriately in the course of the book. Our theme
is not a defence of the faith, but a testimony to the nobility and kingship
of man.

That is why we have not discussed the Biblical creation-narrative in the
first, but in the fifth part of the book. The king of the earth takes precedence over the earth, his kingdom. Nevertheless the latter must not be
overlooked in its rightful place.

The scientific references in the book, particularly those taken from
astronomy, geology and atomic physics, are therefore in no sense superfluous deviations from its real object. Rather, if man is really appointed to
be the king of the earth, and if the earth is really the principal scene of
God's redemptive acts, then there belong together: spirit and material
nature, the universe and the earth, creation and revelation of salvation, the
temporal and the eternal, the human king and his earthly kingdom.

The purpose of this book is to be a "testimony," not a theological or
scientific treatise. It endeavours to help seekers and thinkers, sceptics and

Christians alike; to remove difficulties from the path of the former, to place some weapons in the hands of the latter in their battle for truth. In addition, it seeks to help them to enlarge the horizons of their own personal knowledge.

How far this attempt has succeeded is for others to decide. It will certainly be judged according to individual attitudes to scientific and Biblical questions. We do not expect complete assent to all that is offered from any, but desire to provoke further thought. Should however any be brought back to faith in the invincible Word of God through the reading of this book, and should others be confirmed and deepened in this faith, that would give the greatest joy to the writer.

With deep gratitude I mention my highly esteemed friend, Mr. G. H. Lang, here. He was the translator of my former books, *The Triumph of the Crucified*, *The Dawn of World Redemption* and *From Eternity to Eternity*, into English. He also helped considerably in the English translation of *In the Arena of Faith*. It was his suggestion that *The King of the Earth* should also appear in English. He made the first beginnings of this translation, but owing to failing strength in his great age he was not able to go on with the work. In October, 1958, after a long life of most fruitful and blessed service for the Lord, he was called home. Through his deep spirituality and his capable and accurate work, he made an unforgettable contribution to the appearance of these books in English.

Making use of Mr. Lang's work as a start, Mr. Michael Bolister, B.Sc., of Bristol, has made the whole of this present English translation, which in turn has been thoroughly revised by Mr. H. L. Ellison, B.D., B.A. My wife and I are grateful to both these friends for their most capable help. As Mr. Bolister was living here at Wiedenest, we could talk over all details, and I gratefully appreciate the keen spiritual interest and ability with which he entered into all the thoughts and problems discussed in this book.

I also feel very much indebted to Mr. B. H. Mudditt, the Proprietor of The Paternoster Press, London, who has always shown such kind and genuine interest in my books and who has done so much to further their circulation. I am grateful to the Lord that He has so blessed our co-operation.

The spiritual and intellectual crisis in which so many now stand is mighty. Modern ideologies of recent growth have revealed their hollowness and have collapsed shamefully. But the gospel of God remains! It proves its own indestructible power in all the crises and catastrophes of the world. It is to this invincibility and universal scope that this book testifies.

May the Lord, who always stoops even to the imperfect, when men set their hearts on Him, not deny His blessing to this work.

ERICH SAUER

Wiedenest, 1959

TRANSLATORS' NOTE

Except where otherwise indicated Biblical quotations are from the Revised Version.

To reduce the number of footnotes, references to minor German works have normally been omitted. In more important cases the reference is given to the page in brackets after the quotation, and the name of the book will be found under the author's name in the Bibliography at the end. Where more than one work by the same author is cited, it is distinguished by Roman numerals, I, II, III, etc., according to their order in the Bibliography. English works cited are given in footnotes, but for full details about them see Bibliography.

INTRODUCTION

THE inexorable march of history turns all to flux. Peoples and kingdoms emerge and vanish. Thrones and dominions rise and fall. The honourable becomes dishonourable and the dishonourable honourable.

Where is the rock on which men may stand? Where is there something eternal, unchangeable? Where is that fixed point from which we may obtain a steady picture of the world? Why do the nations rage and swell like the stormy sea? Mankind—from where has it come and where is it going?

This problem is as old as man; the endeavours to solve it are innumerable. The greatest minds have been drawn to it, but there is no agreement in their answers.

Antiquity could not even formulate the question, for it did not possess a conception of universal history. Apart from the Stoic philosophy it was unable to rise to the idea of "humanity." In Greek historical thought each people, unconnected with any other, had grown up out of its own soil.[1] This meant that even to ask whether there was an objective meaning in universal human experiences and in a developing history of mankind was meaningless.

Only Christianity, with its world-embracing view, the heir of the early chapters of Genesis and of Old Testament prophecy, was able to bring about a change. "In the process of the development of human thought true reflection upon the nature of history came for the first time with Christianity" (Dr. H. Lilje).

The treatise by the church father Augustine (354–430), *The City of God* (*De Civitate Dei*), was of great importance in the shaping of history. But here too for the time being there was no real advance on the first beginnings. Roman Catholicism, which soon became dominant, quickly clapped free Christian thinking into the iron fetters of rigid dogma and dead scholastic hair-splitting.

This is a fact, even if we recognize that the Middle Ages were far from being that obscuring of culture we so often think them to have been. They produced great achievements of the human mind, like the theological-philosophical and scientific works of the South German Count Albertus Magnus (1193–1280) and of his still greater Italian pupil, Thomas Aquinas

---

[1] According to the Greek doctrine of *Auto-chthonism* (Gr. *autos*, self; *chthon*, earth, land).

(1225–1274). Their contemporaries, in their admiration of their intellectual power and comprehensive knowledge, gave them the title of "Doctor Universalis," and to Thomas Aquinas in addition that of "Doctor Angelicus."

A decisive revolution for mankind as a whole came only with the reawakening of free research at the Renaissance and in the Humanism of the fifteenth and sixteenth centuries, and still more with the powerful rise of the historical sciences at the turn of the eighteenth and nineteenth centuries. The most varied philosophical systems of history were now put forward. Men like Voltaire, Rousseau, Herder and Kant, each from his own particular standpoint, attempted to fathom these deep problems. Fichte, Schelling and Hegel advocated idealistic systems. Marx and Engels proclaimed their materialistic philosophy of history. Schopenhauer and Spengler taught their atheistic, pessimistic interpretation of history. But irrespective of the philosophy of humanity under consideration, all these trains of thought leave the deepest problems unsolved. The study of history first begins to emerge into the light, when Alexander von Humboldt's words are accepted: "World history is incomprehensible apart from world government." World history is merely the scaffolding for the history of salvation. Its true meaning lies in that which is behind and above the senses. Only when we view the temporal from the standpoint of the eternal, all earthly activity and being are illumined by the light of heaven, and events in time gain their meaning from that which is beyond time.

But this realm cannot be attained by natural thought, because this is earth-bound and finite. The eternal must, therefore, reveal itself to man's understanding. In other words, only the Divine revelation enables us to comprehend the eternal background of the development of history in time, with its forces and aims. Only when a ray of light from God falls upon us do we begin to gain luminous vistas through the turmoil of this world; only then do we understand the heart of the manifold phenomena presented to us in history.

The Bible gives us this revelation. It follows that a true interpretation of history must be a Biblical "theology of world history." For the goal of all that is earthly is its transfiguration in the eternal. It is the self-glorification of God in the unfolding of salvation and the blessing of His creation.

PART I

ETERNITY AND UNIVERSE AS BACKGROUND FOR THE HIGH CALLING OF MAN

CHAPTER I

THE NOBILITY OF MAN?

"THE Nobility of Man? How can any one use a phrase like that today, after two world wars with their devastating effects and innumerable crimes committed by all involved?" This was the comment by one who saw the title of an earlier German edition of this work, and was drawn by it to read the book.

One might well ask whether a true human nobility has ever existed in practice among men as a whole. Do not the savage customs of primitive peoples demonstrate the contrary? Even among the more advanced and most advanced peoples, is not the whole history of the world, so far as we can follow it back into the mists of prehistory, a story of blood and iron, of atrocity and oppression? In every nation, on every continent and at every time we find an incalculable volume of falsehood and deceit, of selfishness and immorality. Who can reckon the religious errors, the mistaken philosophies and ideologies, the thoughtlessness and apathy among the masses?

We grant that there has also been much that has been noble; much love and faithfulness between man and wife, between parents and children; much sacrifical devotion between friends and selfless service to nation and country! In addition there have repeatedly been innumerable individuals whose thoughts and efforts were directed towards the good, the true and the beautiful, and whose intellectual powers have produced outstanding achievements in cultural development. But when we look at them against the background of the whole we see they have always been a mere fraction; in addition even their lives have not been free from error and therefore they have not been a complete realization of true, human nobility.

Thus if we consider the whole development of mankind, the statement of the great apostle of Jesus Christ retains its terrible validity: "All have sinned, and fall short of the glory of God" (Rom. 3: 23).

Where, then, is the nobility of man?

1. THE BALANCE SHEET OF TWO WORLD WARS. STILL GREATER DANGERS THROUGH THE MISUSE OF ATOMIC ENERGY

In the first world war there were more than 8,500,000 fatal casualties in the armies involved.[1] In the second world war there were over 27,000,000 deaths among the fighting forces and nearly 25,000,000 among civilians; that is, a total of over 52,000,000 fatal casualties between 1939 and 1945,[2] to say nothing of the wounded and prisoners of war.

Indeed, the question is fully justified, whether we have any right to speak of the nobility of man, especially today in the twentieth century, today, in the atomic age. Fear and horror have seized all thinking people when they have considered the future. A mad decision by an individual or by a criminal or desperate government can, by the use of atomic weapons and H-bombs, annihilate millions and millions of human lives and irretrievably destroy the results and relics of centuries and millennia of human culture. Today, in our period of history, mankind is playing with the possibility of an indescribable mass-murder, which under certain circumstances could lead almost to the point of suicide for all the cultural leaders of the world. According to the latest information at the end of 1958 the nuclear weapons now in the possession of the great powers already suffice to depopulate the whole earth.

Would it not be much better, in view of these terrifying symptoms of decline in the twentieth century—of our *own* present day—to speak of the age of disintegrating humanity, of "The Decline of the West" or, indeed, of the collapse of civilization; to speak, not of moral nobility but utter moral inability, not of a high call but a deep fall, not of kingship but slavery, not of success but failure, not of progress but catastrophe, not of hope but despair? Has not the increasing dethroning of God in Europe and America led to the dethroning of humanity in man?

Man was formerly held to be a torchbearer of a divine reason underlying the world, but now has become a riddle, indeed, an abyss. "The belief in the personality and the humanity of man has fallen to the ground and has been broken in pieces in the disturbances of the past decades. Through the atrocities which man has committed against man the very face of man has been dishonoured and distorted."

Despite outstanding technical advances, man has brought a self-humiliation and destruction of the human image to pass without precedent in the history of his race. Is it not far truer to reality, instead of speaking of man as the "king of the earth," to say with Schopenhauer, the atheistic, pessimistic philosopher, "Men are the devils of the earth"?

[1] *Encyclopaedia Britannica*, 1947 edition.
[2] According to the data collected by the Swiss Red Cross. In addition, over five million were reported missing and have not been heard of since, a large proportion of these being soldiers and civilians who had been taken prisoner.

Again and again—particularly in our generation—man has used the technical achievements, through which his life can be advanced and improved, to produce the most terrible weapons to destroy life. "Out of cars grew tanks, out of aeroplanes, bombers, and even the miracle of wireless was degraded into a means for the incitement of nation against nation. Whatever science and technical progress have created for good has been misused, and out of blessing has come a curse. If mankind cannot do better with atomic energy in the future, then the power of the atom will become the greatest danger which has ever hovered over our globe" (Gail).

"The beasts are harmless compared with men. Man, the beast of prey, has broken loose! Brutal egoism demands its rights! One man becomes his neighbour's devil!" (K. Heim).

One scarcely dares to speak today of the greatness of man. His patent of nobility has been torn to shreds. The dignity which he received from his Creator has been lost. "Man devours man like a wolf." We see not ethical nobility but moral degeneration, not ascent but fall, not sovereignty but slavery, not success but failure, not progress but collapse, not hope but despair. We may ask, whether man, the king of the earth, is not on the point of turning his sceptre into a sword on which he will finally run himself through.

We agree; man has fallen deeply indeed. Only the superficial, ignorant and illogical can without faith in God still look with confidence into the future. For everyone who is able and willing to think, it is clear that the end of humanism has arrived! The illusion of faith in human progress has collapsed since 1914.

2. THE CONFLICT BETWEEN SCIENTIFIC PROGRESS AND MORAL DEVELOPMENT

Mankind is clever, *very* clever. But it is also evil, *very* evil, and it is more evil than it is clever. Its wickedness is greater than its intelligence. Its moral development has not kept pace with its technical and intellectual development. Its science has improved but not its conscience. Therefore this growing knowledge actually increases the general distress of mankind. The end of the man who, without God, penetrates the secrets of God's creation is despair and destruction.

The philosopher Professor Diltey expressed it thus: "The ethical possibilities of modern man are not equal to the technical forces he has released. The unity of man is breaking up. The tension between science and the arts, between the religious-moral and the physical-technical world has placed too great demands upon the unity of man and its resultant harmonious polarity between the intellect and the ethical will. The military application of atomic energy has led us to a point where the separation of physics and ethics has become extremely dangerous" (see Howe, p. 51).

At the same time it becomes clear how justified is the literal interpretation of the New Testament prophecy of the last world war before the return of Christ, which foretells that in this struggle between the nations a third of mankind will perish. "By these three plagues was the third part of men killed" (i.e. at the present level of world population, over 800 million: Rev. 9: 18, cf. v. 16). "Armies . . . twice ten thousand times ten thousand," i.e. two hundred million soldiers!

Particularly impressive is the warning given by Dr. Albert Einstein, the world-famous physicist, in a lecture in 1948: "The true problem lies in the hearts and thoughts of men. It is not a physical problem, but an ethical one . . . What terrifies us is not the explosive force of the atomic bomb, but the power of the wickedness of the human heart, its explosive power for evil. In the Name of God, if you believe in Him, take Him seriously, and control and restrain scientific discoveries; if not, we are lost."

Yet, for all that, we continue to speak of the nobility of man. We do so in the light of the high vocation and destiny of man, ordained by God and revealed in the Bible.

3. BIBLICAL REVELATION—THE ONLY WAY OUT OF IMMINENT CATASTROPHE

God gave mankind a royal task. As the Eternal and Omniscient He foresaw all decline and disaster from the very beginning. Therefore He also determined a way of salvation in Christ His Son. This was accomplished in the history of His self-revelation and is authenticated and testified to by Holy Scripture.

It is dependable, for it is the way taken by the love and holiness of almighty God. God has never changed His goal for man. Over against human failure He triumphantly sets His Divine plan of salvation. Therefore, despite all man's decline, he remains called to human nobility, a call that finds its fulfilment in all those who in faith lay themselves open to the Divine saving activity.

The Bible is the book in which God unfolds His royal plan of salvation. It is the only document of lasting value in which the high call of man has its roots. This finds its clear expression right at the beginning of this Divine book, "Fill the earth, and subdue it; and have dominion" (Gen. 1: 28). All true nobility of man will stand or fall, therefore, with our acceptance or rejection of the Bible.

Man has irrefutably demonstrated his failure as he has sought to reach his goal by the development of civilization. Through true scriptural faith God offers him in Christ salvation and the fulfilment of his high destiny.

This being so, man, especially modern man, in the midst of all the catastrophic shocks caused by his own false development, is placed before this ancient book and challenged to take up some attitude towards it.

4. MODERN MAN'S CRITICAL ATTITUDE TOWARDS THE BIBLE

Our age is one of seeking and questioning. Unsatisfied by the untenable ideas of a cold, outworn, materialistic philosophy of life, many are striving after new and higher ideals. They are trying to grasp the true meaning of existence and to become conscious of the nobility of human existence. Only then is it possible to mould our life in practice to conform to its real meaning. Though so many strive after a new content for their lives, most heedlessly pass by the Bible. From the very outset modern man generally approaches it with an attitude of doubt.

This is very largely due to the cultural intoxication of modern progress. Men think that they have superseded the Bible where history and science are concerned. They even claim that its supernatural, transcendental pre-suppositions are untenable, especially its doctrine about the Trinity, the angel world, the existence of a personal devil and its belief in revelation and miracles in general. Heaven and hell are said to be astronomical impossibilities. Indeed, not a few think that modern man has evolved beyond certain basic moral and legal concepts of the Bible. The modern sense of justice is supposed to move on a higher plane than the Scriptural doctrine of redemption, at least in thought and principle. For it is claimed to be legally and morally inadmissible to reckon the punishment suffered by an innocent person as subsequently valid for the guilty in order that he may go free, hence the rejection of the Scriptural doctrine of substitution and with it the kernel and heart of all Christian preaching of salvation.

In such a situation a return to the Bible is considered to be intellectual and cultural retrogression. Belief in the Bible and continued evolution upwards are said to be incompatible. Only by mounting higher than the Bible can one reach true "nobility of man."

In this turning away from the Bible man rejects the patent of nobility given him by God Himself. In spite of the fact that this attitude has in practice failed to fulfil its claims and promises, man supports it with a rejection of the Bible on theoretical grounds based on a natural philosophy.

The peoples of the West have not held this view so strongly at every period of their history. There have been centuries when the Bible was regarded much more positively. What has led to this basic change in mental attitude? What new questions, linked with the high calling and kingly position of man, are associated with this?

It was very soon after the beginning of the modern era that this development became acute.

5. DOUBTS CONCERNING MAN'S CENTRAL POSITION IN THE UNIVERSE PANTHEISTIC INFERENCES FROM THE COPERNICAN SYSTEM. MINUTE MAN AND THE "INFINITE" UNIVERSE

The voyages of discovery in the transitional period between the Middle Ages and modern times were in themselves epoch-making. Some of the ancient Greek philosophers had already inferred that the earth was a sphere, and this was confirmed beyond all doubt by the voyages of

Christopher Columbus (the discovery of America, 1492) and the first journeys around the world by Magellan (1519–1522) and Sir Francis Drake (1577–1580).

In addition to these there came the new planetary system of Copernicus, which revolutionized the whole concept of the world, placing the sun in the centre with the other planets, including the earth, revolving about it. Professor Diltey considers that this Copernican recognition of the heliocentric system, together with the convincing scientific arguments for it, is "the greatest scientific achievement of mankind."[1]

With the recognition of the spherical form of the earth and especially with the new astronomical conviction that the universe is "infinite," an apparently logical conclusion from the Copernican system, the problem of "above" and "below" emerged in a completely new form. This raised a question as to the world beyond, as to the existence and "place" of heaven and hell.

What had become of God, who reigns "over" His creatures? Where did the souls of the saved and of the lost go? Indeed, what and where is "above" and "below?" Was not pantheism the only possibility remaining, that is, the identification of God and the universe? Was not the belief in a personal, transcendent God to be regarded as an exploded idea?

Further, how could one, in view of the newly discovered, immeasurable vastness of the universe, still hold at all to the pre-eminent position and kingly calling of mankind in God's world-plan, as taught by the Bible? The earth had become so small, and man so insignificant!

Do not modern geography and astronomy refute all Biblical theology and teaching on salvation? Must not a conflict arise between Christianity and science, a conflict not only on certain isolated questions but especially

---

[1] Nikolaus Kopernicus, or more accurately Coppernicus, as he usually wrote his name, was born in 1473 in Torun or Thorn in Poland, of a family that had moved from Cracow.

In fact ancient Greek astronomers had already had presentiments of this truth. *Aristarchus* of Samos (310–250 B.C.) had suggested that the sun did not move around the earth, but the earth around the sun. He had been led to this conclusion very strongly by his insight into the fact that the size of the sun was so great as to surpass everything earthly. A hundred years later the Bythinian *Hipparchus* of Nicea (in north-west Asia Minor, not far from Byzantium or Constantinople) drew up a catalogue of stars which showed the positions of about 1080. Through it Hipparchus (c. 160–125 B.C.) proved himself to be the most important observer of antiquity, and became the real founder of scientific astronomy. *Anaximander* of Miletus (sixth century B.C.) and *Pythagoras* of Samos (fifth century B.C.) had also conjectured the spherical form of the earth. But all this was obscured by the Alexandrian geographer and astronomer *Ptolemy* (born A.D. 150), who taught the geocentric system with the earth as the centre of the universe and thereby concealed the correct ideas of Aristarchus for centuries, right until the beginning of modern times.

Thus it was through *Copernicus* that these ancient insights—almost two thousand years after their first expression—were at last able to exert a real influence on human history.

on the decisive foundations and central doctrines of revealed Christian faith? Is it not clear that no educated man can still believe in a personal God or speak of the high calling of man in its Biblical sense?

Even before the time of Copernicus the infiniteness of the universe had been suggested by Cardinal Nicholas of Cusa (1401–1464), who was led to the idea by the *theological* consideration, that the universe as God's creation must share in the greatest possible degree in the attributes of God and therefore also possess His infiniteness.

The infiniteness of the universe was then convincingly demonstrated *scientifically* and *astronomically*, for his time, by the planetary system of Copernicus.

Building upon the ideas of Nicholas of Cusa and Copernicus the Italian-born Dominican father Giordano Bruno carried over this idea of the infiniteness of the universe without an "above" and "below" into the *religious* and *philosophical* fields, thereby taking a final and decisive step. Giordano Bruno recognized that the fixed stars were suns, just like "our" own sun. This, however, put an end to the belief of the ancient Greeks and of the Middle Ages in the crystalline vault of the heaven of fixed stars arching over the disc of the earth like a great sphere to which the stars (apart from the "wandering stars" or planets, among which the sun and moon were also reckoned) were fixed. "Thus Giordano Bruno was the first man to experience the infiniteness of space and to gaze with drunken eyes into a sea of nothing but suns."

Logical deductions were applied to the concept of God. It seems that now one can speak of "God" only in the sense of "Deity," in the sense of an impersonal "world-spirit," which permeates the universe and reveals its omnipresence in every place, in every thing and in every living creature, equally in the beauty of the flowers, the majesty of the mountains, the radiance of the sun, the light of the stars and the nobility of the human mind. At the same time this seems to lead to the collapse of the whole Biblical revelation, with its belief in a personal God, in answers to prayer and in miracles, in redemption in the Scriptural sense and in the personal glorification of the individual soul in a coming kingdom of God. One can still be convinced of the present mental greatness of man, despite his insignificant bodily size; but when the individual only rises and disappears like a wave in the universal ocean, how can one still speak, so far as eternity is concerned, of a real, lasting, personal nobility of man?

6. THE INADEQUACY OF EARLIER CONCLUSIONS IN THE LIGHT OF TWENTIETH-CENTURY MATHEMATICS

Today we see things differently from the men of 300 years ago. Through the recognition of four-dimensional space-time the whole question appears in a completely new light.

In addition modern physics and astronomy doubt the infinity of the universe and speak of a "curved" space-time continuum, that is, space closed in on itself. Just as the surface of a globe this can be considered as both endless and limited, only that the former, as a surface, is merely two-dimensional (length, breadth). This four-dimensional space can even be mathematically calculated, though it lies beyond the limits of our perception and understanding (length, breadth, depth and time). In the popular mind these theories are normally linked with Einstein's theory of relativity, which postulates a space-time continuum.

No one—not even Einstein himself—can picture to himself a curved space-time continuum. But Albert Einstein was able to calculate the curvature and to draw conclusions from it, and even to predict certain events, such as the change of path of the planet Mercury in its course around the sun.

"Our mathematical thinking can surpass the limits of our perception. For the mathematical formulae, in which we express the structure of a three-dimensional space, may, by appropriate modifications, be readily applied to more than three dimensions" (K. Heim, cf. IV, pp. 106–112; III, pp. 145 f.; II, pp. 158–162). As a result of this, mathematics, this so "abstract" science, becomes the connexion—the only connexion—which we can make with the four-dimensional world, just as it is the only key which has unlocked the gate into the strange world of the atom.

With this new knowledge the problem of the location of the world beyond has disappeared. The doubt about God's heaven and the "dwelling-place" of saved souls is seen to be pointless. And it is just the physics, astronomy and mathematics of the twentieth century which have cleared the path for faith.

7. INCREASING TENSION BETWEEN NATURAL SCIENCE AND BIBLICAL FAITH

All this was unknown to the men of the sixteenth and seventeenth centuries. This explains the bitter conflict between the Church and the natural sciences, the result of which was that far-reaching, growing estrangement from the Church and the Bible of countless people in the dawning new age, which was a characteristic of the transition period between the Middle Ages and today.

Copernicus, a pious Roman Catholic, sensed a coming opposition and possible persecution by the Church and exercised extreme reserve in making known and spreading his new astronomical theories. He imparted his daring theory only to his scholarly friends. Only shortly before his death did he decide to publish his principal work, and he was on his death-bed when the first copy of it was handed to him (1543). In fact, this book was in 1616 put on the Index by the Roman Catholic Church, and not until 1822 and 1835, 292 years after its first appearance, was this prohibition annulled by papal decrees.

Galileo, the famous Italian physicist and astronomer, was one of the principal champions of the Copernican system. At the age of 70 he was tried by the Inquisition in Rome, imprisoned for 23 days, and forced to abjure his views in spite of his own scientific convictions (1633). In spite of this he was kept under the supervision of the Inquisition to the end of his life.

The most tragic fate—in the period between Copernicus and Galileo— was that of Giordano Bruno, the most important Italian philosopher of the dawning new age. He also was a defender of the Copernican system. Unfortunately for him he linked with it pantheism, i.e., the identification of God (Deity) and the universe. He was seized by the Inquisition in 1592, transferred to Rome in the following year, held there in imprisonment for seven years and then finally burnt at the stake (1600).

With such a general tension between science and the beliefs of the Church the only too understandable result was that many advocates of this newly gained scientific knowledge emptied out the baby with the bath-water and together with outdated ideas about the natural world threw Christianity also overboard.

This antagonism between Christianity and science was made even more acute by the firmly rooted alliance between the theology of the Middle Ages and the world-picture of classical antiquity. Those who continued to hold the old views were sincere in their beliefs and were able to support them with powerful arguments. It was generally believed that the world-picture of the Bible was in fact the same as that of antiquity. But in reality a fusion of essentially different elements had taken place. This is especially true of the philosophy and the concept of nature held by Aristotle and Ptolemy, of certain basic conceptions of Roman law and of the adoption of many ideas from the mysticism and symbolism of Hellenistic-Oriental religions. But also, quite apart from such details, the alliance between Christian theology and Greek philosophy was in its very foundations something self-contradictory and therefore incapable of lasting. Essentially this was not a matter of simply adopting certain more or less important scientific and philosophical ideas and interpretations from Hellenism into Christian thinking, but of a most unnatural association of two completely different conceptions of God.

"God or Deity for the Greeks meant absolute, metaphysical being, that which really exists, eternally unchanged and immovable, the highest good. God in the Biblical revelation is the Almighty, acting, revealing Himself in acts of salvation, the personal, triune Lord of the world, both transcendent and immanent, who lives in the fulness of the life which is God's alone and out of this fulness creates history" (Howe).

"The emphasis (in the name Yahweh) lies not on existence in its mere being but on its activity."[1]

The Biblical revelation leads us to God as the Father of Jesus Christ, the

[1] Prof. W. Eichrodt, *Theologie des Alten Testaments*[5], I 1957, p. 119.

God of redemption; human reason leads to the inactive prime cause of Greek philosophy, to the "immovable" mover of the world (Aristotle).

Such a union of classical antiquity and Christianity was from the very outset doomed to collapse and had to dissolve one day. A kingdom—even a kingdom of ideas—which is divided against itself cannot stand (cf. Mt. 12: 25). But for many thinkers such an unavoidable process of dissolution of two contradictory ideas of God was of necessity a source of utmost danger for faith itself.

This amalgamation was completed by the Fathers of the Church especially between the time of Origen and Augustine (A.D. 250–430). It was then introduced into North-Western and Central Europe by monasticism.

Its most perfect expression is found in Albertus Magnus and in the system of his great pupil Thomas Aquinas (1225–1274), which, regarded purely from the intellectual point of view, has been called "one of the greatest achievements in the history of human thought." The intellectual moulding of the West was based on this alliance between classical antiquity and Christianity. Nevertheless, when free research and science awoke once more towards the end of the Middle Ages, it became one of the principal causes for the rejection by the general public of Christian dogma.

"The intellectual development of the West in the last 300 years can best be understood as a growing out of the *naïveté* of the Middle Ages, as a freeing of personality. Western man becomes increasingly conscious of his reason and uses this more and more as a standard for evaluating and understanding all human relationships, including his relationship to God" (Rohrbach, I, p. 2).

Aristotle (*c.* 350 B.C.) had taught the geocentric picture of the world, *viz.* the earth was the unmoving centre around which the sun and the stars moved. He had further advocated the theory of the four elements, according to which nature was composed of fire, water, earth and air. The Church of the Middle Ages had taken up these ideas into its dogmas, and so they came to be considered as part of Christian truth.

The result, however, was that as scientific research progressed, every refutation of Aristotle's scientific errors lowered the prestige of the Church. Every blow dealt at the authority of Aristotle by scientific discoveries inevitably fell indirectly upon the Church.

Thus "the scholastic attempt to use the philosophy and scientific system of Aristotle as the foundation, framework and conceptual tool of theology" ended with a strong threat to the Christian faith from modern science. The effects of this were all the more serious as the representatives of Christianity were not able to free themselves from the heritage of antiquity in time.

This development grew stronger from century to century. More and more of the sciences became conscious of the laws of their own nature. Increasingly the conviction was reached that these were independent of the Church's claim to control the minds of men. There was a somewhat milder repetition of this process, when the importance of geology began to be realized in the nineteenth century.

This meant, however, that the pressure of secularization on science grew ever greater. A conflict arose between theology and physics, the arts and the natural sciences, between belief in God and the study of nature, which from the end of the Middle Ages was to lie for centuries like a dark shadow over the whole history of the West. Although the great creators of modern physics, Kepler, Newton and also Galileo, had been faithful sons of their churches, the science they had moulded very soon against their will trod the path of hostility to God, and was finally used again and again in the extremest manner in all civilized countries as a weapon by the most radical godlessness (cf. Howe).

"The ever-multiplying adherents of science increasingly separated themselves from a Christianity, which they regarded as tradition-bound and hostile to progress. The conflict has, taking a long view, affected Roman Catholicism and Protestantism equally."

8. MAN'S SELF-EXALTATION AND SELF-HUMILIATION IN THE INTELLECTUAL DEVELOPMENT OF THE WEST

During the course of recent centuries the question of man's nobility has repeatedly been stressed. Although the continually increasing general unbelief rejected the Bible, and with it the patent of nobility which God Himself had given to man, it attempted, on the basis of its own presuppositions, to attain to *its own* affirmation of the dignity of man.

Admittedly, the central position of man in the universe could, on the basis of his conclusions from astronomy and science, no longer be maintained. For the universe was so big, and man and the earth so small and insignificant.

But what about the majesty of the human *mind*? Were not its science and art, its progress and cultural achievements, its thinking and striving, in short, its "reason," an irrefutable testimony to this majesty and dignity?

Even at the beginning of the modern era Humanism and the Renaissance had tended to a *self-glorification* of man. In the Rationalism of the eighteenth century we can find an almost religious overestimation, even a self-deification of the power of human reason. During the French revolution, at a special ceremony in the cathedral of Notre Dame in Paris, religious homage was paid to a girl as a symbol of the "goddess of reason." In the nineteenth century, in fanatical opposition to all belief in God, Friedrich Nietzsche proclaimed the ideal of the "Superman;" the influence of his ideas, especially of "the will for power," "the right of the stronger," "beyond good and evil," of "If there were Gods, how could I endure it to be no God?", can be traced into the historical catastrophes of the twentieth century.

Of course there were also numerous moderate, truly noble, idealistic philosophies and intellectual movements.

The problem of the dignity of man was raised in acutest form in the middle of the nineteenth century. The sciences of geology and palaeontology formulated about 1800 led to the theory of evolution. Particularly as developed by Darwin (died 1882) and his pupil Ernst Haeckel (died 1919), it fitted man's genealogical tree into the animal kingdom, or at least spoke of animal-like pre-hominids, which during the course of hundreds of thousands of years had evolved to man's present level.

If at the beginning of man's history there stands not Paradise but the animal kingdom, where is his uniqueness and special position? If he did not come immediately from the hand of his Creator, but only mediately through untold animal-like intermediate stages, how is this to be reconciled with his nobility? Is not the assertion of the first pages of the Bible, that man was a special creation of God who from the first received a central position in God's plan for the world—to use an expression of Haeckel's—only "anthropistic megalomania"?

In 1939 in the Natural History Museum in New York the writer of this book saw a large genealogical table of the human race. In it the descent of man was traced back through the mammals to the fishes. According to this view the origin of man goes back to the first living organism, so that everything originates in one common root. Thomas Carlyle's attitude to this view was not unjust. "Thomas Carlyle was once at a meeting of learned men in which the problem of man's descent was being discussed, and was asked to give his opinion. 'Gentlemen,' he said, 'you place man a little higher than the tadpole. I hold with the ancient singer: Thou hast made him a little lower than the angels (Psa. 8: 6)'" (Neuberg, I, p. 101).

We grant that by no means all the advocates of the evolutionary theory have drawn these extreme conclusions. In the gradual development of man there was also seen a slow but lasting progress onwards and upwards to his present level and kingly position on earth. But millions of people have interpreted these teachings in the way we have suggested. Ultimately, they have seen in man something not much higher than a more perfectly organized and also mentally more gifted "man-animal," which was far superior to the general animal world, but had still proceeded from it.

Darwin tried to explain the formation of species not by repeated, Divine acts of creation or by a Divinely controlled (theistic) evolution, but by natural selection in the struggle for existence. This evolution was without a goal and controlled by "chance." Professor Emil Brunner[1] has rightly emphasized that Darwin has shaken modern man's acceptance of Christianity far more than did the developments of the Copernican world-system. Modern man senses a much greater contradiction between belief

[1] Dr. Emil Brunner, *The Christian Doctrine of Creation and Redemption* (*Dogmatics*, Vol. II), 1950.

in the Bible and the study of fossilized human remains, i.e. between theology and palaeontological anthropology, than between belief in the Bible and astronomy and geology in general.

These doubts of natural philosophy about the Bible were strengthened by the influence of Biblical criticism, which first became prominent at the beginning of the nineteenth century. For many, the historical criticism of the Old and New Testaments signified a *reduction of the Bible to a book of legends.* And why should the general public continue to confess belief in this book, when many representatives of the Church itself—both theologians and clergy—to a great extent doubted it?

Of as far-reaching importance as the theory of evolution was the almost simultaneous "mechanistic picture of the world" taught by physics.

9. MAN'S SELF-DEGRADATION IN THE MECHANISTIC THEORIES OF THE NINE-TEENTH CENTURY. DOUBTS CONCERNING MORAL FREEDOM, THE BASIS OF ALL HUMAN NOBILITY

The more scientific research developed, particularly in chemistry, physics and astronomy, the more men became convinced that the whole of nature was subject to natural law. Everything depended on a chain of cause and effect. Every event is a necessary result of its antecedents. Everything is controlled by "invariable natural laws." Everything is rigorously causal and mechanistic.

It is clear that *pantheism,* the identification of God and the universe, can associate itself with such a picture of the world. It also leaves room for *deism,* i.e. the belief in the existence of a Creator-God, who called the world into existence, much as a watchmaker starts a watch, but who did not then intervene further in the course of nature.

But in such a picture of the world there is no room for the *theistic* and Biblical concept of God with its belief in God's rule of the world, in miracles and answers to prayer, and in its history of revelation and salvation. For every miraculous act by such a God would be a "breach" of the natural laws, which He Himself had established. The God of revelation would stand in contradiction to Himself as the God of creation. The unity of the idea of God would be smashed.

Millions fell a prey to *atheism.* The universe and matter were said to be without a beginning and eternal. Space and time were claimed to be absolute dimensions, and matter, solid substance. The universe was not only spatially, but also temporally endless. A God and a Divine revelation could not exist. Materialism had triumphed.

Just as devastating are the moral and ethical consequences of the mechanistic picture of the world for the dignity of man. For if it were true that everything in the world—and therefore also human life—were subject to invariable natural laws, which determine the whole course of *all* inward and outward events, so that everything could be exactly calculated from the very beginning, then there would be no possibility of free choice for man. He, too, in his activity would be subject to powerful and inevitable natural laws. Then he would be nothing more than an insignificant speck of dust in the universe without a will of his own, and moral freedom would not exist. But without freedom there can be no personality. The mechanistic theory of the world therefore destroys the moral core of all human nature. It lowers him to a level of a small machine, of a tiny wheel in the cosmic mechanism. It makes him a slave of more powerful forces. It robs him of his moral sense of responsibility, destroys his ethical being and delivers him over to fatalism, i.e. to a belief in a "fate" to which one has to bow. In this way the mechanistic theory of the world destroys the nobility of man most effectively in practice. Man is not "the king of the earth," but the slave of the cosmos. Acceptance of the mechanistic theory of the world carries with it the self-humiliation of man.

"Thus the destruction of respect for God and for nature as His creation meant the loss of respect for man himself, and the West became a desert without a goal for life and without a God, such as the world had hitherto not known."

To this we must add the propaganda of new, great, social, economic and political movements with ideological goals. With the rapid progress of technical knowledge and industry these were able to develop extremely quickly. They appealed to the just mentioned theories of history and especially of natural science and sought to popularize their own free-thinking, anti-Christian, indeed, often anti-religious ideas among the broad masses of the people.

"For the first time in the history of the West the Church experienced that a newly arising class, the working class, could no longer be incorporated into it and that it became a historical force without being moulded by the Church" (Howe, p. 42).

At the same time the Christian front was weakened by divisions within its own ranks. In addition not a few in their defence of belief in the Bible showed personal ignorance and clumsy, extreme and at times obscurantist, and therefore completely untenable apologetics.[1]

At the same time important progress in natural science was to a great extent the result of work by men who took up a negative attitude to Christianity and who strove to influence the great mass of students in universities and colleges, thereby winning the intellectual leaders of the coming generation for their views.

The result was empty churches and full lecture rooms, an apparent conquest of Christianity by modern learning, an ever increasing turning away of Europe and the New World from the Bible and belief in God.

[1] For the whole of this section see G. Howe, and Ramm, pp. 15-18. We are indebted to these two excellent books for many valuable suggestions.

To a great extent this development went far beyond the bounds of a denial of true Christianity and aimed at a universal turning from all religion.

10. MAN IN FLIGHT FROM GOD, YET HELD FAST BY THE CONCEPT OF GOD

At this point the development we have sketched encountered certain barriers erected by the human spirit and soul. In spite of all his deliberate godlessness the secularist does not become completely freed from all "religion." Even in his flight from God the godless is held fast by the concept of God. Even the atheist remains somehow—unconsciously and unwillingly—in the grip of a certain concept of God. Repeatedly the atheist speaks of "Nature" with a religious colouring, and in his language and emotional life brings about a kind of identification of "Nature" and God (in the sense of an impersonal Deity), of "fate" and the idea of God.

Thus the mechanistic picture of the universe has become for many of its adherents virtually a substitute religion. However much a belief in the other world is rejected, a religious attitude is maintained towards this world. This creates a self-contradiction in man. In his conscious he is an atheist; in his sub-conscious there exists a vague pantheism.

In his will and thought the Divine has been completely excluded; in his sentiments and feelings there is left a certain uneasiness at the possibility of the existence of a Deity, a possibility which cannot be completely refuted.

In outward propaganda and in outward, personal behaviour we often find a self-confident, even arrogant self-assurance and emphasis on "progress;" where knowledge is concerned, millions of adherents of this "religion of this world" are often appallingly bogged down in regress. An example of this is how the propaganda of atheism so often uses "scientific" arguments of the last century which have long been outdated by modern research. This also is a self-humiliation of man.

So we see that even anti-religion is "religion." Indeed, to a considerable extent unbelief lives on certain fundamental principles of faith; it not seldom uses the religious phraseology of the Bible and the Catechism, e.g. "eternal" values, "salvation," (self-) "redemption" of mankind, the "coming kingdom" of prosperity, "peace on earth." The result is a secularization of Biblical conceptions, and the technical terms of faith—for modern man's want of ability to create new expressions—are misused by the religion of this world by being applied in a completely different sense.

This leads to the philosophical thought of unbelief about life becoming increasingly foggy. "Abstract realities like art, science, state, society, associations of super-personal powers resemble patches of fog which prevent a clear view of reality. They cannot be grasped; they throw a veil over the realities of history and social life; they threaten freedom. Modern man is less than ever capable of coping with them" (Howe, p. 50). More and more man sinks into mass-humanity. The number of real individuals, who think independently and seriously remains small.

II. THOSE WHO PROCLAIM CHRISTIAN TRUTH MUST HAVE UNDERSTANDING FOR THOSE THAT SEEK AND QUESTION

We shall get nowhere, if we simply ignore these questions which have arisen in this way. In all civilized countries they are being asked by contemporary man, by young and old, in schools and colleges, factories and offices, on the wireless and in the press, in public lectures and literature; in some countries they form part of popular propaganda and politics. There is no use telling oneself and the honest seeker after God, who is often genuinely troubled by doubts, "You must not ask such questions. You must believe even when you cannot see." For the problems are there. Once science has proved that twice two is four, no one would believe the Bible, if it asserted that the answer was five! While we must bring our reason "into captivity to the obedience of Christ" (II Cor. 10: 5), it may never and under no conditions be eliminated. After all it is the Bible itself that says: "Thou shalt love the Lord thy God with all thy heart, and with all thy soul, and with all thy *mind*" (Matt. 22: 37). Despite all their battles against the wisdom of this world and philosophy (I Cor. 1: 18–31; Col. 2: 8), the Lord and His apostles never issued a charter for laziness of thought. "However much we inveigh against an evil intellectualism, however correctly we assert that the Divine mysteries are beyond our comprehension and that the misunderstood possession of a simple, believing heart is more valuable than the cold knowledge of a shrewd head, it remains true that knowledge strengthens faith. It cannot replace it; but it can give it light and greater confidence."

The slogan of the new age at its dawning was well chosen, "*Sapere aude!*" Dare to think! Have the courage to use your reason!

The German mathematician Professor Hans Rohrbach tells of the following conversation between Cardinal Faulhaber, Archbishop of Munich, and Professor Albert Einstein.

"I respect religion, but believe in mathematics;" said Einstein, "doubtless for your Eminence the reverse is true."

"You are mistaken;" replied Faulhaber, "religion and mathematics are for me only different ways of expressing the same Divine exactness."

Einstein was astonished. "But what if one day mathematical research should show that certain verdicts of science contradict those of religion?"

"I have such a high regard for mathematics," replied Faulhaber, "that in such a case you, Professor, would be under obligation never to stop looking for the error in calculation."

Professor Rohrbach goes on to say: "This answer rests upon the certainty that mathematics are not a product of the human mind, but are cleverer than man—a discovery which the mathematician and the theoretical physicist can fully endorse" (I, p. 16).

Experience shows that faith in God's Word has nothing at all to fear from serious thought. It would be useless to reject faith for the sake of natural science, or to abandon thought for the sake of faith. Faith does not need to prune the assertions of science nor does science need to bend the confessions of faith into shape. A sacrifice of one's reason (*sacrificium intellectus*) is not demanded. On the contrary, it is just the Bible which sees both together: creation and Creator, nature and revelation, the visible and the invisible, man as the king of the earth and the earth as his kingdom.

Today, however, the progress of modern research comes as a direct help to the seeking mind.

We can see this first in the historical sciences. Starting shortly before 1850 and continuing ever since, the excavations in Egypt and the Near East, combined with the deciphering of the hieroglyphics and cuneiform characters, have tremendously broadened the historical horizon of modern man. They have proved the existence of highly developed civilizations already in the ancient East and have quite simply cut away the ground from under many preconceived assumptions of earlier Biblical criticism. It had accused the Bible of numberless historical errors, but the historical statements of the Bible have repeatedly been proved correct by the excavations in the valleys of the Euphrates and Tigris and of the Nile. The Bible constantly emerges from battle and discussion as a royal victor. Here may be particularly mentioned the excavations at Nineveh, Babylon, Ur and Uruk in Mesopotamia, and the discovery of the tombs of the ancient Pharaohs near Luxor and Karnak, the discoveries at Tell-el-Amarna and the excavations in the region of the pyramids in Upper, Middle and Lower Egypt [and latterly at Ugarit, Jericho and Hazor. H.L.E.].

To these more recent results of the historical sciences there may now be added a new thinking and orientation in the physical sciences. This is true particularly in the twentieth century.

12. THE SUPERSESSION OF THE MECHANISTIC THEORIES OF THE UNIVERSE BY THE "DYNAMIC" PICTURE GIVEN BY MODERN PHYSICS, PARTICULARLY BY ATOMIC PHYSICS

After the revolution in the study of the universe in the sixteenth and seventeenth centuries by geography and astronomy and in the nineteenth century by geology and palaeontology, a third and decisive revolution has now taken place in the first half of the twentieth century. The contemporary period, from the standpoint of the development of human thought, is one of the most important eras that man has been permitted to experience.

The chief impulse has been the triumphal march—without parallel in the history of science—of modern physics, and especially of atomic

C

physics. All science has been deeply influenced by its recent discoveries.

It has become clear that the phenomena discovered by the research of the present century cannot be explained by the teachings of Plato and Aristotle and the other great thinkers of the past. Physical research found itself compelled to change its whole system of thought and to admit that reality around us is other than that taught up till now by varying philosophies and concepts of the universe (Rohrbach, III, pp. 2, 3).

The materialistic, mechanistic, nineteenth-century concept of the universe has collapsed. Earlier ideas about the nature of matter have been refuted. The so-called "modern" picture of the world, which claimed to be valid right up to our time, and which is still regarded as such by millions of the uninitiated, has been scientifically overthrown, and since it is out of date, it belongs to the past. A completely new, "dynamic" picture of the universe has come into being.

Formerly it was universally believed that the ultimate components of matter were solid, rigid, unchangeable, material particles; now it has been shown that certain rays pass through all matter, even the densest, without difficulty. It follows therefore that matter must be without solidity and porous, rather like a spider's web with a wide mesh and with single, sparsely distributed "particles," between which the still smaller particles of these other rays can freely pass.

It has also been realized that these fundamental components of matter are moving at unimaginable speeds. It has become apparent that nature is everywhere at work.

The atom was considered inactive and stationary, so far as it could be conceived by itself; it is now seen to be a world of frantic, whirling movement. It was earlier regarded as something "indivisible," impenetrable and indestructible; it is seen to be an association of electrons moving freely in space around a nucleus, a "system of connected events" (Prof. A. Titius). It continues to be called by the ancient name "atom," but it has lost its original meaning of indivisibility. It can disintegrate. The old solidity has disappeared.

It follows that the name "atom," as it is used today, is no longer a true designation. The expression "atomic fission" (fission of something indivisible) is, regarded physically, a contradiction in terms. Nevertheless this expression has become so popular that, despite its physical incorrectness, it will probably continue to be used. It preserves, however, a recollection of an error of many centuries ago. As early as the fifth century B.C. the Greek philosopher Democritus of Abdera (460–370 B.C.) had drawn up his fundamental atomic theory.

We now know matter is radiation. The universe, of which the Biblical creation-narrative speaks, is a giant field of oscillations. According to Rutherford (1911) the negatively charged electrons speed in elliptical paths around the positively charged atomic nuclei. The electron of the hydrogen atom, for instance, rotates one thousand million million times around its nucleus in a single second! Matter is something that is continually coming to pass.

This discovery was followed by closer investigation of the movements in these atomic foci of energy and electrical fields. Especially significant was the observation of atomic *disintegration* and the possibility of nuclear *fission*. It was not long before these discoveries were applied to military and peaceful ends, and so we entered into our own present time, the "atomic age."

All this has led to completely new thought about the universe. The observation of atomic disintegration and nuclear fission led of necessity to a reconsideration of the problems of beginning and end, of the temporal finiteness or infiniteness of the universe and, inevitably, of a *creation* and of the existence of a Creator. The great, cosmic problems of the origin and end of the universe, of the beginning and end of time, were seen in a completely new light. The position of man also in the universe and on the earth had to be reconsidered.[1]

At the same time the new knowledge about nature has become a testimony to the irrefutability of Biblical faith, the faith in which the high calling of man, his nobility and royal position, have their foundation. For what the unbelief of the nineteenth century, in its certainty of victory, had trumpeted abroad as the unshakeable refutation of Biblical faith has now been called in question and scientifically denied by the results of twentieth-century research.

The basic concepts of the mechanistic view of the universe were the infiniteness of the universe, the absoluteness of space and time, the invariable causality behind all natural events, determination by unchangeable natural laws, the solid nature of matter and its eternal existence. These ideas, which had become the idols of modern western man, are now seen to be mere structures of human thought, which cannot be scientifically established. Physics was permitted, after wrestling for fifty years to grasp its basic principles, to conquer the mechanistic theory of the universe, to overthrow and break to pieces its idols, to remove the foundations on which its substitute religion was built, and thus to free the way for faith once more.

Dr. A. Neuberg has well said (II, p. 7): "When we meet those who even today look down on believers in what they call an 'outdated view of the

---

[1] On a purely scientific level also a complete revolution took place. "That which had hitherto been regarded as the final and basic element, to reduce everything to which had constituted the whole sense and meaning of research, that—the atom—had now become the most questionable, the most in need of explanation of all.

"That which had hitherto been declared to be the key to the solution of all the riddles of the world, had now become the great riddle.

"The *final* point, in which all previous questioning had come to rest, had now become the *starting* point of a new and much more radical inquiry" (Heim, IV, p. 35).

world' and base themselves on the science of the eighties, we must be prepared to tell them in the minimum of words that it is they that are living in an antiquated system." Another German physicist, Professor Pascual Jordan, declares: "The new discoveries of physics deny the old picture of the universe, which on its part denied God."

Whether this double negative leads an individual to an acceptance of God will depend on his own, free, moral decision. Through scientific knowledge alone no one finds his way to God. Nevertheless it may be a help to some to know that modern science is increasingly not denying the foundations of the Biblical view of the universe.

"It is amazing," says Professor Rohrbach, "to what extent modern natural science and modern theology, two sciences which even a few decades ago were still looked on as hostile brothers, are now beginning to think or rather have already begun to think along the same lines and now hold discussions with one another, in which they increasingly discover that they both bear witness to the same truth."

13. THE COLLAPSE OF THE THINKING MAN'S WORLD OUTLOOK IN THE ATOMIC AGE

We are raising the question of the nobility and the high calling of man just at a time when the whole question of the nature of the universe, the foundations of faith and man's position in the universe is being posed anew. We are living in a period whose importance in the history of thought may be compared only with that some 300 years ago, when the giants of science, Galileo, Copernicus, Kepler and Newton created a completely new picture of the universe for Europe.

In their time the concept of a stationary earth disappeared; today, that of stationary matter. Then man discovered solar systems in the macrocosm, today, "solar systems" in the microcosm. Contemporary discoveries of movement in nature are just as tremendous and momentous as the Copernican recognition that the earth moves forward in space at an astounding speed (25 miles a second, i.e. over 600 million miles in a year in the course of one revolution around the sun).

Emotionally, too, we are in much the same position as those of 300 years ago. Atomic physics declares that matter, apparently so solid, consists in fact almost only of empty space. We are told, that if we were to pack the constituent parts of the atoms in 30 cubic feet of lead with no space between, they would take up less space than a pin-head (Titius). In the same way we could compress the earth to go inside a moderately large building (Riem).

"Our human body too is merely an electrical 'swarm of gnats' and in the main is just empty space. One could press the thousand quadrillion[1]

---

[1] i.e. 1,000,000,000,000,000,000,000,000,000.

atoms of the human body together to make—a single microscopic speck of dust" (Neuberg, II, p. 18).

So we too, seen as material bodies, are virtually nothing floating in nothing. *Within* us there is virtually only empty space, and *around* us and *beneath* us everything is a virtually completely empty world—an immeasurable, tremendous, gaping abyss.

"The shock we receive, when we recognize these facts, is like that experienced by men at the end of the Middle Ages, who were suddenly forced to realize that the earth was only a little globe, revolving about itself and the sun, suspended above nothing in empty space" (Rohrbach, III, p. 19).[1]

14. THE PROBLEM OF THE NOBILITY OF MAN RESTATED. THE BIBLE—GOD'S ANSWER TO ALL MAN'S SPIRITUAL QUESTIONS

At the beginning of this chapter we asked how one could talk of the nobility of man today. We considered it in the light of man's moral failure, then in that of astronomy, geology and palaeontology and finally in that of atomic physics. So we ask again, "How can one still today, in the atomic age, in the light of such facts, speak of 'the nobility of man'?" How shall men, these "nothings," these tiny creatures born of dust, in whom moreover almost everything is empty space, some day and somehow attain the highest honour in the universe which has been created by God, the All-Sovereign, and reach eternal nobility and kingship in all worlds and ages? Where can be the nobility of man in his position midway between the stars and the atoms?

For all that, the Bible says: "Know ye not that the saints shall judge the world?" (I Cor. 6: 2), "They shall reign for ever and ever" (Rev. 22: 5), "Fear not, little flock, for it is your Father's good pleasure to give you the kingdom" (Luke 12: 32).

We shall approach our problem from three view-points:

We shall investigate it as men of the *twentieth* century, whose whole surroundings cannot any longer be separated from the intellectual and philosophical development of the West, which we have briefly sketched; in other words as *modern* men.

We shall investigate it at the same time as did the men of the *first* Christian centuries, who, just as the Apostolic Church, believed in the

---

[1] Twentieth-century physics is, however, judged by its starting point, going the opposite way to that of the sixteenth and seventeenth centuries. The latter began with the macrocosm (Copernicus, Newton); the former has been built up from the microcosm. The older astro-physics dealt in millions of "light years" (one light year is about six million million miles). The measurements of modern atomic physics are unimaginably small. In a single speck of dust there are more atoms than the population of the whole earth, that is, over two thousand five hundred million. A hydrogen atom has a very small mass. Thanks to the experimental accuracy of modern physics it can be exactly stated. It amounts to 26.4×10^{24} grams.

revelation of the Old and New Testaments, which God had begun to give thousands of years earlier; in other words, as men of the *Bible*.

And we shall investigate it as men who treasure God's Word *above* all human discovery, as those for whom the eternal and unchangeable is more important than all man's temporal and changing science and philosophy.

Thus present and past, today and antiquity, natural science and faith in revelation are all combined in our inquiry.

But the decisive factor will continually be God's Word. In its indestructibility, its eternity and its living power it is God's message equally suited for every era. God's Word is always contemporary, and He keeps His promises, however "old" or "young" they may be. Therefore the high calling of man, rooted in this Divine revelation, can neither be destroyed by the most revolutionary discoveries nor by the crises and catastrophes of today. God is carrying out His royal plan with man as the king of the earth. "The gifts and the calling of God are irrevocable" (Rom. 11: 29).

It is our duty to make all this the subject of serious reflection. Pythagoras, the ancient Greek mathematician and philosopher, rightly said, "Perception of the truth begins with silence," that is, with quiet, inward surrender to it. Truth lives in the depths, for God lives in the depths. He stands behind all things. Therefore only he will attain the knowledge of Divine truth who seriously and honestly immerses himself in it.

CHAPTER II

GOD'S GLORY IN NATURE

IN the beginning was God. He is the Originator and Lord of all creation. He is King and Sovereign over the universe. All glory and all true values have their origin in Him. Only where God is, is there true greatness. Only in Him does man attain to true dignity and real nobility.

But creation as a whole is also an expression of the glory of the great King. It is God's will to let His life and love shine out into it as well. Therefore *everything* is to be ennobled: heaven and earth, spirit and nature, man and his kingdom.

God is the source of all authority. He alone has full freedom and absolute dominion. In His freedom and sovereignty He has put everything in relation to Himself, the All-Highest.

The true value of all creation lies in its relationship to the Lord of the universe. This value becomes a reality wherever the individual creature participates in the life and the power of God. The character and extent of this participation is determined by the position assigned to the individual by the Creator within the framework of the whole.

It follows that above all the high calling of man has its origin alone in God. All nobility of man is derived from the free, sovereign will of the Lord of the world.

In God both have their common source: spirit and nature, man and the universe, the earthly king and his earthly kingdom. Therefore the high calling of man must be considered in its connexion with God's great plan of creation and redemption, the product of His sovereign will.

I. GOD—THE INFINITE, THE ABSOLUTELY INDEPENDENT CREATOR, THE KING OF THE UNIVERSE

God is the Absolute, unconditioned by anything outside Himself. He is purely self-determined, and all His acts have their origin in Him alone. In other words, He is completely independent and free. Constrained activity would be an act proceeding, at least in part, from another independent, external cause. But God is determined in His actions by no one else.

The creating of a universe is therefore not necessary for the perfection of the Divine being. For God's perfection and blessedness do not depend upon the existence of a universe. God exists for His own sake and needs nothing else in order to be true God. He has always reached His purpose in Himself and is the completely Self-sufficient and therefore absolutely Blessed One. All that He does He does "for *His* Name's sake" (Psa. 23: 3; Col. 1: 18b; I Cor. 15: 28).

Freedom from external constraint is however not the same as freedom from internal compulsion. Otherwise it would be the same as arbitrariness. This, however, may never be said of God (cf. I Cor. 14: 33). Though He is free, He is absolutely determined by His own nature. Therefore the creation is a *free* product of the Divine will and has God Himself as its goal.

Nevertheless there must have been inner motives in God's nature, which caused Him to undertake this creative activity. These motives, however, are not revealed to us. "The secret things belong unto the Lord our God" (Deut. 29: 29). God remains, despite all His revelation, the Unfathomable. With all His condescension to His creatures He does not forsake His unique eminence as Creator. He remains eternally *above* us, and therefore we shall eternally stand before Divine mysteries. Only lack of reason and weak thinking can reject faith in God simply because it includes mysteries.

After all can we explain the most fundamental experiences of earthly life? Do we know what life and death are? Can we explain what electricity, gravity and mass are? Are these in any way "unreal" because they are inexplicable and hence mysterious?

The well-known natural scientist Professor Dubois-Raymond wrote: "Before the question of what is matter, we stand as helpless as the first ancient Greek, Ionic philosophers (*c.* 500 B.C.). Since the time of Epicurus (*c.* 300 B.C.), who already knew of the conservation of matter and energy, we have made no progress in understanding the nature of spirit."

In the same way, faith also knows that it cannot explain the Ultimate. It bows, however, before the Infinite, conscious of the limitations of the finite; in its humility it is truest to its nature. Humility is here honesty, modesty is a sense of reality. All mere desire to know more is a foolish overestimate and ignorance of oneself, a thoughtlessness out of touch with reality. Faith knows, "I am the Father's child and not His privy counsellor" (Tersteegen). Therefore we stand in silence before the Infinite and worship Him, who once uttered the great "Let there be." "He spake, and it was done; He commanded, and it stood fast" (Psa. 33: 9).

If, however, the world is exclusively God's work, then it is also His exclusive possession, and He has the right to dispose of it as He wills. From God's glory as Creator we deduce His kingship. He is the creative origin and kingly goal of all creation.

But wherever God's will makes itself known, there is also a revelation of His Divine nature. This is at once evident in the works of His creation. "The invisible things of Him since the creation of the world are clearly seen, being perceived through the things that are made, even His everlasting power and divinity" (Rom. 1: 20).

II. The Self-revelation of the great King in the Works of His Created Kingdom

Once the universe had been created by God it had to be, since it was His work, in harmony with His nature. The existence of a universe developing in space and time is, so far as its origin and meaning are concerned, a revelation of the innermost nature of God, with its holiness and love.

The world then, being an effluence of the Divine will, must be a concrete expression of the thoughts of the Creator. The spiritual laws of Eternal Being must be reflected in the natural world. Between the infinite and the finite, the ideal and the real, there must exist such a basic parallelism that the visible becomes the clothing of the invisible, a symbolizing, graspable by the senses, of the transcendental. This is a fact underlying all symbolism, both in Divine revelation and human thought.

That is "natural revelation" in its widest sense. By virtue of it, all created forms of life become concrete expressions of definite thoughts of God, and the universe becomes a universal "reflection of the majesty of the Eternal in earthly matter" (cf. Rom. 1: 19, 20). Within this mighty cosmic framework man should become conscious of human nobility. To experience God Himself in holiness and love and to radiate His nature in power and majesty is therefore the content of our human vocation, the goal and crown of our nobility as man.

The creation has as its purpose the revelation of the Divine glory in the entire life-process of the universe. This everywhere reaches its goal as it brings forth and perfects spiritual life in the likeness of God. On earth this must be achieved in man, God's image, God's representative and the God-appointed ruler of His creatures.

How wonderfully this world has been made by God! In its construction, involving millions upon millions of suns and solar systems, He has used only *two* basic kinds of building-material—electrons and the atomic nuclei which, in turn, consist of protons and neutrons. And He has so related them to one another, that the electrons revolve around their nuclear "suns" in circular or elliptical paths, just as do the planets in the solar systems.

How inconceivably small these atoms are! The diameter of a hydrogen atom measures only one hundred-millionth part of a millimetre! On the top of a drawing-pin there is room for so many atoms that if they were carried by an army, marching four abreast, an atom to a man, it would need over twenty thousand years for a march-past (Neuberg, II, p. 14).

All is movement in free space—tremendously fast, whirling movement, a mighty, vast field of vibration. We have solar systems in the world of the stars but also "solar systems" in the world of the atom! The same, uniform principle rules the whole universe, the principle of circling movement both in the microcosm and the macrocosm.

One of the greatest wonders of creation is that it is so harmonious in its structure, that the great Master-Builder has applied the same principle in the whole universe. "This principle is heard in countless variations through the whole universe like the leading theme in a symphony." This amazing, systematic construction of the universe is thus a testimony to the greatness of the Creator as an omnipotent, universal Builder.

The universe is held together by tremendous forces. The formula for energy put forward by Albert Einstein[1] shows us that *one* gram[2] of any substance, if completely reduced to energy, would do the work of 25,000,000,000 kilowatt hours.[3]

The German physicist Otto Gail, writes (p. 101, also p. 88): "If we succeeded in changing matter completely into energy, i.e. not merely in splitting the atomic nucleus, but in completely dissolving and dematerializing it, then a single gram of fuel in a motor-car would suffice for 400 journeys around the world. That would be a total distance of ten million miles, more than twenty times the distance from the earth to the moon and back."[4] He uses also another comparison: "Two hundred truck-loads of coal have the same calorific value as one gram of dematerialized matter. What an abundance of energy is hidden in every gram of matter, in every fragment of stone, in every piece of wood! We cannot utilize these riches, but they are everywhere around us, in the earth, in the water, in the air."[5]

In all this we can only admire the power of the great Creator. The inquiring mind which looks into the depths of God's workshop is led by these incomprehensible energies to the source of the universe, the Almighty Himself. It is just the smallest things that point us to the Greatest of all. Thoughtful consideration of nature leads a believing mind to adoration and worship of God.

Professor B. Bavink, a contemporary scientist, is fully justified in saying, "Modern physics achieves today what astronomy has always done; it fills the mind with ever renewed awe. It gives to him who has become

[1] The energy value (or energy equivalent) of a mass is equal to the product of the mass and the square of the speed of light, i.e. $E = mc^2$.

[2] 28 grams = 1 ounce.

[3] i.e. the work of about sixty-five million foot-pounds. One foot-pound is the work required to raise one pound through one foot.

[4] The mean distance of the moon from the earth is approximately 240,500 miles.

[5] Some idea of this energy, in fact a terrifying demonstration of its power, has been given our generation through the atomic bomb. "The energies of disintegrating atoms over the Japanese city of Hiroshima on August 6, 1945 produced a pressure and heat wave which within seconds destroyed everything which came within its range—houses, plants, animals and men; over 230,000 were killed. At the centre of the explosion, which took place 2,300 feet above the city, the temperature rose to ten million degrees Centigrade. The effects of the bomb, which contained only a few pounds of active atoms, were equivalent to the explosive force of 20,000 tons of dynamite." The hydrogen bombs, developed since then, have an explosive power a hundred times greater than this first bomb at Hiroshima!

absorbed in it a completely immediate and magnificent, but in no way forced or artificial impression of the glory of God in creation."

To these wonders in the physical realm we must add the innumerable wonders in the realm of plant, animal and human life, in the secrets of mental life, the riddle of memory, the mystery of human personality with its thought and will, its longings and ideals, its moral aptitudes and its strivings after the infinite and eternal.

Thus everything unites in a grand, sublime testimony—the world around us and in us, giant stars and atoms, the animate and the inanimate, matter, soul and spirit. The book of nature joins the book of the written Word of God in its song of praise: "The heavens declare the glory of God and the firmament showeth His handywork!" "Lord, how manifold are Thy works! In wisdom hast Thou made them all: the earth is full of Thy riches . . . Let the glory of the Lord endure for ever; let the Lord rejoice in His works . . . I will sing unto the Lord as long as I live: I will sing praise to my God while I have any being!" (Psa. 19: 1; 104: 24, 31, 33).

III. THE BIBLE AND NATURE IN THE HARMONY OF THEIR REVELATIONS

One of the outstanding Christian leaders in the third century, widely known for his wisdom, was once asked—so we are told in old records—whence he had derived his wisdom. He said, "The source of all I have learnt is in two books. The one is outwardly small, the other is very large. The former has many pages, the latter only two. The pages of the former are white, with many black letters on them. One of the pages of the big book is blue and the other green. On the blue page there is one big golden letter and many small silver ones. On the green page there are innumerable coloured letters in red, white, yellow, blue and gold. The small book is the Bible; the large one is the book of nature.

"The book of the Bible has many pages with many inspired texts. The book of nature is heaven and earth. Its blue page with its one big golden letter and the many small silver letters is the dome of the heavens, with the sun by day, and the moon and the stars by night. Its green page is nature as we know it on earth with its living garment of green, its countless coloured flowers and blooms in mountain and valley, in field and wood."

These two books belong together. Both testify to the revelation of the one, living God; their testimonies are in harmony and point to the power, greatness and love of the Lord of the world.

In spite of this, nature does not reveal God straight away. It unveils and veils God at the same time. It is a veil, even though a transparent one. "All things hide a mystery. They challenge us to unveil this mystery. The final mystery is God."

Only he who seeks God will find Him. Those who do not want to know anything of God will not find Him in nature either. For them nature becomes only an occasion for doubt. Or, as Pascal, the great French mathematician, expressed it, "Just as all things speak of God to those who know Him and unveil Him to those who love Him, even so they hide Him from all those who neither seek Him nor know Him." To all those who strive after Him He will reveal Himself. "Ye shall seek Me and find Me, when ye shall search for Me with all your heart" (Jer. 29: 13).

Over and over again leading scientists have testified to their belief in God. W. Herschel, the astronomer, the "Columbus of the world of fixed stars," as he was called because he had discovered so many stars,[1] once said, "The broader the field of science grows, the more manifold and irrefutable become the proofs for the eternal existence of a creative and omnipotent Wisdom. Nothing can be more unfounded than the reproach made by well-meaning but narrow-minded people, that the study of science leads to doubt in the immortality of the soul and in revealed religion."

"No true scientist can be an atheist. Whoever has looked as deeply into God's workshop as we have, and has had as much opportunity to admire His omniscience and eternal ordering of nature, must bow the knee in humility before the rule of the holy God," said von Madler, Professor of Astronomy in Dorpat (died 1874). "I pray during my work in the laboratory," testified Pasteur, Professor of Chemistry at Strasbourg and Paris. Linnaeus, Professor of Medicine and Botany at Uppsala, said triumphantly, "I have seen the footsteps of God," and John Kepler, the greatest astronomer of the period that followed Copernicus, said, "In creation I grasp God, as it were, with my hands."

"Both ways to knowledge, scientific research and Biblical revelation, correspond to one another and belong together; only when taken together do they open up the whole of reality around us" (Rohrbach, II, p. 16).

Similarly the Nobel prize winner, Professor Max Planck, said in a lecture held in Osnabrück in 1942, "Religion and science are not mutually exclusive. The difference between them lies only in the paths which their adherents follow. If the believer follows a path which leads *from* God, whom he needs in all his activity and work, the scientist, when all is said and done, follows a path which leads finally *to* God as the perfection and crown of all natural law."

Sir James Young Simpson, who by his discovery of chloroform became one of the greatest benefactors of mankind, has been described by Professor Rendle Short as "a Christian of the most enthusiastic and Evangelical type." He goes on to say of him, "He knew his Bible from cover

---

[1] Herschel was the builder of giant telescopes, the discoverer of the moons of Saturn and Uranus, and in addition of 700 double stars and nearly 1,900 nebulae and star-clusters (died 1822).

to cover, and one of his last utterances was, 'I have unshaken confidence in Jesus only'."[1]

There is something wonderfully liberating about all this. No blind chance stands at the beginning of the evolution of the universe. No heartless play of overwhelming natural powers, no arbitrary despotism of uncontrollable forces governs the cosmos, but eternal conformity to the laws of holy love. At the beginning stands God. He is *above* and *in* the world. He is Creator, Sustainer, Ruler and Perfecter. Never since He finished His creative work has He severed His connexion with His creation. The whole world lives in God. "In Him we live and move and have our being" (Acts 17: 28). "The sun would not long remain in the heavens giving light, no child would be born, no ear of corn, blade of grass or anything else would grow on earth or renew itself, were not God continually at work" (Luther).

Only so can nature be a glorious cosmos, the universe an ordered system. The Divine work shows the Divine Master-worker. Only on this basis can we triumphantly welcome life. Were it otherwise the world, despite all its apparent conformity to law, would be only chaos. Therefore only on the basis of a living faith in God can there be a true optimism.

Here we see clearly the superiority of Biblical thought. The Christian philosophy of life does not fear comparison with any other view of things! It is far superior to all the solutions of the riddle of the world, which do not take God into account. It is not speculation but reality, not imagination but wisdom, not a deception but the truth, and therefore it does not paralyse but liberates, it does not humiliate but exalts, it does not degrade but ennobles.

IV. THE GREAT SYMPHONY OF CREATION

It is in this way that in creation God has harmoniously revealed the concepts of being and living which exist in His eternal power and divinity. Everything in heaven and on earth consists of an organically related variety of pure, created images of the eternal originals within God Himself. Since God, however, never created anything that is a contradiction of His own nature, everything which proceeds immediately from His hand must be also something already eternally willed and conceived by Him. Therefore it must also later, once it has begun its existence in space, bear the characteristic mark of His holy existence in light. Since God knows reality before it is created, there are present to Him timelessly as many ideal forms and ideas as there will be finally created realities.

Professor Rendle Short says very beautifully: "We see Him active, not six thousand years ago merely, but thousands of millions of years ago. His hand stretches out to stars so distant that our arithmetic cannot find figures

[1] *Modern Discovery and the Bible* (Third Edition), p. 18. Simpson was Professor of Medicine in Edinburgh; died in 1878.

for them. The imagination staggers both at the vastness and the minuteness of His work. The beauty and the infinite variety of nature show Him to us as the superlative Artist and Craftsman. 'O Lord my God, Thou art very great. Thou art clothed with honour and majesty.'" (II, p. 83).

Thus all creation radiates in its *own* fulness of life and yet at the same time living and moving in *Him* (Acts 17: 28), His uncreated glory. In a harmonious rhythm of degrees and ranks, in an organic unity of aeons and spheres, the whole cosmos is a great symphony of indescribable beauty and eternal harmony. A mighty organism of the most *differing* worlds bound together in all its parts by the *same* creative concept, the whole universe is a ceaseless song of praise, a psalm of creation displaying millions of variations, yet bound together by the same basic theme. "For of Him and through Him and unto Him are all things. To Him be the glory for ever. Amen" (Rom. 11: 36).

This is then the great cosmic setting in which the high calling of man must find its realization.

CHAPTER III

MAN THE CROWN OF CREATION

"Ιν the beginning God created the heaven and the earth." As if cast in
bronze these words stand there defying all atheism, pantheism and
materialism, whether originating from heathen or modern philosophical speculation. Even the liberal theologian Hermann Gunkel found
himself compelled to acknowledge, "There is no statement in the cosmological teaching of other peoples which equals this first sentence of the
Bible." In the beginning was not chaos; in the beginning was God. Spirit
has precedence over matter. This is the first thought contained in this
wonderful Biblical account, about which the German poet Jean Paul once
said, "The first page of the Mosaic document has more weight than all the
folios of scientists and philosophers." When we compare this prophetic
account of creation in its backward look with the conceptions of the
heathen, we find blowing through it "the morning breeze of a new
outlook on the world which with its fresh breath scatters the shadows of
the night like the morning mist."

God called the world into being out of nothing. The present creation
was not to arise out of something open to sense-perception (Heb. 11: 3).
He, God Himself, is the beginning and as such is the absolute ruler over
matter. Everything is His, and everything coheres through Him (Heb.
1: 3; Col. 1: 17; Jn. 1: 3).

After the first verse follows the narrative of the six days' work, through
which God brought a wonderful world into being out of the *tohu-wa-bohu*,
the "without form and void."

I. THE SPIRITUAL MESSAGE OF THE BIBLICAL CREATION-NARRATIVE

The real interest in the creation-narrative is throughout religious. Its
purpose is less to give a scientific doctrine of the origin of the world, as
the heathen religions tried to do, than to reveal certain great, Divine
principles of creation and rule.

God is the *Creator*. He created the world out of nothing. It follows that
the world is His work and as such belongs to Him and He has the right
to dispose of it as He wills (Acts 17: 24, 25). But since the world is His
creation, He alone, to the exclusion of every thing and person, is to be
worshipped, for everything derives its existence exclusively from Him.
The fact that the world was created out of nothing, excludes all heathen

deification of nature, and so at once, with its very first sentence, the Old Testament rises incomparably, indeed infinitely, above all the religions of its heathen environment, however much or little its cultures and civilizations may have been developed.

Contemporary scientific investigation has also reached the concept of a possible beginning of the universe. The conception of a creation out of nothing cannot, however, be reached by purely scientific methods alone. Only faith can do this. "By faith we understand that the world was created by the word of God, so that what is seen was made out of things which do not appear" (Heb. 11: 3 RSV.). Nevertheless faith is capable of fully appreciating the testimony of nature.

Modern scientific thought is also opposed to the atheistic materialistic assertion that the universe and matter have neither beginning nor end. The establishment of the fact of atomic disintegration and of radio-activity leads of necessity to the idea of a beginning of the universe.[1] Thus from the scientific point of view the first words of the Bible are inviolable; "In the beginning God created the heaven and the earth."

God is *Lord of the universe*. He is subject to no restrictions. He is God of the universe, not only God of a nation. He called everything into existence, both in heaven and on earth. Thus right at the beginning of Holy Scripture the Biblical creation-narrative denies the very conception of national gods. God is like the sun, which gives light to the whole earth; just as there is no extra sun for Babylonia, Assyria, Egypt or Persia, so there can be no extra god for each single nation. No, if there is a God—and the Bible, nature and personal experience are witnesses to His living, undeniable existence—then He must be the God of His *whole* creation, the God of *all* men, the Ruler of the universe, the "God of heaven and earth."

God is *Ruler*. He rules over matter. He forms and shapes and moulds it into a well-ordered whole. He is therefore the Lord of all development, the God of history. Just as in the creation He formed order out of chaos,

---

[1] "A material is radio-active if it gives off small atomic particles which fly away from the active substance at great velocity. Radium and uranium are the most commonly known of such substances. The atomic bomb has made the public very conscious of radio-active phenomena. As uranium gives off high-speed particles it disintegrates till eventually it becomes lead. The speed of this process of disintegration is known and is the same no matter what temperatures or pressures the substance is subjected to. Hence . . . (by the degree of this disintegration) physicists can tell how old a uranium sample is and therefore get some idea of the age of the strata in which it was found" (B. Ramm, *The Christian View of Science and Scripture*, pp. 122, 123).

By further measuring, reasoning and calculation we reach the idea of an original beginning of all existence, earthly and cosmic. Whether this original beginning took place three or four billions of years ago, as some physicists think, or whether these figures should be markedly smaller or even greater, is of no essential importance in this present setting. What matters here is that modern research postulates the idea of an original beginning of the universe, so that nature is not eternal but temporal, and must have had a definite beginning at some definite point of time.

so too, as the history of the world unfolded, He is the God of all progress, the God of revelation, who lets His salvation unfold in natural growth, the God of the history of redemption, who brings it to its goal.

God is *Judge*. He judges His own work. When we read seven times in the creation-narrative that "God saw that it was good," these words of approval appeal at the same time to our conscience and solemnly ask us whether it can be said of our work, "God saw that it was good."

God creates everything through His *Word*. "He spake, and it was done" (Psa. 33: 9). This demonstrates the ease of His activity, the omnipotence of His power. Ten times we read, "And God said." His word is no empty sound. His word is creative energy. "In the king's word there is power."

God is the *God of growth*. He creates through evolution. From the lower we pass to the higher, from the elements to individual entities, from dead matter to the living king of the earth. But the goal is perfection. The whole ends with the Sabbath, with God's rest and God's joy, with the celebration of the finished work. "And God looked on all that He had made, and behold, it was very good."

God is especially the *God of mankind*. The whole creation-narrative is "anthropocentric," that is, it places man in the centre of the whole and makes him unmistakably appear as the goal of the entire creative activity of God, as the head and crown of all visible, created beings. Even Nietzsche said, "Man is the reason for the world." He is the keystone and the goal of creation. Thus the very first page of the Bible is a reference to the dignity of the human race, a testimony to our calling to man's nobility.

II. MAN AS THE GOAL OF THE SIX DAYS' WORK

Conservative expositors of the Biblical account of creation do not completely agree on all questions of interpretation. The basic question is differently answered, i.e. whether the first chapter of Genesis records the one, universal, original creation, or whether it describes a restoration of the earth after its destruction following on the fall of Satan, so that God then raised the earth anew out of its *tohu-wa-bohu* condition ("without form and void") to a state of beauty and harmony.[1] Almost as basic is whether the six "days" were literal 24-hour days—perhaps "days of revelation"—or longer periods or, very generally, "days of God," which bear no comparison with chronological, earthly measures of time, neither with days of 24 hours nor with longer periods. Here too there is no agreement.

It is not the task of this chapter to discuss these varying interpretations. They are discussed in Part V, especially in chs. 14, 16, 17. But it is important for us to note the following. All conservative exposition agrees that the Scriptural account of creation emphasizes that man is the goal and crown of the creation process. Here there are no differences amongst the expositors of the creation-narrative.

[1] For an account of this view see ch. 17.

D

Modern science also comes, quite independently of all Biblical considerations, to the same basic conclusion. From the point of view of geology, man is the *final* link in the chain of creation.[1]

The South African palaeontologist R. Broom wrote, "There is no doubt that evolution, as far as new groups are concerned, is at an end. No further biological progress is now possible except in man. That drives us to the conclusion that the aim has been the production of human personalities, that there was no need for further evolution after man appeared, and that the evolution of man must have been deliberately planned by some spiritual power."[2]

Here is a geological attestation that man is the crown of the earthly creation, and that, in consequence, it is fully justifiable from the scientific point of view to speak of a nobility of man. Man is the summit and conclusion, the creaturely centre and peak of the development of all life upon the earth.

Baron von Huene, Professor of Palaeontology in the University of Tübingen, has rightly said, "Earthly development has reached its summit and its goal in man; here in man the imperishable and spiritual is able to link on. Both spheres meet in man."

Thus the whole plan of creation has a kingdom as its goal. The course of evolution is not characterized by a principle of equalitarian levelling, but everything has as its purpose that a definite creature, chosen for the purpose, should have rule over the earth. This creature is man; and so he forms the triumphant crown of the richly articulated tree of life of the organic, earthly world.

One can follow Karl Heim and compare the creation-narrative with the building of a pyramid, in which each layer supports the next erected upon it. "At the summit of the pyramid man appears. The whole creation builds the gate for its king to enter by. It erects the throne which man finally occupies. Thus all creatures work together to make the existence of this unique being possible, in whom the creation of the earth finds its completion" (II, pp. 46, 47).

The writer of the Biblical record of creation is fully conscious of the grandeur of his theme. The concise brevity of his presention shows this. There is not a word too many. Everything is clear and definite, sober and simple. Nothing is artificial or affected. And it is just in this sublime simplicity that the solemn dignity shows itself. It is just in this objective brevity that the highest poetry lies.

Thus the chief and essential interest of the creation-narrative is a spiritual one. Its real concern is not to give a report about cosmogony but rather a manifestation of revealed truths, not to give a *history* of creation but to testify to its *meaning*. This must never be forgotten in our scientific study.

[1] For a brief synopsis see ch. 15.
[2] *The Coming of Man* (1933), pp. 218, 221.

It is necessary to look at both together and to see the harmony of both Divine revelations, the book of nature and the book of the written word. In this way we shall come to recognize God as Lord of all, as Creator and Redeemer, as the God of nature and the God of the revelation of salvation, as the God of the universe and the God of man.

The botanist Philipp von Martius, who conducted a well-known correspondence with Goethe, had his shroud made during his life-time and had a green cross sown on it. He said that the cross was because he was a Christian, and green was to the honour of botany.

Dr. Arthur Neuberg wrote, "I consider that one of the things for which our Bible should be specially praised is that it begins with such a glorious chapter; it is just from the scientific point of view that I feel this" (I).

All this makes the Biblical creation-narrative a kind of confession of faith. It exalts the majesty of God in our eyes and frees us from the danger of limiting our conception of Him by the range of our own, small, personal experience. It makes us tremble before the mighty greatness of the Creator and makes our heart shout with joy that He, this infinitely great Lord of the universe, has yet become our heavenly Father in Christ.

CHAPTER IV

WITHOUT FREEDOM OF WILL—NO NOBILITY OF MAN

IN spite of all written in the last two chapters this glorious world, which the eternal Creator made in such beauty and harmony, impresses us as it is today as a battlefield. A mighty struggle between opposing powers fills the history of the universe. It is the gigantic battle between good and evil, light and darkness, Satan and God! And man, destined for kingship and nobility, has become a combatant. How often has the king become a servant! Instead of mastery there is slavery, instead of kingship the service of sin, instead of nobility, dishonour.

How is this possible? How could God possibly tolerate such a situation in the universe? Why did He not prevent the appearance of evil from the first? At least so far as our earth and mankind are concerned, is not to permit imperfection and evil in the world automatically to prevent, indeed to destroy true, practical human nobility?

Is not the presence of sin a crying contradiction of the very idea and existence of a living God?—of His *omnipotence*, which surely could have prevented its origin and continuation; of His *love*, which could never have willed all the sorrow that sin has brought; and of His *omniscience*, which must have foreknown in eternity that many of His potentially free creatures would take the way of apostasy and destruction? Was not the only possible way to refrain from the first from creating such beings? But why has God nevertheless given man, created pure and good as he was, the possibility of sinning? Does it not mean that, even if He did not will the actual existence of sin, He did quite clearly will its possibility?

We agree, and we do not hesitate to say clearly, that though God has not *willed* sin, He has *not* denied its possibility and permission. Indeed the very fact that He allowed it to happen and did not prevent it shows that He willed its permission.

But do we not in saying this stand before the abyss of atheism? Does not the very idea of God simply disappear?

For many this problem has been a stumbling-block. Some even find here the rock on which the whole message of the Bible is shattered; after all the fall of man is one of the hinges on which the whole Christian history of redemption turns. Others again have in faith acknowledged that the reason why the fall of man was permitted lies in God's own nature and all-wise decree, but they have regarded it as inscrutable. Let it suffice that the wise and almighty God of love has considered this to be good; man should not inquire at all about the inner reasons.[1]

But this willingness to leave the problem unanswered has not satisfied all, and there have, therefore, been attempts, in spite of the difficulties involved, to solve the problem. We consider this justified, so long as the thinker refrains from vain human philosophy (Col. 2: 8; I Cor. 1: 19, 20) and brings every thought into obedience to Christ (II Cor. 10: 4, 5). Reflection, if redeemed by Christ and tied to the Scriptures, is not philosophy. Indeed we believe that such reflection, starting from the presuppositions of revelation, and always checking its inferences by Scripture as a whole, can lead us to the heart of the question. If we then find that this lies in God Himself, so that everything finite is lost in the infinite, then of course we must humbly confess that God, who must remain a mystery, is always incomprehensible for the limited understanding of the creature; but at least we shall have gained the knowledge that the permission of sin, in no way, considered intellectually, contradicts the idea of God.

One thing must, however, be stated clearly before we begin our study of the problem. *The origin of sin itself is utterly inexplicable;* we cannot explain how, unprovoked by any temptation from without, evil thoughts and evil deeds could take their rise in a being created pure and good (cf. Rom. 11: 34; Job 8: 9; 38: 4). Therefore, if we now attempt to probe deeper into these problems, we can only concern ourselves with the reasons for the Divine *permission* of sin.

The question divides into three parts: What is the relation of the permission of sin to God's omnipotence, to God's love, and to God's holiness?

I. GOD'S PERMISSION OF SIN AND HIS OMNIPOTENCE

It must be emphatically emphasized that to speak of God's omnipotence does not imply that He does everything that lies in His power; the term is not inconsistent with God's voluntary self-limitation. Erroneously to equate God's omnipotence with His actually *doing* everything would lead to pantheism, i.e. to the doctrine that God and the universe are one. Then, of course, there would be no possibility of a free will apart from God; rather the whole of reality, including "evil," would be the logical outcome of an unconditioned development within God Himself, which would come under the law of absolute necessity.

If we are true to Scripture, however, we must teach that God *can* indeed do everything, but He does not *will* everything and therefore does not *do* everything. He wills only that which accords with His own nature. The only law that governs Him is His Self. Outwardly He is absolutely free; but inwardly His freedom is at the same time of necessity limited by His

---

[1] e.g. Luther and the older Reformed theologians. "*Hoc tam excelsum, ut nihil responderi possit, nisi quia placet Deo.*" (This is so high that no other answer can be given than, that so it has pleased God.—Luther).

own nature. If then He granted to angels and men the possibility of sinning, i.e. moral free will, and thereby subjected Himself to a voluntary self-limitation, this can under no circumstances contradict His omnipotence. Obviously this raises the question of the Divine, inward *reason* for His self-limitation. By the nature of things such a question can be answered only from the inner nature of the Divine existence, which is holy love, and so we are automatically led to the second part of our discussion.

II. GOD'S PERMISSION OF SIN AND HIS LOVE

First it is to be noted that God desired in His moral creatures servants, not such as were under compulsion to do nothing but "good," since they could not do otherwise, but such as would honour Him of their own free will, though they could act otherwise. His kingdom is no realm of endless slavery; His rule is no compulsory servitude, but the highest harmony of spiritually related souls. But where there is no freedom everything is slavery, even all the apparently "good." Only on a foundation of freedom can there be true dignity and nobility of man. That is why God wanted to crown the ranks of His creatures with a being capable of becoming conscious of the difference between good and evil and of choosing the good. In so doing He wished to show man the highest form of kindness. He wished to render the supreme victory possible to him, to grant him the noblest joy, to adorn him with the most glorious crown.

This can hardly be challenged; and from this angle we can see a certain harmony between the love of God and the permission of sin, for the latter presents itself as the necessary way to the supreme blessing and ennobling of the moral creation. The doubter, however, is apt to ask, whether, even granting that the endowment of angels and men with free will could lift them to an exceptional condition of blessing, it would not have been more consistent with *perfect* love to have left them with a less exalted blessing rather than to have given them such a perilous possibility of ascent, which, as God knew from the first, would only too soon cast them down into misery and destruction. Or for that matter would not God's love have been still greater and more perfect, if from the first He had created angels and men as He had planned them to be at the final perfecting of all things?

Such questions are in so far justified as they force us to realize that our problem can only be solved (in the measure possible for the human mind), if the possibility and permission of sin are seen as an *essential and necessary element* of holiness and love.

Love is the will to fellowship, "a life striving after union."[1] Its full development can be reached, therefore, only in mutual life and experience. Its nature is whole-hearted partaking and imparting. Its goal is perfect

[1] Augustine: *Vita quaedam copulans vel copulare appetens.*

interchange through giving and receiving. In its full and ideal sense it can be predicated only of a conscious, personal being; for since it is a volition, it presupposes a conscious will. The *personality* both of the lover and of the beloved is thus the foundation of all love's intercourse. Only a "self" can love; the truer and richer this self the fuller is the blessing imparted to the loved one by his life and love. Therefore the unimpaired preservation of personality is both foundation and limitation of all true intercourse of love.

Further, love is not only the will to fellowship, but also its highest living form. This can be found in perfection, inwardly and all-pervading, only between cognate beings. Therefore *spiritual relationship* is the second condition for all true communion in love. This relationship must, moreover, not merely exist, but must be seen and recognized by both sides. Thus *respect* enters as a further essential requirement. But this automatically includes preserving the other's integrity. "However much love imparts itself, it must never impair the freedom of the other nor suspend his independence. His nature may not be forced to take into itself any foreign element, nor may his individuality be suppressed" (Prof. Schoeberlein). This means that love, as a bond uniting personalities whose basic nature is individuality, must be a bond of *freedom*. When we apply this to the relationship between the Creator and His creation, it leads directly to the answer to our question.

All intercourse of love, by its very nature, involves completely free fellowship on both sides. In the relationship, therefore, between God and His moral creation, it would cease to exist in any ideal and true sense the moment one of the two parties, i.e. the creature, no longer had freedom of will. For if that were to happen, he would lose his spiritual relationship with God and, therefore, his capacity for true responsive love. We could no longer talk of a real *intercourse* in love.

If in spite of this this relationship is to exist—and we know that the necessity for it is based on God's own nature—then we must take creaturely freedom of will absolutely seriously. Not until there is freedom of will does the creature possess the ability for spiritual relationship with God. If this ability is to have reality, existence and full development, the creature must also be *positively good*, i.e. he must choose the good for himself. Only through the holiness of the creature does the potential spiritual relationship with God, made possible by freedom of the will, become a reality. This involves the necessity, that an opportunity of exercising this freedom to decide for the good be granted him. Thus we have shown the *unavoidability of some form of temptation in God's world-plan*.

Since God is love, He must protect the independent individuality of the creaturely objects of His love, *viz.* of men, in order to promote a true relationship of love. The creature also, to create a mutual and active relationship of love, must love God, i.e. be able to will freely while loving. Thus the free will of the moral creation is an essential and necessary element in this requisite fellowship of love. From this it follows as a Christian doctrine that, precisely *because* God is love, and a fellowship of love is the necessary goal of His creating, He *must*, in order that His moral creatures may be capable of true responsive love, grant them freedom of will and therewith the possibility of sinning. Thus the permission of the possibility of evil is a logical law of love which expresses its very nature. Only on the basis of freedom can mutual love exist, and with it true morality, dignity and nobility of man.

III. GOD'S PERMISSION OF SIN AND HIS HOLINESS

We reach the same conclusions when we consider the holiness of God. This determines that the Divine purpose in creating the universe must reach its climax in the self-glorification of Him whose holy nature is eternal love; it follows that this can be realized only through an essentially ethical development. This demands the creation of intelligent beings, who, by the fact of their creation, are destined and fitted to sympathize with God's moral attributes. God's holy nature can be glorified and shine out in His creation only in and from such beings. Thus, applying this to ourselves, the moral will of God as it reveals itself will lead of necessity to man's appointment to bear His image.

Moreover, it follows automatically that creatures that share in God's holy attributes will be capable of the ethical antithesis, *viz.* the antithesis of good and evil. First they must *discern* what the difference between good and evil really is; then they must *decide* for the good and reject the evil. By discernment and decision they will have made the ethical antithesis part of themselves.

This *knowledge*, however, could not have been given man. He is a created and therefore finite being, with a beginning, and so he finds the world already there as an external fact, when he enters it. Discernment for him could not mean knowing everything at once, but learning from that which is already there. So his whole thinking divides into a *discerning* of what he has not yet known and a *retaining* of that discerned; it is not omniscience but *learning* in the temporal antithesis of before and after.

How then could man have known of the antithesis between good and evil if he had not come upon it as something external to himself to be learned? Further, how would this have been possible except through a prohibition against doing something? Finally, how could such a pro-hibition be given if no possibility of its transgression were granted? Thus Adam and Eve—and similar principles must have existed for the angels, even though Scripture is silent as to details—had at first no knowledge of what disobedience was and could not know until a definite command was given them; the concepts of disobedience and evil were made concrete by non-obedience to it. Till then their "discerning" could in fact be only an immediate intuition, an instinctive feeling. Feeling will have far surpassed their ability to discern, and only through an express prohibition could the intellect obtain the superior position which was its by right.

A bare command would indeed have sufficed for purely *external* knowledge; for an *inward* and *experimental* knowledge of good in contrast to evil, an opportunity for participating freely in one or the other was necessary. Only so could the Divine objective for the moral creature become subjective experience. Only so could what was his by natural disposition truly become the possession and experience of his spirit. With the nature of man, both finite and appointed to holiness, there is therefore linked the necessity of a temptation, so that his capacity for discernment should not remain undeveloped but should be completely transfigured in God and as a result God in it.

Exactly the same is true of man's *will*. Had the will to do good been from the first an innate, necessary capacity in man, then it would not have been "will" at all but only a natural instinct. Its love for God could have been only an attachment, which was felt, and not something consciously willed and chosen, and just as feelings would have dominated man's capacity for discernment so they would also have his "will."

Most important of all is that, where there is no possibility of doing evil by omission or commission, the doing of good is no longer an ethical act but the mere inevitable, determined consequence of natural laws.[1] "The possibility of evil lies thus in the basic relationship of the rational creation to the Creator. By the nature of things ethical good cannot be forced upon any rational creature, nor can evil be restrained from impinging on him externally" (Dr. Th. Haarbeck). Innate holiness is a contradiction in terms. "Ethical development includes as an inalienable characteristic self-decision and self-determination, i.e. under normal conditions self-determination for the good, for God and for the eternal content of His will. No one can make this part of his own life unless he of his own free choice decides for it and obtains it by his own personal act. It follows that the *possibility* of evil in God's plan for the universe is *grounded in His own will*. This cannot be worked out without a choice between good and evil and with it the possibility of deciding for the evil. The fact that this possibility again and again becomes a *reality* is caused by the free decision of the creature. Evil, as a historical fact, arises wherever and whenever the creature misuses for evil the Spirit's imparted freedom to choose the good" (Prof. J. Kaftan).

One might term this temporary lack of necessary holiness an imperfection in creation. This is true, when one is speaking of a final goal not yet attained in normal development. But this relative imperfection of a temporary stage in development is determined by the absolute perfection of the final goal, and must therefore itself be regarded as perfection.

[1] It is self-evident that this may not be extended to cover the holiness of God. For the law is the expression of God's Being, and He stands, as the Eternal and Absolute, above all creaturely comprehension.

The freedom of a created personality is the basic condition for its perfection. But the very conception includes the abstract possibility of a wrong decision. Therefore God, if He were not willing to leave this possibility open, would have had to renounce perfection and—this being an impossibility—the creation of man altogether.

If He were not to allow ethical creatures the possibility of exercising their free choice, they would no longer be ethical personalities. They would be mere passive toys of His sovereignty, mere creatures governed by instinct, in reality nothing more than more highly gifted and more complexly controlled animals. There could be no more talk of a *nobility of man*. Their "morality" would in truth be a forced, only apparently moral mechanism, and they would be nature-bound beings without a will, puppet-like, living morality-machines. The holy nature of God could never have glorified itself, and with this the chief object in the creation of man would have been missed. But precisely because this object is of necessity grounded in God Himself as holy love, we must say: *God's own nature requires that He should of His own free will limit Himself so as to leave room for the unhindered self-determination of His ethical creation.* His will to create a realm of freedom outside Himself belongs to His basic nature. It is necessary for Him freely to limit Himself. "Even that we are *able* to do evil, is something *good*."[1] So far then from the temptation of man and the possibility of sin's being a contradiction of the almighty, omniscient, loving God, they are rather a necessary stage of development in the Divine order for the universe, and this in turn is in harmony with the Divine nature.

It should be obvious that we are not teaching that God's plan could not have been realized without evil. That would lead to the idea, half-bordering on pantheism, that without the devil and evil God could not have reached His goal. We are still further from teaching that God willed evil; it is rather that He has not not-willed its possibility. For because there can be nothing ethical without the possibility of the unethical, God, however contradictory it may sound, had, precisely on account of the holiness of His purpose for the universe to permit the possibility of unholiness.

When all has been said, however, He Himself remains to the finite understanding of the creature the Incomprehensible and Unfathomable. Here we must desist from all further questioning and searching. We must have the courage to confess our ignorance; and the humility to perceive that the finite cannot comprehend the infinite and that our reason often sees the things of eternity full of contradictions only because it is sinful,

---

[1] Pelagius, the celebrated opponent of Augustine (*c.* A.D. 400). So likewise Richard Krämer: "It must be unconditionally maintained that the capacity and possibility of moral decision, and therefore of a 'free' carrying out of the Divine will, belongs to the *good* endowment of man; but with this is also given the possibility of choosing evil" (p. 72).

fallen and enslaved, and therefore in contradiction to the laws of the Divine world above.

There is nothing more irrational than 'Rationalism'. Indeed our reason tells us that like can only be understood by like, therefore God only by God. Therefore Martin Luther said rightly (and he was certainly no simpleton), "In God's commands and affairs we must lay aside our wisdom and think thus: Does it appear foolish to me? Then in truth the only reason is that *I* am a great fool who cannot comprehend the Divine wisdom." He who would look into God's secrets must be adorned with the triple ornament of humility, reverence and faith. Where these are found, light from the throne of the Most High falls into the heart of the creature, and, in spite of all consciousness of minuteness and insufficiency, he will cry out joyfully, "The Lord is God, and He hath given us light: Bind the sacrifice with cords, even unto the horns of the altar" (Psa. 118: 27).

CHAPTER V

SATAN, THE PRINCE OF THIS WORLD—THE ADVERSARY OF THE NOBILITY AND KINGLY POSITION OF MAN

I. THE EXISTENCE OF A PERSONAL DEVIL

THE Bible teaches the existence of a personal Devil. This doctrine has been much derided, but in numberless cases without any serious thought. All too often to be a "free-thinker" is almost equivalent to being "free" from thinking! The truth is that the Biblical world outlook here also towers high above the criticism and lack of thought of its opponents. A brief philosophical reflection on nature will suffice to show this.

I. THE TESTIMONY OF NATURE AND HISTORY

It is undeniable that the order in nature as known to us is imperfect. Absolute harmony does not exist in the world. Nature presents to us a puzzling hybrid of happiness and unhappiness, wisdom and folly, plan and ruin. Gladness and grief, kindness and cruelty, the joy of life and the pain of death—all these convulse the world organism.

(a) Disharmony in the world

All this does not immediately prove the existence of powers hostile to God. For imperfection is not necessarily of itself a consequence of opposition to God. It is clear that the principle of development is among the laws given to the world in space and time by the Creator Himself. The world, as God wills it, must *develop*. It belongs to the concept of development that that which develops must develop from a relatively lower condition to a higher and more perfect one, till at length the goal of the whole process is reached. Absolute equality in perfection in all its stages would destroy the whole idea of development. If then there is and must be a difference in degree between the relatively imperfect and the relatively more perfect stages of creation, then in a world planned to develop, a relative imperfection is something willed and imparted by God so long as the development lasts.

But this is not the imperfection which obviously characterizes the present world. It does show many such *normal* imperfections, which are of necessity associated with the conception of any form of growth. What does predominate, however, is a different and *abnormal* imperfection, which inhibits true development. No one will assert that death is only a lower degree of life, that lies are only the first step to truth, that murder is the initial stage of love for one's neighbour! Hence the idea held by pantheism, that all we feel to be "bad", even evil and death, is no abnormal but a *normal* imperfection, i.e. a necessary stage in the evolutionary development of the divine world-stuff (just as cold is not a contradiction of heat, but only a lower degree of it), is meaningless and a denial of the facts.

Nature reveals a different and far greater cleavage. Behind the war in nature there is obviously some form of revolution. The state of the small section of the universe accessible to our experience sets a problem for every observer. "On the one hand it shows too much intelligence, wisdom and happiness to justify a denial of God; on the other hand it shows too much lack of intelligence, malignity and unhappiness to make belief in God probable. It gives the impression of a magnificent temple in ruins in which its inscriptions expressing profound truth have been maliciously and skilfully caricatured by some unknown person" (Dr. von Gerdteil).

It is beyond question that there are things in the world which we feel to be wicked and evil, such as the disturbance of the balance of the forces of nature, the sufferings and death of conscious, living creatures. But when we inquire after their cause, it becomes equally clear to us that the presence of wickedness and evil contradict the concept of a personal, holy, perfect God. We have already seen that good is not possible in God's plan for the universe without the *possibility* of evil (see pp. 54–58); but the *reality* of evil and the disturbances in nature connected with it, which we experience, can never be a necessity appointed by God. For if this had been a necessity at the *beginning*, then we cannot comprehend why it should not remain so *for ever*.

One could suggest that God was obliged to create a disharmonious multiplicity of beings and principles, so that He might have the greater opportunity of revealing the might of His wisdom and goodness which would be seen the more clearly as He reduced these contradictions to harmony and subjection. Without these disharmonies His might would not have been revealed so clearly, for the government of harmonious creatures would have been substantially easier.

But if this were the case, then in the same measure that God leads the universe to perfection He would also have to increase evil and imperfection in it infinitely! For He could reveal His wisdom absolutely, only if absolute disharmony reigned in the universe! This would mean that the perfection of the Divine self-unfolding could be attained only in a completely chaotic universe. Evil would thereby be perpetuated for ever, and the very concept of perfection destroyed. The fact, however, that it will one day be possible for the government of the universe to be without disorder (cf. Rev. 21: 4) is sufficient proof that its nature does not make it impossible for it to exist without disorder.

Apart from all this, such a theory involves such a separation of the omnipotence and wisdom of God from His holiness and love that God would cease to be a uniformly harmonious being. This objection would still remain valid, if one said that evil is necessary so that God's glory as Saviour and Redeemer might have the opportunity of displaying itself in its full brightness. Moreover this would involve us in the immoral principle against which Paul fought: "Shall we continue in sin that grace may abound?" (Rom. 6: 1). But above all, all these theories involve God in using a devil, or willing sin and calling it into existence Himself, had it not otherwise arisen.

(b) The reality of the demonic

The world has become the victim of corruption from the crown of its head to the sole of its foot. It is impossible to regard God as the immediate and sole cause of it as it is, if we are serious in taking the creation as a revelation of the nature of the Creator and the concept of revelation as a self-revelation of a holy and perfect God. But it is also impossible to conceive of wickedness and all evil as being necessary transition-stages in the development of the universe, as merely a temporary absence of the more perfect, as something purely abstract and negative.[1] They must rather be regarded as actual obstacles and counter-workings, which means something real, concrete and positive opposing the God-willed development of the world. To sum up: the existence of sorrow and evil throughout the world proves the existence of a transcendental, real, dynamic, hostile power, not willed by God. This must be thought of as a *personality*, since the ethical and unethical can only be predicated of a conscious, free being.

The concept of an absolute and eternally perfect God involves His being *unique* and as such the origin of *all* that exists beyond and beside Him. Therefore this opposing power, so far as its existence is concerned, must be traced back to Him. God can indeed create something incomplete viewed as a historic process but not that which is directly contrary to His world purposes. Therefore this opposing power must originally have proceeded from the hand of the Creator pure and spotless. Thus there remains only the possibility of *apostasy* as an explanation of its present hostility towards God.

This argument has shown that the existence of the devil is a necessity for natural philosophy.

---

[1] As Pantheism would have it. Pantheism—the doctrine that God (actually the impersonal deity) and the universe are one—must, by its very nature, regard all evil, including sin and death, as only a relative (not an abnormal) imperfection, and thus as an unavoidable transition-stage in the evolutionary process of the divine world-stuff. But this at the same time destroys the concept of true, ideal Deity; for the idea of Deity without self-harmony is a contradiction in terms.

The natural sciences offer no possible grounds of objection to this belief. They teach that in the world there are the most diverse kinds of living creatures. On our small earth alone there are well over two million living species.[1] There are fishes which can live only in the depths of the oceans, and birds which can exist only in the air of the highest mountains. There are animals which can live only in tropical heat, and others only in arctic cold. But they are all real, living beings, although so different in their nature. In the same way, speaking purely from the standpoint of natural philosophy, there can be beings without a material body, just as on our earth all beings must have material bodies. There can, therefore, be no talk of belief in the existence of good or evil spirit beings being scientifically out of date.

Modern man for the most part rejects *a priori* the concept of the devil, because he almost always thinks at once of the coarsely material, vulgarly horrible, ludicrously grotesque and foolishly fantastic, medieval representation of the devil. Professor Ebrard rightly says: "All the objections raised by philosophy against the devil are not against him as portrayed in the Bible, but against the false conceptions of him invented in the past." We must agree with Dr. von Huene, Professor of Palaeontology at Tübingen, that "the comical figure with horns and cloven foot, attributed to the devil during the Middle Ages and frequently even today in speech, art and literature, is at the least playing with fire; it is sheer flippancy. The danger is far more serious, and his power even today much more threatening, than most suppose." "God, willing and representing a good cause, *reveals* Himself; the evil one, seeking the opposite, *hides* himself" (Prof. E. Schäder).

The fact is that the devil is a spiritual being gifted with the highest intelligence, and though fallen, exceedingly powerful, whose existence cannot be in any way assailed by philosophy nor natural science. Since it is just in our world and in the universe immediately surrounding it that we observe disharmony, death and destruction, even a purely speculative contemplation of nature forces on us the conclusion that this world, and presumably the solar system connected with it, are the domain of this world-ruler and potentate.

2. THE BIBLICAL PROOF

All these conclusions find their confirmation in Holy Scripture. Beyond all doubt the belief in the existence of a personal devil is the belief of Jesus and His apostles.

(a) The testimony of Jesus and His apostles

At the very beginning of His public ministry Jesus knew that He was

[1] e.g. 20,000 *species* (!) of birds, 20,000 of butterflies, 250,000 of beetles, 300,000 of fungi and 250,000 of plants.

involved in a direct conflict with His arch-enemy, the devil. The whole story of the temptation of Jesus proves beyond all doubt that we are here concerned with a factual and personal conflict between two protagonists. The accounts of the evangelists and the behaviour and words of Jesus show clearly that we are not here concerned with a mere "principle" of evil, but with a real, factually present, speaking and active person, not "the evil" but "the evil one." "The tempter came to Him and said" (Matt. 4:3). "Then the devil taketh Him . . . and he set Him on the pinnacle of the temple and saith . . ." (v. 5). "Then the devil leaveth Him" (v. 11). "The devil . . . departed from Him" (Luke 4:13). Similarly, in reverse: "Jesus said unto *him*" (Matt. 4:7). "Jesus answered *him*" (Luke 4:4). "Then saith Jesus unto *him*" (Matt. 4:10).

Other words of Jesus also testify to His belief in the existence of a personal devil. He says that Satan has a "kingdom" (Matt. 12:26). "I beheld Satan fallen as lightning from heaven" (Luke 10:18). He calls him the "prince of this world" (John 12:31; 14:30; 16:11). The unbelieving Jews are said to be his children. "Ye are of your father the devil" (John 8:44). Golgotha is for Him a personal and decisive battle against this personal, hostile power; "The prince of this world cometh;" "The prince of this world hath been judged;" "The prince of this world will be cast out."

The same belief is shared by His apostles. Hence Paul speaks of the "prince of the power of the air" (Eph. 2:2) who has his "devices" (II Cor. 2:11), and his "servants," who disguise themselves as servants of righteousness just as Satan himself takes on the form of an angel of light (II Cor. 11:14). The purpose of his own missionary task was "to open their eyes, that they may turn . . . from the power of Satan unto God" (Acts 26:18), and, assured of victory, he declares to the Romans, "The God of peace shall bruise Satan under your feet shortly" (Rom. 16:20).

John testifies to a similar belief. "The devil sinneth from the beginning" (I John 3:8). "The whole world lieth in the evil one" (I John 5:19). "To this end was the Son of God manifested, that He might destroy the works of the devil" (I John 3:8). The number of such proofs from the Gospels and Epistles could be multiplied without difficulty.

Whoever does not share this original Christian belief cannot possibly understand Jesus and His apostles. Faith cannot accept the implications of the theory that Christ erred in accepting this view and shared certain purely transient conceptions of His time. For quite apart from the fact that Christ, in spite of His self-emptying (*kenosis*, Phil. 2:7), was, as the incarnate Son of God, exalted above every error, error on *this* question would mean in addition that Christ deceived Himself as to the powers against which He had to contend and which He had to overcome, and therefore also as to the background, the historical presuppositions and the goal of His whole personal work as Redeemer. Professor Erich Schäder has rightly said: "This assumption is intolerable for the faith which is spiritually bound up with Jesus as the Redeemer and the Bringer of the kingdom of God . . . With the thought of God's judgment on evil, i.e. sin, is associated belief in judgment on the *evil one*, who stands behind human sin as tempter and inciter."

(b) World destruction and cosmic revolution

More must, however, be added. According to the Bible, not only the earth but also the heavens associated with it will one day disappear in a violent, catastrophic judgment. "The heavens shall pass away with a great noise and the elements shall be dissolved with fervent heat. The earth also and the works that are therein shall be burnt up;" in other words, all shall be destroyed (II Pet. 3: 10; Rev. 20: 11; Matt. 5: 18). But if creation showed merely a relative but otherwise normal imperfection, linked to an ever-advancing process of growth, it would be inexplicable why it could not reach its goal by a gradual upward evolution without such a dreadful catastrophe. Further, since it is impossible to see how this judicial catastrophe, including as it does the *heavens*, should be the result of the fall of man, an earth dweller, the only remaining possibility is to think of an original, pre-Adamic sin, a cosmic revolution, which must have taken place in the spirit-realm.

(c) The testimony of Genesis

There seems to be a hint in Scripture pointing in this direction. Man was to till and to keep, i.e. guard (so Moffatt) the garden of Eden (Gen. 2: 15). It follows that there must have been danger present which made such a "guarding" necessary. The story of the temptation that follows proves this inference a fact. Even in those first days of the development of mankind an evil power existed opposed to the kingdom of good (Gen. 3). In addition, this hostile power must have stood in some relation to the earth, because it was just there that it exercised its seductive skill.

(d) Angelic organizations in the kingdom of light and in the kingdom of darkness

From the prophecies of Daniel we know that certain regions of God's creation lie at any given time under the control of particular angels. It is their task to rule over and administer the regions, which God has assigned to them, in His Name. Therefore they are at the same time "watchers" and guardians of God's world order (Dan. 4: 13). On the basis of their "decree" kingdoms, and even empires can be shattered. "Behold, a watcher and an holy one came down from heaven. He cried aloud and said thus, Hew down the tree (Nebuchadnezzar's rule). . . . The sentence is by the 'decree' of the watchers, and the 'demand' by the word of the holy one" (Dan. 4: 14, 17). Similarly Stephen says that Israel received the law "as it was ordained by angels." (Acts 7: 53).

The outward form of organization of the kingdom of darkness is basic-

E

ally the same. Thus the Book of Daniel speaks of an (angel) "prince of Greece" (Dan. 10: 20) and a "prince of the kingdom of Persia" (v. 13). Doubtless these refer to demonic spiritual powers which inspire and lead these peoples. On the other side, in the world of light, the archangel Michael is the angel prince of the people of Israel, "the great prince which standeth for the children of thy people" (Dan. 12: 1), "your prince" (Dan. 10: 21).

The Revelation of John shows that both in the invisible world of light as well as in the world of darkness there are even *armies* of angels, each of which is commanded by a particularly eminent angelic prince. Thus Michael has "his" angels, and the dragon has "its" angels: "And there was war in heaven: Michael and his angels going forth to war with the dragon; and the dragon warred and his angels; and they prevailed not . . . And the great dragon was cast down, the old serpent, he that is called the devil and Satan . . . he was cast down to the earth, and his angels were cast down with him" (Rev. 12: 7–9).

All this shows that angelic organizations exist, "thrones, dominions, principalities and powers," as Paul calls them, not only in the visible, but also in the invisible world (Col. 1: 16; Eph. 1: 21). From this fact we may be able to infer further links in the prehistoric background of the history of the universe.

(e) Satan as a fallen angelic prince of God

When he tempted Jesus, Satan offered our Lord all the power and glory of the kingdoms of this world, if He would only fall down and worship him. He justified the possibility of his offer and his ability to carry it out by claiming that the rule over the world had at some time been conferred upon him. "It hath been delivered unto me (Gk. *paradedotai*); and to whomsoever I will I give it" (Luke 4: 6).

This whole offer would have been unreal from the first for the Lord as a temptation, if some such legal basis for Satan's dominion in the world had not existed. Otherwise Jesus would only have had to point out that the necessary presuppositions for Satan's legal claim to and ability to dispose of the glory of the world simply did not exist. The Lord however left this claim of the devil's uncontradicted and merely declared that man should worship and serve God alone (Luke 4: 8). With this He recognized in principle the tempter's right to dispose of the kingdoms of this world in this present age.

The same thought lies behind the various sayings of Jesus in which He calls Satan "the Prince of this world" (John 12: 31; 14: 30; 16: 11).

The testimony of the Book of Revelation is in harmony with this. For when it says of the end of the present age that "the kingdom of the world is become the kingdom of our Lord, and of His Christ: and He shall reign for ever and ever" (Rev. 11: 15; cf. 19: 6), it implies that until that moment the kingdom of the world is under the jurisdiction of another, even the prince of this world. Now we can also understand why the archangel Michael, when contending with Satan over the body of Moses, dared not bring against him a railing judgment but only said, "The Lord rebuke thee" (Jude 9).

The fall of this mighty prince of light, as already the Rabbis accepted,[1] appears to be in view in Isaiah's description of the overthrown king of Babylon: "How art thou fallen from heaven, O day star, son of the morning!" (Isa. 14: 12). Also Ezekiel obviously borrows his description of the fall of Tyre from that same primeval event: "Thou wast the anointed cherub that covereth: and I set thee, so that thou wast upon the holy mountain of God; thou hast walked up and down in the midst of the stones of fire. Thou wast perfect in thy ways from the day that thou wast created, till unrighteousness was found in thee. . . . Thine heart was lifted up because of thy beauty, thou hast corrupted thy wisdom by reason of thy brightness" (Ezek. 28: 14–17).

Without doubt these two prophetic passages do not refer directly to the fall of Satan! Obviously these words of Ezekiel are concerned with the literal, human king of Tyre and those of Isaiah with the literal, human king of Babylon. Therefore these two passages cannot be regarded as decisive, doctrinal foundations for the fall of Satan. Doctrinal conclusions may not be deduced offhand from pictorial and poetical passages but must be based on literal and immediate statements of Scripture. The significance of pictorial and poetical passages in Scripture lies principally in their illustrative power, so as to increase the effectiveness of the message in the heart and feelings of the reader and hearer. Nevertheless it is unmistakable that the way these descriptions are here given goes beyond the boundaries of the purely human and the purely poetical. Just as king David is a type of Christ, his heavenly Lord, so here these two heathen kings are types of their demon lord.

Repeatedly in the Psalms the way in which David's experiences are described goes far beyond the boundaries of his earthly personality (e.g. Psa. 16; Psa. 22) and becomes entwined with the story of the heavenly "David." Of the same type—only in the reverse sense—is the relation of the kings of Babylon and Tyre to Satan, their master, who controls and inspires the history of the heathen empires as their real lord.

So in such poetic descriptions we can see both the fall of these heathen, earthly kings and the fall of the ruler of the kingdom of darkness; both Isaiah and Ezekiel can draw the illustrations for their description of the fall of Babylon and Tyre from that terrible, primeval event which in reality lies at the root of all human sin, all human revolt and all human collapse. A contemporary English expositor, Dr. J. H. Baxter,

[1] This is incorrect; the identification is first found in Church Fathers in the third century. (H.L.E.)

rightly calls the kings of Tyre and Babylon "mirror images of the majesty of Satan in his fall. A latent mystic significance is, in these passages, interwoven with their more immediate reference to local and historical persons and happenings."[1]

(f) The silence of the Bible

If Holy Scripture does not speak openly, in detail and immediately about these questions, it is because of its whole character and purpose. It is the record of salvation, and so its purpose is to show man through prophetic history the way to redemption, not to give him through philosophy a systematic view of history, of the world or of eternity. If that were its object, no man would understand it. Therefore it speaks only briefly and mediately of the origin of evil, only in incidental, figurative hints, but never in direct doctrine, and nowhere in continuous, unveiled form.[2] It does not wish to give us the history of the angels but rather that of human salvation. It sets out to tell us what we must know to find the way of redemption.

When all is said and done, it is always Himself alone that God reveals. And His purpose in so doing is by word and deed to make a way of salvation possible on earth, along which sinful mankind can be led back to Him. Hence the goal of His revelation is not theoretical but practical. Therefore the Bible does not give us a theological and intellectual summary of religious dogma, such as we find in a catechism or a treatise on systematic theology—valuable as such works may be in their own spheres—but absolutely simple, prophetic-historical records about the activity

[1] J. H. Baxter, *Studies in Prophetic Texts*, 1949, p. 191.

[2] Luke 10: 18 and I Tim. 3 : 6, 7 are almost the only passages which speak somewhat more clearly of the fall of Satan, and even there, as not a few expositors believe, other considerations play their part.

Thus Luke 10: 18 refers also to the victories gained by Jesus in His temptation and in His miracles over the power of the devil during His days on earth: "I beheld Satan fallen as lightning from heaven."

I Tim. 3 : 6, 7: The "bishop" should not be a novice but already proved in the faith, "lest . . . he fall into the condemnation of the *diabolos* (accuser, slanderer) . . . into the snare of the *diabolos*." The Greek word *diabolos* can, so far as its actual meaning is concerned, signify either the satanic or a human accuser (cf. the verb *diaballo* in Luke 16: 1). According to some notable expositors we are here concerned with the *human* accuser and slanderer, under whose malevolent judgment, criticism and evil report, the young Christian could come. The context can quite fairly lead to this conclusion, since the very next sentence says that the "bishop . . . must have a good testimony from them that are without," that is, from the world. Also the Greek word *diabolos* itself, as we have seen, permits the possibility of this interpretation.

On the other hand it is important to consider that in almost every occurrence of the word *diabolos* in the Greek Bible it refers to the devil himself. Thus most of the Church Fathers (e.g. Jerome) and many well-known modern expositors explain this verse with reference to the prehistoric fall of Satan.

I Pet. 2: 4 and Jude 6 refer in our opinion to Gen. 6: 1–4.

and government of the Most High in the life of this world. Their purpose is that our eyes should be opened by them and a new world unlocked for us, in which we may see God Himself living.

But when the sun of the true concept of God rises in the sky of our understanding, it pours down the brightness of its eternal light also on the whole world in and around us. And as the Divine revelation would be simply incomprehensible apart from its primeval background, Holy Scripture must also briefly mention this, but merely as a background. And since the origin and the activity of the evil one belong essentially to this background, the Bible permits his existence and history to show through the veil that hides them, at least by allusions.

II. THE FIRST SIN AND THE CONDITION OF THE WORLD

With the fall of Satan, however, there was associated the ruin of his realm, as was the case with the fall of man, only on a smaller scale (Gen. 3: 18). As did later sinful man, so Satan as the first result of his fall drew the part of creation entrusted to him into alienation from God.

This explains the presence of death in the pre-human, geological periods. The Biblical record of creation may be interpreted in different ways. It may be regarded as an account of the one, continuous, original creation of the earth, that is, as a creation-narrative in the strict sense, or it may be explained as a record of a "restoration" of the earth after a destruction caused by the fall of Satan.[1] Further, the geological periods may be fitted in different ways into the Biblical creation-narrative: either in the time before or during the *tohu-wa-bohu* condition of verse 2 or parallel with the six "days" of creation, themselves considered as periods. The fact is, however, that *both* types of explanation agree with one another and with the testimony of science in saying that death was already present upon the earth before the appearance of man.

It is just this agreement which is of decisive importance in our context. Death in the primeval world is not a geological hypothesis but a palaeontological fact. For anyone who knows anything of the facts it is completely incontestable that fossils that are definitely pre-Adamic exhibit traces of death and decay, indeed often of horrible destruction of life.

This fact has been confidently exploited by unbelief in its battle against the Biblical revelation. Already Karl Vogt, professor of geology, a materialist and follower of Darwin, said triumphantly, "No boasting about faith or pious break-neck leaps will help you to get over this stone which lies in your garden. Death has existed from the very beginning, and be it clearly said in the cruellest forms. Generally speaking, scarcely any more dreadful torments have been invented by perverted human ingenuity, than those by which nature destroys its creatures." Nature is, as another of Darwin's adherents expressed it, "red in tooth and claw."

[1] Concerning the restitution theory see pp. 195f., 230–242.

But this shout of triumph raised by enemies of the Bible, prematurely certain of victory, and also all similar objections raised by serious doubters are silenced, when we recognize that the existence of death and destruction upon the earth before the fall of man is fully compatible with the teaching of Scripture. Only it must all be traced back to the primeval fall of *Satan*. The original root of all suffering in the creation is that cosmic revolution, the revolt of Satan against God and the consequent introduction of disharmony and destruction into the region of the universe which the Creator had entrusted to him who had at the first been a prince of light.

Man was later in his fall not the originator of sin and death in the universe, but the *door* through which already existing sin entered into the world of man descended from him. In his explanation of Romans 5— especially of verse 12, "*through* one man sin entered into the world and death through sin"—Karl Heim points out that the apostle here does not use the Greek proposition *dia* ("through") with the accusative but with the genitive. The Greek "through" (*dia*) with the accusative denotes the origin or the originator of a thing, with the genitive it means a place "through" which one goes, e.g. a door "through" which one enters into a house.[1] Thus at the fall of man the satanic power of evil, already in existence before his creation, penetrated "through" this entrance into the world of man. The word *kosmos*, "world," is frequently used by Paul to mean not the universe but the world of man, e.g. I Cor. 1: 20, 27; 4: 13, etc.

Evil, as a satanic power, was thus already in existence before the creation of man. "The dominion which death exercised over the whole creation already in the pre-human primeval age had its foundation in the fact that the satanic revolt against the omnipotence of God had already had its effects in the whole living creation before the formation of man. A curse lies therefore over the whole creation originating from the satanic power which has brought the living world of creation under the slavery of mortality."

When and how this disastrous, primeval event itself took place, no one can say. The prehistoric point in time in a past age at which the fall of Satan occurred remains completely unknowable for us. Therefore it is not possible to place it with any certainty within the Biblical creation-narrative. Did it take place in the period between the first and second verses of the Bible, as the supporters of the restitution theory assume?[2] Or was it at some later point of time in the development of the cosmos, perhaps between the creation of the world and the beginning of the first plant-and-animal-life, the fossils of which are now to be found in the

[1] Though K. Heim may well be correct in his exegesis, he goes beyond the evidence, cf. Arndt and Gingrich: *A Greek-English Lexicon of the New Testament*, pp. 178 f., Moule: *An Idiom-Book of New Testament Greek*, pp. 54 ff. (H.L.E.)

[2] Cf. pp. 195f., and Ch. 17.

deepest strata, and which therefore perished and died in those early ages? That would mean—if the period theory of creation is correct—at some indeterminate time between verse 1 and verse 11 of the Mosaic record? Who would dare answer these questions with assurance? Certain is only the fact—and we are surely justified in using the term—that it took place before the first appearance of suffering and death in the universe.[1]

In any case the history of the earth from that point onwards has been decisively influenced by the conflict between destruction and further development, death and life, evil and good, darkness and light, Satan and God.

Also *after* the creation of man important results of this primeval catastrophe continued to exert their influence. The kingdom of darkness maintained its existence, and access to the earth was not forbidden to it.

However we may interpret the work of the six days of creation and correlate the geological periods with the creation-narrative, it is clear from the indications in Scripture that the earth was not immediately withdrawn from Satan's sphere of activity by virtue of the work of the "six days" of creation. Its preparation for man did not effect its absolute perfection. No immediate banishment of the demonic powers from the earth and its surroundings was associated with the conclusion of the work of creation. In the time that followed also they were able to continue their activity in some way or other upon the earth. Only so can one explain God's instruction to man that he should not only till but also "guard" the garden of Eden (Gen. 2: 15). Only so can one explain the appearance of the "subtle" serpent and the story of the temptation as a whole.

At the same time this opens out mighty perspectives, when we seek to answer the question as to the purpose and goal of the creation of man within the framework of the universe. Through the victory of man over the great adversary of God these conditions were to be overcome. Here was a high task for the new lord of the earthly creation.

At this point we realize a connexion between the history of man and the history of the invisible world and of the universe as a whole. The history of nature is linked with the history of salvation. The primeval history of the earth becomes an important commentary upon the historical goal of mankind that followed, and the earth, man's kingdom, throws light upon the nobility of man.

[1] Concerning the lack of more direct, exact statements in the Bible about the fall of Satan cf. E. Sauer, *The Dawn of World Redemption*, London, 1953, p. 34.

PART II

MAN AS THE KING OF THE EARTH

CHAPTER VI

THE EARTHLY KINGSHIP OF MAN

GOD set man on the earth He had prepared for him. He planted the wonderful garden in Eden which was to be the joy and delight of its possessor. Paradise was the beginning of the ways of God with man. God's wisdom, love and power wished to unfold itself in everything on the earth and change everything here below into an ever-blossoming paradise. In man, as the crown of creation, all the blessings planned by His grace were to be brought together and perfectly exhibited. In him, the one free and moral creature on earth, God's moral nature wished to glorify itself and to make man an image of his eternal Creator.

It seems that we should add another factor to the preceding. When He created man, God evidently had not only the intention that he should glorify and worship Him like the angels in heaven, as a pure and happy being, but also when He entrusted him with sovereignty over the earth, He delegated to him a special task linked with this his dwelling place. What exactly this task was seems to us clear from the earlier history of the earth.

I. God's Plan of Salvation for the Earth

From the realistic standpoint of Holy Scripture, God's cosmic, universal kingdom of worlds is, it would seem, divided into a number of "provinces" and world-regions over each of which an angel prince is set, as it were, as feudal lord and governor for God. Yet Lucifer, one of God's world rulers, to whom our earth and probably our whole solar system was subordinate, renounced God by apostasy and rebellion. Catastrophes affecting both the universe and the earth struck the area under his rule as the counter-working of the righteousness of God against this cosmic revolution.

But God did not view the fall of these angels and its effects on their region of the universe under their control with indifference. As the perfect, holy and supreme Ruler of all the worlds He could not be willing to leave this part of His cosmos desolate and ruined. On the contrary, if His will to glorify Himself had of necessity led Him to create a world in which He could glorify His Divinely perfect person, so now that same principle of self-unfolding necessarily moved Him to win back this portion of His universe, so that His plans might be carried through in it also. Purely physically He, the sole Deity, obviously had the power to wrest this area of the universe from Satan, the rebel, simply by force. But this would have contradicted His own moral principles of government. His fundamental nature is innately moral, and so the laws governing His cosmic world-order must also be of a purely moral character; and because Satan's area of power was legally granted him before his fall, God desired now, after he had fallen, to recover it only by means conforming to the fundamental law of His being.

This could be effected only through a moral confrontation between the power of God and the power of the devil. This demanded a free, moral being to carry this out as God's representative. His task involved both his remaining subject to God as an act of free self-decision and his spreading over the earth as its ruler. No further or more specific conflict was required. The progressive extension of rule over the earth by a being who remained faithful to God would automatically involve a gradual reconquest of the earth for God. The practical accomplishment of such a double task, to be both servant of the Lord and ruler of the earth, involved the actual deliverance of the earth from Satan's power.

We might possibly think that God would have entrusted this commission to some of the unfallen angels; but it would appear that they had all long since passed their moral testing and had reached the state of being no more able to sin, of being of necessity holy and no longer temptable.

If God had appointed such beings as His instruments to deliver the earth, Satan would have had no possibility of a real moral confrontation with God. The gradual extension of rule over the earth by a deliverer insusceptible to temptation, and therefore beyond attack, would have been, however it had worked out, a gradual but none the less forcible wresting of the earth from Satan's power. But this would have contradicted the principles of Divine justice. Since this could never be, because God is God, the liberation of the earth could be accomplished only by one whose home was the earth and who was at first *neutral*, i.e. one who was committed neither to God nor to the devil, but would have in due course to decide for himself on whose side he would stand. This cosmic calling of the new inhabitant of the earth as its deliverer demanded that he should have freedom of will, i.e. as well as the possibility of a temptation the capacity for being tempted.

God, as the Holy One, allows precisely His enemy both the right to unfold his innermost nature and to pursue his plans. This is the only way He could make it clear that Satan, despite all his trickery, can achieve only bankruptcy, and that God alone is wise, mighty and good. Thus Satan must work out the full implications of his rebellion and in so doing condemn himself.

In saying this we have been throwing light on the temptation story in the first chapters of the Bible. The possibility and fact of such a temptation of the new lord of the earth was doubly a necessity:

a *general, ethical, subjective* necessity, for only by a free decision of will could this, God's new creature, become in truth a moral personality, and

a *cosmic, objective* one, for only so could the earth be won back from the power of Satan in a way corresponding to God's will, i.e. in a truly moral manner.

The Swiss expositor Samuel Limbach expressed this as follows: "God possesses a stronger power than the mere external force which destroys its opponent. His power is justice, and therefore He grants justice even to His enemies.... But Satan is the prince of this world. Faced by him man was to represent God's justice on earth. He was to rule over creation in the name of God and to work God's works within it. Thus the enemy would be driven back legally. But if the liberation of the world was to be effected wholly according to justice and righteousness, then an opportunity had to be given Satan, God's foe, to extend his world rule of evil over man as well by being permitted to tempt him."

II. THE SMALL EARTH AS THE STAGE FOR THE REVELATION OF THE GREAT GOD

God chose man as the being for His work of deliverance. He is therefore peculiarly an object of the Divine plans and decrees. He is the instrument chosen by God for His mighty work of winning back part of His universal kingdom. Only in the far-reaching context of primeval events can man's origin and work, his purpose and goal be rightly understood. We have no intention of losing ourselves here on the shoreless sea of theosophical speculation; but we should for all that observe the signposts and indications given in the word of Divine revelation.

From it we see that it is in the world of men that a mighty battle between light and darkness is fought out. The earth is the point where the great drama takes place, which involves good and evil angelic powers, heaven and hell. The earth has thus become the stage for a mighty confrontation, for a Divine revelation, the results of which stretch out beyond the earthly and influence God's universe as a whole.

If this were not so, how could the Scriptures say that through the sacrifice of Christ, which after all was offered upon earth, on Golgotha, not only the earthly, but also the "heavenly" things are cleansed (Heb. 9: 23), and that in the coming kingdom of God the *sun* and *moon* will shine more brightly than at present? "Moreover the light of the moon shall be as the light of the sun, and the light of the sun shall be sevenfold, as the light of seven days" (Isa. 30: 26). How otherwise could the Bible's last prophecy proclaim that when all is perfected there will not only be a new earth but also a new heaven (Rev. 21: 1), indeed, that then even the throne of God will be upon the renewed and transfigured earth (Rev. 22: 3)? How otherwise could the Bible testify that "the earnest expection of the creation waiteth for the revealing of the sons of God" and, as it were, "groaneth and travaileth in pain" until that time (Rom. 8: 19, 22)? And finally, how otherwise could we explain that a new heaven and a new earth are not brought into being until *after* the conclusion of the story of man's redemption?

Only so does the sublime relationship between heaven and earth, presupposed throughout the book of Revelation, no longer appear as an unanswerable riddle. Only so also does faith grasp that the earth is the stage for the most glorious, Divine revelations, indeed, for the incarnation of the Son of God, and that the blessings they create benefit not only this poor earth but also radiate their influence into the celestial world.

We grant that in such contexts Scripture often uses poetic and pictorial expressions, e.g. the "throne" of God, the "travail" of creation, "precious stones" and "pearls" of the heavenly "city," the "water" of life, "leaves of the tree of life." It is clear from the outset that for us men in the present age no immediate "description" but only an intimation of the eternal world can be given, and even this can be done only by using pictures and symbols. But it must be just as clearly stated that behind all such picture-language there exists an eternal, factual, transcendental reality.

It is to be noted too that exacter details concerning the content and extent of these super-terrestrial influences of the redemptive work of Christ achieved upon earth are not revealed in Scripture. Nevertheless, the Bible clearly shows that our earth as the stage for the revelation of God has an importance in the history of salvation which far surpasses its material and spatial, "astronomical" significance.

But how is it conceivable that our tiny earth, this speck of dust in the ocean of suns that make up the universe, should have such a vast, indeed, inconceivably great significance? Does not the modern, astronomical picture of the universe refute *a priori* such a belief based on the Bible, so that no modern man who knows anything at all about Copernicus and Kepler can still believe in the Bible? Is not this whole idea of the nobility of man and his royal position in creation something out of date, indeed just "a megalomania based on human hopes" (E. Haeckel)?

Our earth is only the 1,297,000th part of the sun's volume. This means it could find room in the sun over one and a quarter million times. The sun itself is only one of countless other suns, indeed a comparatively small one. Some other suns have a diameter between ten and thirty times as great, and thus a volume between 1,000 and 27,000 times that of our sun. That means that their volume is as much as 20,000 million times that of our earth!

Together with 400 other suns our sun forms the "solar cluster." This is a part of the Milky Way System, a flat, discus or lens-shaped star-system of inconceivable extent. The number of luminous stars in this "our" galaxy is estimated at 500 million; its diameter is about 100,000 light years. A light year is the distance travelled by a ray of light in a year, i.e. about 6¼ million million miles. Light travels namely at about 187,000 miles per second, or 7½ times the length of the equator of the earth (24,000 miles).

Our Milky Way, however, is only *one* island-universe in the midst of numerous other similar (though mostly somewhat smaller) ones. These appear to us, from their immense distances from us, as spiral nebulae, e.g. the mighty Andromeda universe.

In the giant 200-inch telescope of the Mount Palomar observatory (U.S.A.) the Andromeda nebula is seen with a diameter of 75 inches, and the human eye gazes with amazement into this mighty abyss of space. Indeed, the photographic plates taken with this, the largest telescope in the world, open up still further, immense distances and worlds.

"The number of spiral nebulae (i.e. Milky Way systems!) up to the twenty-first magnitude detectable in a photograph is now estimated at 60 million. The maximum measured distance of a spiral nebula so far is 500 million light years" (Heim, II, p. 15).

From the consideration of photographic records of stars down to less luminous, smaller magnitudes, the English physicist Sir Arthur Eddington, one of the most important astronomers of the last generation, arrives at still larger figures. In his work *The Expanding Universe* he writes of 100,000,000,000 island systems, each believed to be an aggregation of thousands of millions of stars with a general resemblance to our own Milky-Way system.

Sir James Jeans, the British astronomer, says in *The Mysterious Universe*, "The total number of stars in the universe is probably something like the number of grains of sand on all the sea shores of the world." And of these stars not a few have a luminosity a thousand times that of the sun! It is due only to their immense distance from the earth that we see them on a clear, starlit night merely as tiny points of light.

Thus the whole cosmos is a giant complex of dozens of millions of spiral nebulae (galaxies). In each of these galaxies are dozens, indeed hundreds, of millions of suns and single stars. Each of these suns is about a million times, many even up to a thousand million times, as large as our earth!

And then, we are asked to believe, in this vast totality of the universe, our tiny earth, smaller than the one-millionth part of just one of this host of myriad suns, should be the stage for such highly important, Divine revelations, indeed for the setting for the incarnation of the Son of God, the Lord and King of this mighty universe. Can we then, confronted by such a universe, the members of which are no longer solar systems but the spiral nebulae (galaxies), still speak of a high calling, indeed, a nobility and kingship of man? Is this not *a priori* completely unthinkable. Is not rather the whole of human history, which we so proudly call "world" history, only a very small, weak, scarcely perceptible pulse beat within the history of this true "world," so infinitesimal as to be scarcely worthy of note by the great and almighty God?

We suggest a fivefold answer.

(1) Spatial and spiritual dimensions are not necessarily comparable. Let us think of two men sitting in the same railway compartment. Spatially they are only a few feet apart, yet under given circumstances they may be from the spiritual standpoint millions of miles apart. Completely different life-stories! Completely different goals! Completely different ideals! Completely different principles in their attitude to the world, religion and faith! On the other hand we can think of two people, e.g. an engaged couple, husband and wife, or close friends, who though separated by thousands of miles (oceans may roll between them), by their love and common interests are spiritually as closely united as if soul stood beside soul, heart beside heart, body beside body. So we see that people can be spatially close together and at the same time, spiritually, infinitely distant from one another. They can be far distant from one another in space and yet spiritually very close together. This proves that spiritual values cannot be measured by spatial dimensions.

(2) The geographical and historical importance of a place are not necessarily identical. Issus, as a place, had no special importance; as the scene of the decisive battle between Alexander the Great and the Persian king Darius Codomannus (333 B.C.) it became one of the most important and world-famous turning-points in the whole of ancient history, indeed of human and world history. Thus it gained a *historical* importance entirely unrelated to its *geographical*. In fact, world history has shown that the places where the most important battles, which have shaped events for centuries, have been fought out, were often themselves very small in size and insignificant in their situation. The inner importance of a place can never be measured by its outward size. The German scholar Professor Kurtz has well challenged the modern sceptic with the question, "How many square miles must a planet have to show appropriate respect for an incarnation of the Eternal One?" This leads at once to our third point.

(3) Quantity can never in itself be regarded as a measure of quality. Quantity and quality do not necessarily stand in the same relationship to one another. Sometimes just the opposite is the case! Does not the smallest space often conceal the greatest wonder? Is not the world of the very small almost more wonderful than the world of the very large? We need only think of the atoms with their solar systems of protons and electrons circling millions and millions of times a second. We grant that the telescope shows us the wonders of the macrocosm and makes us aware of how tiny our earth is in this vast universe, just like "a grain of sand in this

world." But the microscope equally reveals to us the wonders of the microcosm and makes us realize how incomprehensible is also the tiny world of the atom, as it were "in every grain of sand a world." Often one does not really know which to admire more: a speck of dust or the world of the stars, the atom or the sun. All this proves that the importance and significance of a thing do not depend upon its size. The smallest organism is of a higher order than the greatest, inorganic mass. The rose in the valley is nobler than the lifeless mountain peak. The quantity of space is absolutely indifferent where revelations of the Spirit are concerned. Just as the small human body is not unworthy of the spirit, which can comprehend the whole world, so the small earth is not unworthy of God, that He should reveal Himself upon it.

All this proves there can be no obvious reason why this earth, in spite of its spatial and astronomical minuteness, could not be the stage for a historic event of decisive importance for the whole universe. Obviously, astronomy cannot with the tools it uses bear prove this a fact—that can only be done by revelation, the historical acts of salvation and prophecy—but it cannot query it. Rather, when it is rightly understood, it fits into the mighty, cosmic framework of the whole Biblical revelation.

(4) Before all else, we must take the relationship between the Creator and creation into account. The human spirit must take the sovereignty of God seriously. *God* is Lord of the universe. And if He, in His wise, absolutely free, omnipotent will determine that this earth, despite its smallness, should become the most important point in the universe, then no dust-born creature has the right to object. We may well apply the psalmist's words, "Our God is in the heavens; He hath done whatsoever He pleased" (Psa. 115: 3). In any case man has to humble himself before the eternal will of the All-Highest. He must in faith accept what He has done and subordinate himself to Him. Then to Him who has so ennobled this tiny earth of man, where he must live out his life, he may with his whole heart *bring thanksgiving*.

(5) In addition this is an activity of Divine *grace*. In His incomprehensible mercy the Highest often bows down to the least. It is precisely in the small things that He reveals His greatness. So too He has chosen this small earth to be the temple of His revelation of salvation. But all has been for His own self-glorification, that all praise might be His alone. He Himself is the goal; not the creation but the Creator, not earth but heaven, not the stage for the victory but the eternal Victor.

III. Primeval Biblical History as a Reliable Foundation for the Kingly Calling of Man

Belief in the historical and literal truth of the first chapters of the Bible is a decisive presupposition for a Biblical understanding of man's appointment to nobility. For here are the fundamental events and reports in which the nobility of man has its roots. We can see this in many ways.

It is the Biblical creation-narrative that contains the affirmation that man was created in the *image of God* (Gen. 1: 27).

In the sequence of the six "days" he appears as the *goal and crown* of creation (Gen. 1: 27–31).

In the story of creation and Paradise we find his calling to *kingship* upon earth and his practical assumption of this office ("subdue it," Gen. 1: 28) by his giving of names to all living creatures (Gen. 2: 19, 20).

With the correctness and reliability of the first chapters of the Bible stands and falls therefore the whole Biblical basis for the vocation of the human race to nobility.

But once more faith stands just here on an unshakable rock-foundation. Here Jesus and His apostles prove to be reliable and decisive authorities. Again and again the Lord and the writers of the New Testament unmistakably profess their faith in these chapters. Some examples will justify this statement.

Jesus established His teaching on the indissolubility of marriage by referring to the Paradise story (Matt. 19: 4–9). Paul proved his instructions about the position of woman in the Christian Church by stressing that the first woman was created *after* Adam and that she had been defeated by temptation *before* Adam (I Tim. 2: 13, 14), just as the first chapters of Scripture literally report (Gen. 2 and 3). James, when warning against the sins of the tongue, referred to the creation of man "after the likeness of God," i.e. to the Biblical creation-narrative (Jas. 3: 9). John called Satan "the old serpent," referring to the temptation of man in Paradise by the serpent (Rev. 20: 2), and he added a warning to his exhortation to true love by referring to Cain's murder of his brother shortly after the expulsion of Adam and Eve from the garden of Eden (I John 3: 12). Paul even established the organic nature of the New Testament Church by contrasting Christ, the last Adam and the head of a new humanity, with the father of the human race, the "first" Adam (Rom. 5: 12–21). In his teaching about the new spiritual body at the resurrection he compares the "first man" who was "of the earth, earthy," i.e. of dust, and Christ, the "second man," who is "from heaven" and will therefore one day grant us His own heavenly glory. "The first man Adam became a living soul, the last Adam became a life-giving spirit. … Just as we have borne the image of the man of dust, we shall also bear the image of the man of heaven (I Cor. 15: 45, 49, the latter from R.S.V.).

Jesus and His apostles could speak and write thus only because they believed in the historical and literal truth of the primeval Biblical history.

Attempts have been made to explain that Jesus was not free from error, and that in any case nothing depends on the historicity of the references which lie behind such statements by Jesus and the apostles but only on the spiritual and prophetical conclusions drawn from them by the New Testament. But how can one still maintain the perfection and deity of the person of Jesus if one holds such a view? How can one ascribe contemporary errors to Him, to Him who is the mouth of Eternal Truth? How can one even explain that, though Jesus Himself knew that these events had never taken place literally, for practical, educational reasons He somehow adapted Himself to the errors of His contemporaries? How could one still believe in the honesty of a prophetic personality who used historical accounts as true, although he knew that, in the form he used, they were historically false! And how can one assert that all this is from the very first a merely symbolical dress for eternal truth, but not the history of what really happened? For no one can dispute the fact that the first chapters of the Bible do not give their accounts as parables, symbols or visions (as does to some extent the Revelation of John), but as literal reports of real events.

No, here we have only one choice:

either to doubt the literal and historical truth of the first chapters of the Bible, and at the same time to deny the full authority of Jesus and His apostles,

or to believe unreservedly in the teaching of Christ and of the New Testament, and at the same time to acknowledge the historicity of the Biblical accounts about the beginning of the human race.

No third possibility exists. And faith, in believing in Christ and His Word, also affirms, together with these first chapters of Scripture, the vocation of mankind to nobility contained in and witnessed to by them.

IV. THE BIBLICAL AFFIRMATION OF LIFE AND CULTURE

The call of mankind to a work of cosmic redemption seems to us to be deducible with special clarity from two main Scripture passages. One is found in the Old Testament, the other in the New. The one refers to man before his fall (Gen. 1: 26–29), the other to man yet to be redeemed after his fall (Rom. 8: 19–22).[1]

The first runs, "And God said, Let us make man in our image, after our likeness: and *let them have dominion* over the fish of the sea, and over the fowl of the air, and over the cattle, and over the earth, and over every creeping thing that creepeth upon the earth. And God created man in His own image, in the image of God created He him; male and female created He them. And God blessed them: and God said unto them, Be fruitful, and multiply and replenish the earth, and *subdue it*; *and have dominion* over the fish of the sea, and over the fowl of the air, and over every living thing that moveth upon the earth." Then God continued, "Behold, *I have given you* every herb yielding seed, which is upon the face of all the earth, and every tree, in the which is the fruit of a tree yielding seed; to you it shall be for meat."

These words plainly declare the vocation of the human race to rule.

[1] For a consideration of the latter passage see p. 97.

They also call him to progressive growth in culture. Far from being something in conflict with God, cultural achievements are an essential attribute of the nobility of man as he possessed it in Paradise. Inventions and discoveries, the sciences and the arts, refinement and ennobling, in short, the advance of the human mind, are throughout the *will of God*. They are the taking possession of the earth by the royal human race (Gen. 1: 28), the performance of a commission, imposed by the Creator, by God's ennobled servants, a God-appointed ruler's service for the blessing of this earthly realm. Only complete misconception of the simplest laws of revelation could charge Holy Scripture with obscurantism and hostility to culture. On the contrary what the Bible rejects, and what is opposed to God, is not culture in itself but the estrangement of millions of its representatives from God, the separation of sinners from heaven, lack of consideration for one's neighbours, the spirit of arrogance and rebellion, in brief, the revolt against the Most High. But the call to be ruler signifies a vocation to advancing civilization and is a God-given regulation in creation.

It is often thought that there can have been no Paradise, because at the very beginning man could not have known a highly developed culture. But this objection rests upon a misunderstanding of primeval Biblical history. The Bible nowhere says that Paradise involved a high cultural or intellectual level. Much rather it speaks quite unequivocally of the later introduction of highly important cultural and technical inventions, e.g. the art of music, metal working, city building, etc. (Gen. 4: 17–22). Just as today there are men poor in knowledge and the outward signs of civilization, but who in every respect stand morally high, just as outwardly simple men often far surpass the "educated" in the fineness of their feelings, so also in our first ancestors morals and culture need not automatically be assumed to have been on the same level. The essence of life in Paradise was not cultural but moral.

Indeed from the Biblical standpoint one cannot even speak of a real moral "height" in the first human beings. They lived in Paradise *before* they had made any moral decision and thus, in spite of having been created pure, they were more like a child in its moral innocency. Hence the outward form of the prohibition, suited to their still childlike thought, not to eat from a tree, the tree of knowledge. Everything was planned for development. The intellectual and moral endowment was present, but had first to unfold itself.

Man was at the first a clean but unwritten page, yet gifted with the latent power to become everything that God had planned him to be. The command to the new lord of the earth to subdue it to himself was at the same time an order to raise himself from a primitive, lower culture and state of knowledge to a universal control of nature and its forces. The rich, intellectual and cultural endowment of man was therefore to be developed as the future unfolded.

F

"It is essentially the vocation of the natural scientist to which God points man in this command. He was to investigate the forces existent in the world and to use this knowledge to raise himself ever higher out of the Paradise of childhood to the highest levels of culture" (Prof. E. Dennert).

We see then that both the story in the Bible, and the outwardly childishly simple form of the prohibition, are in complete harmony with the concept of the advance of the human race. Far from resulting in contradictions, this apparently objectionable serves rather to the mutual confirmation of the Bible and the modern study of nature and history.

In the same way it is inexcusably superficial to allege that the Bible regards idleness as an ideal and work as a punishment. Scripture certainly does say that it is part of the punishment of sinful man that he should eat bread in the sweat of his brow (Gen. 3: 19). But this does not refer to the work itself, but the *drudgery* of the work, the often fruitless toil in the fields which bring forth "thorns and thistles" instead of wheat and corn. It means also the pressure of his activity, the unceasing strain, the necessity of chasing from task to task, if he is to earn enough to support himself. Not only is he to earn his daily bread with the sweat of his brow, but the sweat is to stand on his forehead when he eats it. So short are to be the pauses in his work!

But this is far from describing work as a punishment. Work is not the curse, but the curse adds weariness and disappointment to the work. Much rather does work belong to the order of life in Paradise. Man was to "dress," i.e. cultivate, the garden (Gen. 2: 15), i.e. he was to *work!* The accomplishment of his work as ruler was not to come without effort on his part. He was to exert himself and to tax his powers. He had to achieve something and thereby justify his royal vocation. If "the nobility of work" is mentioned anywhere, it is here at the beginning of the Bible, where it is presented as a programme for the future. Through work the noble race of man was to fulfil its royal vocation. Work bears the stamp of Paradise!

All this is equivalent to saying that man's actual entrance upon his God-given rights was not to be forthwith complete, but gradual and progressive. "*Subdue* it" (Gen. 1: 28). Man was to extend his kingship little by little, beginning at Paradise, until he had drawn the whole earthly creation into the sphere of his activity and rule. His dignity as ruler in Paradise was therefore not immediately complete but was only potential and in principle. From the very beginning God's revelation of His will had development as its purpose.

Therefore corporeally the first man was not at the first created in a condition of absolute perfection. Paul says of Adam's body that it was only "psychic" (soulish), not a spiritual body. He said this—as the context shows—of man's original corporeal condition by creation, not of the corruption introduced later by the fall. Only in the measure that Adam, in the moral realm, raised his created *purity* to a conscious, voluntary *holiness*, could his natural, soulish body be physically transformed into a spiritual body. "The first man, Adam, became a living soul, the last Adam (Christ) became a life-giving spirit. Howbeit that was not first which is spiritual, but that which was natural, then that which is spiritual" (I Cor. 15: 45, 46).

Before the fall man's body was not exactly "mortal," for it did not have to die. But neither was it "immortal," because it could die, if sin entered, as was actually the case. Through enjoyment of the fruit of the tree of life the "psychic" (soulish) body of man, capable of dying, though not "mortal," should have been transfigured by sacramental, organic means into a pneumatic (spiritual) and, in the full sense of the word, immortal body (Gen. 3: 22, 23). However great and inconceivable the glory of Paradise, it was only the beginning of a yet mightier upward development. Adam's path began in glory, but it was to have gone on "from glory to glory."

V. BIBLICAL FAITH AND THE CONTROL OF NATURE[1]

Man's appointment as the ruler, indeed, as the liberator of the natural world creates for him a positive relationship to nature. Nature also takes its origin from God. It is the work of His power. It is the great, majestic temple of creation, in which He makes known His divinity (Rom. 1: 19, 20). "God is a God who forms the bodily, the earthly, the visible. He does not create a mere world of ideas, not merely soul-flames and immortal spirits, but also a world with colour and form . . . The bodily and earthly did not arise from the depths but was originally glorious and good. Therefore nature also may await with joy an eternal Easter Day" (Köberle, pp. 49 f.).

Despising nature and denying the body are in no sense Biblical or Christian, they are derived from heathen, especially Hellenistic-Greek, speculation. If man, however, has been appointed king of the earth, this implies an appreciation of the earth as his kingdom, and it belongs further to the dignity of his calling that he, the king, should gain the right relationship to his kingdom. A ruler may not neglect and flee from his kingdom but must rule royally therein.

Thus man's dominion over nature is derived from his kingship. We must not interpret it to mean that he is gradually to gain his position as king by applying his rule over nature in practice, as though his position of dominion depended upon his technical mastery over nature. No; this kingship was conferred upon him directly by God from the very outset. Right at the beginning God gave man, whom He had created in His own image, a share in His own rule over the earth. Man, however, by the application in practice of the technical ability given him, by conscious deliberation, by systematic calculation on the basis of recorded observa-

[1] Cf. the section, Biblical Faith and the Affirmation of Nature, p. 109.

tions and experiences, and by his own, inherent, creative power of invention, is to draw the powers of nature into his service, and in so doing into the service of God.

Thus man's vocation to nobility, which was made known to him in Paradise, has also an earthly and moral aspect. Man should not be a *tyrant* over nature. He should not misuse it by senselessly destroying beautiful landscapes, by the predatory exploitation of field and forest, by harnessing the strength of animals so ruthlessly, that it becomes sheer cruelty. Equally he should not become a *slave* to nature—through pagan deification of nature, through the vague, modern enthusiasm for nature, in pursuing gold and possessions as though true happiness were dependent on the possession of material goods. He should be its *lord*, and as lord should guard his kingly dignity. True, we cannot yet eliminate the universal suffering of nature, but we should not increase it, and indeed, whenever possible we should lighten it. Let us not forget that the whole creation waits for *our* perfecting. One day it will share in the liberty which the glorified children of God will possess (Rom. 8: 19–22). That being so, its human redeemer must not, while it waits, make its chains heavier!

We cannot rule over nature without first discovering its laws. It is a fact that only after the pagan deification of nature had been conquered did true inquiry into nature enter the history of the sciences. For as long as men, even in classical antiquity, believed that nature was animated by good or evil spiritual powers, awe in the face of these gods and demons was a restraint on the objective study of nature.

A characteristic example of this is the fate of the philosopher Anaxagoras, a personal friend of Pericles, the great Athenian statesman, and of Phidias, the most outstanding Greek sculptor and artist. Despite his relationships with the highest political and artistic circles of Athens, Anaxagoras became involved in great difficulties because of some of his new scientific and natural philosophical teachings.

He had examined a large meteor, which had fallen near Aigospotamoi in Thrace, and came to the conclusion that the sun was in fact a glowing mass of stone, and that the stars also consisted of stones, which were subject to the same gravitational force as earthly bodies. At the same time he taught that the moon received its light from the sun. He further asked himself why, if he were right, the stars did not normally fall to the earth but remained in the heavens in their courses. He concluded that there must be a dominating, purposeful, intelligent power, independent of matter, which caused the celestial globe to revolve and which prevented the heavy masses of the stars from falling as had that meteorite. Thus Anaxagoras arrived at the idea of a spiritual power which moves and governs the world, and so faith in a world-control through a divine reason triumphed in his conception of the world over the astral myths of the common, heathen religion of the masses, for which the sun, moon and stars were the divine lords of the world. This implied at the same time a conflict with the gods of Greece. So Anaxagoras was accused of atheism, brought to trial, exiled from Athens, and died abroad (428 B.C.).

Things being so, most of what was achieved in science, even in classical antiquity, was the work of men who were regarded by their people and time as "atheists." Even the Emperor Nero, although undoubtedly personally irreligious, had to capitulate in an important plan in face of the nature-deifying superstitions of his subjects. He stopped the very important cutting of a canal through the isthmus of Corinth, by which the voyage from the Adriatic to Athens (the Pireus) could have been shortened by about 200 miles, because many of his contemporaries felt it to be an unwarranted intrusion into the secrets of the earth and a desecration of spirit-animated nature, and so feared the wrath of the gods. It is true that the news of a conspiracy had caused him to return to Rome and to attend to other affairs. But it was officially announced that Egyptian geometricians had declared that evil events would occur as soon as the canal was opened. And yet Nero himself had cut the first sod with a golden spade and had carried away the first load of earth in a gilded basket! In addition nearly a mile of the canal had already been dug by the use of Roman soldiers and of 6,000 Jews, who had been taken prisoner in the first battles of the Jewish war. In actual fact, even earlier the rumour had got about that Julius Caesar, and, later, the Emperor Caligula had met their terrible end by assassination just because they had planned to cut through the isthmus of Corinth, and so had incurred the wrath of the gods for this outrage.[1]

When the inhabitants of the small Greek city of Cnidus in Asia Minor inquired of the oracle of Apollo at Delphi, whether they might cut through their isthmus and join their two ports by a canal, they received from Pythia, the oracle-priestess, the warning answer, "Hard indeed it is for man to offer violence to the divine" (Uhlhorn, p. 57).

Those who deify nature are always, through awe of the mysterious spirit forces that rule within it, kept from looking more deeply into the life of nature and from penetrating into its laws. As long as there was a popular religion which saw nymphs in field and wood, naiads in springs, Neptune with his trident in the sea, and the sacred herd of Helios in the sun, scientific thought could never become the possession of all, even if the upper classes were more enlightened. Only "by the side of religion, *purged* from nature gods and demons could natural science blossom and flourish."

It follows that natural science in antiquity was primarily only an external *description* of nature. The Indians, Chinese, Babylonians and Egyptians, gifted representatives of great civilizations though they were, achieved surprisingly little in the development of the natural sciences. For them too

[1] Cf. Uhlhorn, p. 57; also G. M. Franzero, *The Life and Times of Nero*, London, 1954, p. 360.

their deification of nature stood in the way of all scientific progress.

Not until Christianity had overcome the deification of nature, so that men saw in it merely the handiwork of the great Creator, was its unbiased investigation possible. Only then was the way open for the removal of the veil from nature, for the investigation of its laws, and for the making of its forces serviceable.

The Old Testament creation-narrative was already a pioneer in this. Its objectivity and clarity, free from all myths about the gods, made it basically different from all the cosmologies of its heathen environment with their deification of nature. Dr. Howe has therefore written, "The demythologizing and de-demonizing of the world we find in the Biblical creation story belong to the most important presuppositions of modern science." For all that the decisive change was brought about by the victory of Christ over the myths and powers of heathendom and by the worldwide spread of Christianity amongst the leading civilized peoples.

"Modern science, paradoxical as it may sound, has to thank Christianity for its origin."[1] These are the plain words of Dubois-Reymond (Professor of Medicine in the University of Berlin), world famous as a physiologist towards the end of last century. Dubois-Reymond made no claim to be a Christian and even betrayed definite materialistic tendencies, declaring that "a supernatural influence did not fit" into his system of thought. Obviously he had no thought of being an apologist for Christianity.

The scientist and botanist Professor Dennert states downrightly, "Christ is the Father of scientific freedom. He it was, who made the way free for scientific research" (II, p. 145).

Such statements have been countered by the objection that the Christian Middle Ages accomplished just as little in the sphere of the natural sciences. The answer is that the blame cannot be put on Biblical Christianity, with its positive attitude to nature, but on the monastic caricature of Christian thought, which was influenced by the Greek-Hellenistic contempt for the body. Above all, as Professor Dennert rightly emphasizes, "it was not the Bible and the words of Christ which in the Middle Ages dominated natural science, but the heathen Aristotle. At that time he was the infallible authority." That is the reason why the Middle Ages failed so dismally in the scientific field.

VI. Man's Use and Misuse of his Sovereignty over Nature

Normally we are inclined to seek the great events of world history where they reveal themselves in great political, international and military upheavals. In fact, however, only few generals and politicians, kings and emperors have succeeded in influencing the development of mankind as strongly and permanently as have physics and the other natural sciences during the past few centuries, especially since Copernicus, Kepler and

[1] Quoted by Dennert, II, p. 145.

Newton; moreover they continue to do so. In the laboratories of scholars, aloof from the noise of politics and war, the world of the future has again and again been shaped, and the physicist of today has always been the father of the technical science of tomorrow and through it the moulder of the outward life of millions.

A new and special advance in physics, technical science and hence in man's practical dominion over nature commenced after the middle of the eighteenth century. It began with the invention of the steam-engine by the Scot, James Watt (1764), through which the whole life of the western world has been revolutionized and directed into new paths.

The nineteenth and twentieth centuries brought mighty advances with mathematicians, discoverers and inventive geniuses like Stephenson, Gauss, Edison, Ampère, Faraday, Daimler, Röntgen, Madame Curie, Max Planck, and Albert Einstein, to mention only a few of the most prominent names. Their number is immense. Their invention of the railway (1825), the study and utilization of electricity (for heat, light and telegraphy), and the discovery of radium ushered in a completely new era for the whole of civilization. The arm of modern technical science now reaches to the most distant regions of all lands and continents, thanks to the control of nature which has been so advanced by these investigators.

In 1919 the English physicist Sir Ernest Rutherford (1871–1937) was the first to break up an atom in a planned and demonstrable experiment by bombarding it with a helium nucleus. "The second in which this happened was the first second of the atomic age." In 1939 the German atomic scientist Otto Hahn succeeded for the first time in splitting the nucleus of a uranium atom and thereby laid the foundation of atomic technical science.

But in earlier times also man could point to splendid achievements. During all the centuries and millennia of his development he was continually striving to make his mastery over nature a practical reality.

He shapes *matter* and creates buildings like the pyramids and the giant temples of Luxor and Karnak in ancient Egypt, the Parthenon in Athens, the Colosseum in Rome. He builds cathedrals, like St. Sophia in Constantinople, St. Peter's in Rome, St. Paul's in London and the soaring Gothic lines of those in Cologne and Milan. He erects great buildings of steel and stone like the Eiffel Tower in Paris (985 feet), the Empire State building in New York (102 stories) and the Merchandise Mart Building in Chicago, this—with its 90 acres of floor space under a single roof—the largest house in the world.

He works with dead marble and forms out of it works of art like Phidias' statues of Pallas Athene and of Zeus, the Hermes of Praxiteles and—at the beginning of our modern age—the David, the Moses and the Pieta of Michelangelo.

He controls the realm of *colour* and creates masterpieces like the Sistine

Chapel and Raphael's "Madonna," Leonardo da Vinci's "Last Supper" and Reubens' and Rembrandt's pictures.

He has mastered *space*. His trains hasten across countries, his aeroplanes speed through the air, his ships cross the oceans. The telephone and telegraph carry his messages over land and sea. Indeed, he is advancing into space, soon perhaps to reach the moon; today this belongs to the practical problems of the technician and his laboratories. The first man-made planet has passed the moon and reached the space between moon and sun (1958).

He rules the realm of *sound* and conjures up the most glorious melodies, e.g. Beethoven's Ninth Symphony, Bach's organ works and chorales, Mozart's violin concertos, Handel's oratorios and the great Hallelujah Chorus.

He investigates the realm of *life* in the natural sciences and medicine. He is mastering, to an increasing degree, even the *invisible powers of nature, viz.* electricity, radio waves, atomic energy.

It is completely impossible to enumerate or to give an appreciation of even his highest achievements.

At the same time, however, man catastrophically misuses his inventions and discoveries. From the earliest times he has used metals and fire as weapons of destruction. With the release and use of atomic energy, a warning has been given of a transformation in human history, apocalyptic in its nature. Man applying technical science, particularly atomic physics, now has powers in his hand which by far surpass everything he possessed in the past. This technical development, once it has made its fresh beginning, can no longer be stopped. Man, however, by misusing his control over nature, intensifies also his methods of battle for mastery over his fellow creatures. As has already been the case with so many inventions in the past, so now also today we see—in a very special, even dramatic manner—the puzzling and fateful double-facedness of his practical application of the powers of nature.

"We are living in the first dawning of a new age . . . Its birth pangs are both horrible and sublime. Within seconds they burnt whole cities to dust, and within days they ended the most terrible, greatest and most senseless struggle between the nations which has ever shaken and devastated the structure of the civilizations of the earth. The atom is the terror and the hope of the world. . . . Since the discoveries of Einstein and Planck, science has had fundamentally to recast its picture of the physical world. Technical science expects that the atomic-powered machine will free mankind from need and suffering. Romantics are warning against the kindling of an atomic fire which could perhaps become inextinguishable and destroy our planet. Philosophers perceive in the penetration of man into the innermost secrets of matter, a presumption which tries to upset the limits which God has set. Statesmen gather at world conferences to discuss how a misuse of atomic energy can be prevented. Generals declare that armies and fleets are on the point of losing their meaning, since there is no possible defence against the power of the atom. The whole world has been brought into a state of excitement by the smallest thing in it—the atom" (Gail, pp. 38, 71).

In addition there is a second factor to be considered. Man now has the possibility through inventions, geographical discoveries and the modern technical science of *world transport* (by railway, motor-car, aeroplane and ocean liner) of a general *exchange of ideas* (by printing, international postal union, radio, the telephone and telegraph) and of an extensive *co-operation* through the mutual purchase and sale of industrial products, so that the nations are drawing ever closer together. For the first time the history of mankind has developed from its former multiplicity of histories of peoples into a unitary "world" history. The globe has become "small." Everything is now one common stage. Under certain circumstances a comparatively insignificant event in some small Near-Eastern state could lead to decisive events for the whole of mankind.

What Friedrich Nietzsche had already foreseen is happening in our day. The struggle between the nations is now not merely for predominance in individual lands or continents, but for the actual dominion of the whole earth. Now the question—in politics, economics, ideology and culture—is who is to be "king of the earth." It is no longer a conflict between single nations or groups of nations, but increasingly a conflict of *everyone against everyone for everything*. For the first time in the history of the human race, since the middle of the twentieth century the stake transcends continents and is global. Our planet earth has as a unity and totality become the object of technical, political and cultural planning for the first time in the history of man.

Finally only *one* shall hold the field as victor; he will then be the "king of the earth," and at the same time the eschatological world-king, the "Antichrist" prophesied in the Bible. Through the misuse of technical science and industry, radio and the press, economics and politics, the nations of today are preparing the literal fulfilment of New Testament prophecy at top speed.

Then, however, Christ will appear and conquer the "universal victor." He will be in truth the eternal "king of the earth" who gives true happiness to mankind, and the kingdom of God will smash the godless world-empire to pieces (Dan. 2: 34, 44, 54; II Thess. 2: 8; Rev. 13: 7, 18; 19: 11-21).

"The breath-taking events of our day point us anew to the prophetic words of Holy Scripture. Above all the happenings upon earth runs God's world-plan from creation to consummation" (Müller).

The real blame for this self-glorifying, suicidal development does not lie on physics and technical science by themselves, but on the failure of morality in the human heart. The physicist and natural scientist in himself is merely an investigator concerned simply in penetrating the secrets of nature for the sake of pure knowledge and truth. It is only when his discoveries are used in the battle of everyone against everyone that they become instruments of destruction and mass unhappiness. "The choice between disaster and happiness, war and peace, is not made within the atom, but in the heart of man" (Gail).

Yet it is precisely our own day that has been presented with inventions and discoveries the implications of which are comparable only with the discovery of the use of fire at the very beginning of human history. It has gambled away possibilities and continues to gamble them away in a way that no other period of humanity has done since Adam and Eve. Despite all our colleges and universities the statement of the American evangelist Billy Graham is completely valid, "Our generation will go down in history as the generation of fools."

So man, taken as a whole, despite the most brilliant achievements in art and science, and the highest and most idealistic aspirations of untold individuals amongst all peoples, has repeatedly treated God's gifts and the powers placed by God in nature disgracefully. He has wished to be king of the earth while rejecting the King of the universe. He has misused the glory and power of God in nature to satisfy his own greed for power and self-glorification. In so doing he has become, not a king, but a rebel; instead of achieving exaltation, he finds himself on the road to self-destruction. The final result is not the happiness of mankind, but universal catastrophe (Rev. 19: 19–21). Unbelief is suicide by the deluded, who consider God's truth a delusion and their own delusions the truth. That is the intellectual position of millions at the beginning of the atomic age.

Nevertheless God, despite all man's failure, holds firmly to His purposes of salvation and in Christ brings them to their fulfilment. Man is and continues to be the object of the highest purposes of His love. Because of this man's noble standing and kingly calling remain.

VII. MAN AS THE PROPHET, KING AND PRIEST OF THE EARTH

Man is an organism combining spirit and body and a free personality. As such he occupies, according to the plan of the Creator, a double position in relationship to God and the world. With regard to the world he is its lord; with regard to God he is His image. Thus he stands between the Creator and creation as a whole, between the world perceptible through the senses and the invisible one, between the temporal and the eternal.

Man is lord of the earthly creation. The very fact of his knowledge and understanding make him this, for understanding is always a prerequisite for the exercise of lordship. Only he who understands a matter aright can really control it, possess it and subdue it.

Man's knowledge and understanding win him a *prophetic* status in creation. His mind penetrates the nature of things and investigates their final connexions and causes. He perceives the spiritual ideas which lie behind all earthly phenomena. He grasps the eternal truths which express themselves in all that is transitory and visible. We see this most perfectly in the parables of Jesus, the Son of God and Son of Man, whose many-sided parabolic language so naturally and profoundly elevates everything earthly by making it an image of the heavenly. Thus man, by his understanding, becomes the interpreter of the meaning of earthly nature, and by virtue of it exercises a prophetic task in his earthly kingdom.

This understanding makes his rule possible in practice. His ability joins hands with his knowledge. The understanding of his mind is the royal sceptre he holds. He can harness the forces of nature like steeds for his chariot, in which he sets out to celebrate his royal triumph over the earth. His thoughts and his will rule over the earth, and thanks to this union of ability and knowledge he adds his functions as *king* to those as prophet.

This world, however, is not only man's royal domain, but also first and foremost the sphere of *God's* dominion. Therefore man does not only belong to this world, but also at the same time to that higher one. Only by virtue of this is he in any sense the crown of creation. Only because eternity towers up into his innermost being can he fill earthly things with an eternal content. It is only his relationship to God that gives his relationship to the world its deepest and eternal significance. Therefore our highest royal dignity is achieved only by dedicating this transitory world to the service of the Eternal.

This, however, makes of man's position as king also a holy vocation to *priesthood*. As prophets and kings of this visible world we are priests of that which is eternal. We dedicate the earthly to the heavenly and lay the created realm as it were an offering upon the altar of the eternal Creator. As God's representatives and priests on earth we have to present and dedicate ourselves and the world to God. In this priestly devotion of everything earthly to God all the activity of our knowledge and ability are perfected, and man's role as prophet and king is perfected by his role as priest. Therefore the highest expression of man's nobility, so far as his duty to the earthly creation is concerned, is that he is this trinity in unity: prophet of the earth, king of the earth and priest of the earth Godwards (cf. Luthardt, pp. 93–96).

CHAPTER VII

THE WINNING BACK OF THE EARTH THROUGH THE RULE OF MAN

G OD had given man a high task. He was to administer the earth in the holy service of the Most High. He was to be the Creator's viceroy in this region of His created kingdom.

I. Man's Royal Commission

As we have seen, the earth outside the bounds of Paradise, which man was to rule and bring into his service, had on principle not yet been withdrawn from the influence and activity of the powers of darkness. Therefore the spread of man's rule over the earth would mean a progressive and increasing dislodgement of Satan. "Man, while he stood in the service of God, should both serve the earth, and take possession of it and transform it for the Divine purpose for which it was created" (Kroeker). Little by little earthly creation would thus have been delivered from the devil, released from his rule and reconquered for God. Thus man's appointed vocation in Paradise consisted in the winning back of the earth for God,[1] and this again was based upon the sovereignty of God over man and the sovereignty of man over the creation.

If man had spread his rule over the whole earth, i.e. if he had reached the goal fixed by God for human development, a complete liberation of the creation, of the plant and animal kingdoms would have been achieved. Even the fact that this miracle will be associated with the setting up of the kingdom of God in the last days proves our contention.

"And the wolf shall dwell with the lamb, and the leopard shall lie down with the kid; and the calf and the young lion and the fatling together; and

[1] We could also say, the "redemption" of the earth. If anyone prefers not to use the word "redeemer" (redemption) of man because of its normal application to Christ, he can say, liberator, rescuer, or even instrument of winning back. The important thing is the fact, not the expression. Nevertheless it is worth considering that the same word "redeemer" (Gr. *lytrotēs*) that refers to God in Psalm 19: 14 and 78: 35 (Septuagint) is nevertheless in Acts 7: 35 applied to a man (Moses). These are the only places where this word is found in Scripture. In the same way the word saviour, deliverer (Gr. *sōtēr*), which is almost always used of God (e.g. I Tim. 1: 1) and of Christ (e.g. Phil. 3: 20), is nevertheless at times applied to God-sent human deliverers, such as Othniel (Judg. 3: 9) and Jeroboam II of Israel (II Kings 13: 5; cf. 14: 25). This shows that in this respect the Bible knows no hard and fast dogmatic terminology.

a little child shall lead them. And the cow and the bear shall feed; their young ones shall lie down together: and the lion shall eat straw like the ox" (Isa. 11: 6, 7). "The wilderness and the solitary place shall be glad; and the desert shall rejoice, and blossom as the rose" (Isa. 35: 1). "Instead of the thorn shall come up the fir tree, and instead of the brier shall come up the myrtle tree" (Isa. 55: 13; cf. Joel 2: 21–23). The difference is that God's purpose, which originally was to be reached by undeviating development *without* sin, will then be accomplished through victory over sin, i.e. by redemption. Thus when Scripture clearly states this *goal* of God's history with man—with the vegetable and animal kingdoms as well—it proves what His original plan was. Otherwise we should fall prey to the error, almost bordering on Pantheism, that God needed human sin to reach through redemption that which could not have been achieved through a development without sin.

It is conceivable, it might be said, that nature could have been redeemed without being involved in human history. The two might have been on parallel lines. But the Biblical description of the last days shows that this is not the plan of God, which shows an interweaving of the redemption of the world of nature with the perfecting of man's development. Thus the description of the *end* becomes a proof of what God had purposed for man, when He first created him.

Professor Bettex has said that originally man was to "reconquer the whole earth as God's viceroy. When God created a world of light, the heavens, Lucifer and his host rebelled against Him. God did not spare the angels. On their dwelling place, however, now 'waste and void'—a chaos that, as St. Martin says, resembled the morning after a battle—God created something new, planting there a garden of Paradise out of which a new being, created in His likeness, should gradually occupy the whole earth, and win it back for God."

Man was, to quote Professor Franz Delitzsch, "to effect the conquest of an evil being who had penetrated into creation," or, as the Swiss expositor S. Limbach expresses it, "the liberation of this world," through Satan's "being legally forced back." Man's calling was to "destroy the works of the devil" and to renew the earth, thus transforming it into an abode of light and life. Just as the kingdom of God, which has drawn near in Christ, is to spread itself over the whole earth and all the kingdoms are to belong again to Him, so the first man also would have received the task, beginning from Paradise, to restore the whole earth to an abode of the presence and revelation of God. His service as ruler consisted in bringing the whole of creation through his mediation into relation with the glory of God and in making the "fulness of Him that filleth all in all" accessible to it. As God's "fellow-worker" he was to "lead the earthly creation towards its renewed glorification and acceptance in the choir of the light-worlds in the heavens, and thereby to the goal of its perfection, when one day the uncreated glory of God will enter into the closest union with the new earth" (Keerl). With *man* a world-wide work of God was to begin; from him "the great process of leading the whole creation back to God should take its start" (von Huene, p. 73). In man's dignity as ruler lay his call to be redeemer.

For all that Paradise was not the scene of man's creation. For the clear statement, that "The Lord took the man, and put him into the garden of Eden" (Gen. 2: 8, 15), is meaningful only if the creation of man took place *outside* Paradise.[1] Before man was placed in the garden he had to see the earth as it was outside Paradise, so as to gain a right and deep appreciation of the glory of Paradise and his calling which extended beyond it.[2] Or, as Keerl says, "When the first man opened his eyes in full consciousness immediately after his creation, the landscape of Eden lay before him, which, as he could not hide from himself, was no really suitable dwelling-place for him. His removal to Paradise was to make him conscious of the difference between the two regions. It allowed him to appreciate with gratitude the depth and height of the grace and love of his God; they were revealed by God's preparation of this place of light and life for him. For these reasons his removal to Paradise is twice emphasized" (Gen. 2: 8, 15).

Thus God had created all the conditions necessary for man, basing himself on his spiritual nature, to fulfil his call, starting from Paradise, the historical base and centre of his rule, "to rule the world and to ennoble it as a kingdom of God, where everything in its service would reveal something of the glory of God."

II. The Symbolism of the Four Rivers of Paradise

This worldwide purpose of Paradise seems to be indicated by the four rivers which flowed out of the garden to the rest of the earth. We read, "And a river went out of Eden to water the garden; and from thence it was parted, and became four heads. The name of the first is Pishon; that is it which compasseth the whole land of Havilah. . . . And the name of the second river is Gihon: the same is it that compasseth the whole land of Cush. And the name of the third river is Hiddekel: that is it which goeth in front of Assyria. And the fourth river is Euphrates" (Gen. 2: 10–14).

We are persuaded that in the Word of God nothing is superfluous or without meaning. So we believe that there is a deeper significance to be found in these rivers and especially in that they are four in number. In Scripture numbers often have a symbolic sense, and four is especially the mark of extension in all directions yet finally limited. It is the number of the world, with its four chief points of the compass, four seasons of the year, four earthly kingdoms of creation[3] and, according to ancient oriental

---

[1] Eve was, of course, formed in the garden.

[2] So also Delitzsch: "The Lord God *took hold* of the man and *set him down* in the garden of Eden."

[3] Human, animal, vegetable and mineral.

thought, four elements[1] and four dimensions.[2] So everything existing in the world—space, time, the world of life, matter and form—is governed by the number four. In relation to the general history of salvation, then, the number four denotes the extension of the kingdom of God over the whole earth, or, otherwise expressed, its "growing oneness."

The fact of the four streams from Paradise indicates then that the blessing of Paradise was to reach out to all lands and that salvation should extend in streams of blessing to all the earth. But since this was to be effected through man, the four rivers symbolize the cosmic calling of man as redeemer.

III. AN ILLUSTRATION FROM HISTORY

An event in secular history gives us a small picture of this high calling of the human race. It is the commission which brought Count Frederick VI of Hohenzollern, burgrave of Nuremberg, in 1411 into Brandenburg. Ever since the death of the Emperor Charles IV (1378), especially under Jobst von Mähren, terrible conditions had prevailed there. Since Jobst seldom visited Brandenburg, the local nobles took the opportunity for robbery and other wild deeds. The two brothers Hans and Dietrich von Quitzow stood out above the other noble families, Schulenburg, Alvensleben, Putlitz, Rochow and Bredow, in this time of anarchy by their plundering and robberies, based on their strong castles of Friesack, Plaue, Golzow and Beuthen, by which they tried to increase their possessions and power. At last King Sigismund (1410–1437) sent his devoted servant Frederick VI, burgrave of Nuremberg, to this eastern frontier region that had run wild to restore order, with the title "Supreme Administrator and Captain of the March." Later, at the Council of Constance (1414–18), the king handed over the province to him, not merely as an area to be administrated but as a hereditary principality, with the title of Elector of the Empire and the office of Lord High Chamberlain (April 30, 1415). This was shortly afterwards legally confirmed by a solemn enfeoffment (April 18, 1417).

The task of this South-German lord in Brandenburg was first of all to bring the land and the refractory nobles into subjection to *himself.* But what King Sigismund envisaged as the chief purpose of sending and later enfeoffing him was obviously nothing less than that, through the enforcement of a rule loyal to him in the country, his *own* royal authority should be restored and the whole region be recovered *for himself.* When Frederick VI brought a province that had revolted against his king under his own sway, since he remained faithful to his lord, he did in fact reconquer it for his overlord and "redeemed" the land from the power of its oppressors. That is what—only in an incomparably greater setting and by other

[1] Air, water, earth and fire, cf. Nah. 1: 3b–6.
[2] Length, breadth, depth and height, cf. Eph. 3: 18.

means—man was to effect within the universal kingdom of God upon this earth.

IV. The Redemption of the Earth through the Redemption of Man

The objection has been raised: How could God in creating Adam have had, as it were, the thought that the earth should be won back through *him*, seeing that in virtue of His omniscience He had from all eternity foreseen the fall of man and had therefore appointed *Christ*, His Son, to be the Redeemer (I Pet. 1: 20; Eph. 1: 4)? For then there would have been, in some sense, *two* redeemers!

The following three points suggest an answer.

(1) God often commands even when He knows that men will not obey. His commands do not depend on the obedience of man. *He* is Lord and Master; His freedom can never be annulled by the free will of the creature. It is *His* will that rules on the throne of the universe, not the pleasure of His creatures. So He gave man the task of guarding the garden of Eden, although He knew that he would not carry it out. Similarly He says in another place, "Look unto Me and be ye saved, *all* the ends of the earth" (Isa. 45: 22), and yet He knew from all eternity that only the "little flock" of His believers would respond to this invitation (Luke 12: 32; Rom. 8: 29; I Pet. 1: 1). God's purposes and aims in grace for the children of men cannot be measured by what they, in their imperfections and finiteness, actually reach. The possibilities which He creates, the fulfilment of which He most seriously intends, frequently, indeed almost always, transcend the reality which His creatures actually attain.[1] Often the most intricate detours and the most varied forms of training are needed to make the creature forsake his false ways and return to the task given him at the first by God. But this does not hinder God from making known at the beginning of a life's course its goal and programme (cf. Jonah 1: 2; cf. v. 3). In any case, however, whether God reaches His purposes with men at once, or by roundabout ways, or not at all (especially in the case of the eternally lost), the saying is always valid, "God is greater than our heart."

(2) Nor is it to be overlooked that, when we speak of a paradisal calling of "man," we mean this in a collective sense of man*kind*. We must obviously not teach that God perhaps purposed or thought, humanly speaking, that Adam, alone or in union with his wife, would perfectly implement the call to be the redeemer of the earth. The task with all its implications applies to him rather as the ancestor and organic representative of his whole posterity.[2] Therefore it says first, "Be fruitful, and

[1] Compare e.g. the boundaries of Canaan fixed by God with those historically reached (Gen. 15: 18).

[2] Cf. Rom. 5: 12–21; I Cor. 15: 22; cf. Heb. 7: 9, 10.

multiply, and people the earth," and only then does God add, "and subdue it; and have dominion . . . over every living thing" (Gen. 1: 28).

Many may be inclined to ask here whether, in these circumstances, we should speak at all of a "paradisal" appointment of mankind. For Adam's posterity, who would have the chief share in carrying out this task, did not yet exist. Nevertheless it is clear at once that the expression is well justified, and indeed necessary. For the human race began after all in Paradise and should have let its activity radiate from there. Further, the aim of this whole development was the transformation of the earth once again into a Paradise. It must surely therefore be unchallengeable, when we describe the *whole* activity of *all* participants as a "paradisal" calling, even though we include those not born in the Paradise period but who were as Adam's posterity already seen "in" him. Paradise was indeed the beginning and end, starting point and goal, foundation, programme and pattern of the collective, total duty of mankind on earth.

(3) Finally, we have a passage in Paul's epistles which shows us most clearly that, even after the fall, the redemption of the earth is most intimately bound up with the perfecting of man. The apostle writes: "The earnest expectation of the creation waiteth for the revealing of the sons of God. For the creation was subjected to vanity, not of its own will, but by reason of Him who subjected it, in hope that the creation itself also shall be delivered from the bondage of corruption into the liberty of the glory of the children of God. For we know that the whole creation groaneth and travaileth in pain together until now" (Rom. 8: 19–22).

What makes this passage so particularly important in our context is its testimony that, even after the fall, the destiny and the redemption of the earth remain indissolubly united with the existence and development of the human race. The redemption of the earth is, in spite of all, still bound up with man. Creation nevertheless still waits for the revealing of the glory of the sons of God. Even though its liberation may in many respects come along other lines than might have been the case had man not sinned; yet the basic thought remains, that *man* is the instrument for the redemption of the earthly creation. And because this remains God's way and goal, there can be a new heaven and a new earth only *after* the great white throne, i.e. after the completion and conclusion of the history of human redemption (Rev. 21 and 22; cf. 20: 11–15).

For all that it would not be right to regard man as the sole object of Christ's saving work. For great and mighty as is the redemption the Lord has brought to man, it goes inconceivably far beyond it. It is true that man stands at the centre of God's purposes of salvation, and it has indeed pleased Him to crystallize in man the mighty thoughts of His loving decrees, so that without man's history of salvation there would be no history of salvation at all; but for all that man is in no way justified in regarding himself as the *only* goal of the redeeming activity of Christ.

G

Rather, the plan of redemption, just as it works through man, so it extends far beyond him. With the redemption of man are linked things in heaven (Heb. 9: 23; Isa. 30: 26), on earth,[1] and things under the earth (Phil. 2: 10); this wholly surpasses our present powers of thought, and is revealed to us in the Word of God gently and through hints. To desire to lift the veil of mystery here would be to wish to eat again of the fruit of the tree of knowledge. Therefore the doctrine of universalism is also not justified Biblically.

V. CHRIST—THE LAST ADAM

Christ accomplished down here the work which the Father also gave Him to do as the Son of *Man*. As *man* He once wore the crown of thorns, which the soil, unredeemed and under the curse, yielded Him, and as *man* He will on the day of cosmic regeneration (Matt. 19:28), as the Head of His body, reign with all His saints over the same soil—now redeemed and free from the curse. The *Divine* Redeemer became *man* and as such redeemed mankind, the ruler of the earth, and bound him to Himself in an eternal, inseparable oneness, and *thus* at the same time effected the redemption of the earth. This is the way discovered by grace. The old vocation of man thus remains, but it has been completely filled with a new content. In Christ as its Head man reaches the goal for which he was created. As the "last Adam" (I Cor. 15: 45; Rom. 5: 12–21) He is his centre, crown and star. The whole race of man is "a circle, and in the course of the history of salvation Jesus Christ is more and more shown to be the centre of this circle."

Thus in the deepest sense there is only *one* redeemer, namely Christ in His oneness with the redeemed, the Head in His organic connexion with His members, the "new man" (Eph. 2: 15), "the Christ."[2] Professor von Huene writes, "The entire process by which the whole creation is brought back to God takes its start from man. In man there meet matter and spirit, God's spirit. The *Man* Jesus Christ, God's Son, has emerged victorious from the decisive battle against Satan, and its results are now being worked out. Therefore the cross stands at the centre of universal history."

"The Middle Ages served God with a devotion worthy of admiration. But God is only to be found in *one* place, in the Man Jesus Christ, and therefore the medieval linking of Christian faith and Greek philosophy was bound to end in weariness and resignation.

"Our modern era is searching for man, man in an entirely new historical realization, but man also is only to be found in one place, in the Man Jesus Christ, and it is precisely here that our age has not wanted to seek Him. Thus our modern era is ending, despite its brilliant cultural achievements,

[1] In the animal world, Isa. 11:6; Hos. 2:18, 22. In the vegetable world, Isa. 55:12, 13.
[2] That is, the Christ-organism, as in I Cor. 12: 12; 1: 13 (in Greek with the definite article).

in the self-destruction of man. But behind the disgraced and disfigured face of man the face of the Crucified is being seen again today, the face of the Crucified as of the one true man" (Howe, p. 17).

Thus everything is gathered together in Jesus, the Son of Man. He is the centre of the whole. He is the greatest of all, indeed, the one before all others. He is "the purest amongst the mighty and the most mighty amongst the pure" (Jean Paul). By the touch of His pierced hands He has brought kingdoms to their fall; He has turned the current of the centuries from its course and the ages obey His command. He is the centre and the turning-point of the whole history of man.

He is, as the Son of Man, the unique one of our race. He is the true Man, the goal of all human history. He is the Representative of mankind itself, the embodied pattern of true humanity. In Him not merely isolated aspects of human nature but the whole of human nature in all its Divinely willed truth and purity receives its perfect expression.

Because He is our pattern He is also our example. In Jesus, the Son of Man, every man equally finds his example. He is for us all—for all men at all times and under all circumstances—the highest, most comprehensive and inexhaustible example. He is the secret of our longing. Though we may not even know it, we all love Him in the depths of our being. We are all concerned with Him. Only in Him does our soul find peace. Therefore He builds up everything on His own person. As the Son of Man He leads mankind to the goal of its vocation.

VI. FROM PARADISE TO PARADISE

"From paradise to paradise," such is the path of mankind according to God's all-loving plan. Created for life and prosperity, for peace and joy, man longs to return to the gates of his homeland. But between the gates of the first and of the second Paradise stands the Mediator, the Man from heaven, "the man Christ Jesus" (I Tim. 2: 5), the Saviour of the world. Therefore, reader, let me ask you: is He already *your* Saviour? Do you already know Him?

Between the garden of the first and of the second Paradise there lies another, that quiet garden, the garden of Gethsemane, where in sternest struggle for you and me Jesus sought the face of His Father. Do you know that garden, the place of His supplication, the place of His struggle for *you*?

Between the rivers of Eden, which watered the whole earth, and the river of life above, beautiful and clear as crystal, flows the stream from His side, His blood which He shed for sinners on the cross. This blood is the price paid for *all*, gaining the riches of heaven for *all*. But faith must lay hold on this personally. Only thus will the work of the Redeemer become yours.

Between the trees of the first and of the second Paradise there stands, silent and sublime, that other tree, the tree of shame, the accursed tree of the cross, upon which Christ once hung. From this cross God stretches out His hand to the lost wanderer in the wilderness, longing to bring him back for ever from his own ways to the heavenly homeland. With his origins in Eden and longing for Eden, the sinner may find his place of rest at the cross. "Blessed are they that long for home, for they shall reach home." "The cross of Calvary is home for the homeless."

Have you come to know this, even as I have?

PART III

THE ROYAL DIGNITY OF THE REDEEMED AND GOD'S WAY OF REDEMPTION

CHAPTER VIII

THE DIVINE NOBILITY OF TRUE CHRISTIAN LIVING

To be a man or woman means fighting, to be a Christian means conquering. Biblical Christianity is endorsement of life and transfiguration of the world in the noblest and most perfect sense. Right at the beginning of the Bible man is described as a royal race: "Replenish the earth! Subdue it! Have dominion!" (Gen. 1: 28). Here is a call to a kingly control of the world and nature, an appointment to a holy, spiritual nobility. Man is master and ruler of the powers of the world of nature, executor of its tasks and goals, fulfiller of its unconscious longing. According to God's plan all men are members of a royal family. They are therefore called to be royal in disposition and conduct, noble in word and deed.

But how can one reconcile certain principles of Christian ethics with all this? Does not the Bible hold up for us the ideals of modesty and humility, meekness and patience, gentleness and yieldingness, goodness and love, self-denial and renunciation of worldly joys and earthly pleasures? Where is there place then for strength of will, self-assertion, self-respect, power of resistance, joy in nature, enjoyment of life?

More than this, the Bible is full of the sinfulness of man, of his moral weakness, even of his complete impotence to improve himself. It even tells him quite frankly that he was born in sin, is a slave of the evil one and cannot in his own strength free himself from this dungeon, so that, if he is to be helped at all, it can be only through the activity of another, a higher being, in short, only through an act of Divine *grace* and *mercy*.

Is not all this an affront to human dignity? Do not therefore the basic concepts of Christian ethics and redemption contradict a vigorous humanity and consequently deny in practice the royal nobility of man? Is not man, according to the Bible, much rather in practice a slave and a beggar, in no way a king or a ruler? Where *is* his dignity to be found?

MODERN CARICATURES OF THE ROYAL NOBILITY OF MAN

These questions are being repeatedly asked by our contemporaries. Earlier too, indeed at all times, the vitality of those brought into contact with the message of the Bible has often felt itself limited, assailed, even challenged by it.

Modern man's tendency to reject Biblical ethics was nourished in the nineteenth century by natural philosophy, especially that of Darwin and Haeckel, in so far as it was applied to the ethics of individual life and racial history. Darwin himself kept his teachings within the bounds of natural research and natural philosophy, but others soon applied his biological principles in the intellectual and moral fields. "Systems of Evolutionary Ethics" arose and were systematically developed by philosophers and sociologists in different countries.

If it were true that the principle of all development is a universal "struggle for existence" in which the stronger holds his ground and the weaker (rightly!) perishes, and if it were true that man and the world can progress only by following the dictates of force, how could one still grant validity to virtues such as love, generosity, goodness, yieldingness, gentleness, sympathy and mercy?

Then surely only the "will to power" would have any value, only the contrast "strong and weak," but not "good and evil" have any validity. Only the "superman" could succeed (Nietzsche)! Might would be right, both in private life, in business and in international politics! Then surely the normal (!) principle of all human progress would be self-assertion, might, indeed force. Would not selfishness be healthy and lack of thought for others good?

Would it not be downright "good" for the continuing development of the whole that the weak perish? What place would there still be for Christianity with its charity and mercy? Would it not rather have to be rejected as disturbing to development and hostile to life? Must we not develop a new, consciously "anti-Christian" ethics, "*Beyond* good and evil" (cf. Nietzsche, *Antichrist*), a "revaluation of all values"?

We know the terrible historical catastrophes these ethical inferences from the theory of evolution and the natural philosophy of the nineteenth century have led to. To a very great extent the intellectual, ethical, economic and political world situation of the present atomic age stands under their influence.

What Darwin taught in the biological field in his theory of "Natural Selection" (survival of the fittest) in the "struggle for existence" as the principle of all upward development, was applied by Fredrich Nietzsche with his doctrine of the "superman" in the field of ethics. The moral philosophy of Nietzsche became one of the chief roots of Nazi ideology. Darwin himself was neither atheist nor theist but a representative of deism (the belief in God as creator, who has neither revealed Himself nor worked miracles). Nietzsche was an atheist. The ideology of Hitler's Third Reich was, in its official utterances, chiefly pantheistic; hence its frequent use of "Providence."

Of course lack of thought for others, violence and bloodshed have been the sombre characteristics of human history amongst all races and peoples and on all continents long before the nineteenth century. World history, so rich in wars, world-conquerors, dictators and mass-murders bears witness to this. The unrestrained master-man had already been glorified by the ancient Greek philosophers and sophists (e.g. Callicles, Thrasymachus, c. 400 B.C.). During the Italian Renaissance especially Machiavelli (1469–1527) and his contemporary Cesare Borgia—the latter subsequently praised by Nietzsche as an example of his superman—advocated this point of view. The evolutionary natural and moral philosophies of the nineteenth century, with their theory of the prerogative of the stronger in the battle of everyone against everyone, gave this whole attitude to life a positive, ideological character and an apparently "scientific" basis. Its representatives in private, economic and political life now for its first time really felt themselves confirmed in their way of life. These theoretical systems, worked out in their studies by the scientists and philosophers of last century, uniting with the rapid rise of technical knowledge, particularly in communications and armaments, have had a real share in the catastrophic consequences in the world situation right down to the present day.

All who can and wish to see will find this proof, drawn from contemporary history, abundantly clear that *this* kind of lording it over others does not lead to kingship but to slavery, not to the endorsement of life but to its destruction, not to honour but to degradation, not to exaltation but to humiliation. Every realistic and objective study of history must recognize that such an ideal of domination is the way to destruction, that unrestricted lust for recognition and will to power are merely a degrading caricature of human dignity, indeed, the satanic, demonic counterpart to the true nobility of man.

But even, where the rejection of Christian morality has not been carried to these extremes, a certain resistance to Biblical ethics is found among the strong and healthy, especially among the young. They will not bow and recognize their impotence and ask for mercy. They will not deny themselves, renounce the pleasures of the world and of life and engage in the battle of the spirit against the flesh. They refuse, to use the popular expression, to say "No" to life. They will not "crawl to the cross."

What answer has the Christian to these objections to Christian ethics?

We have seen that the general, "*cultural*" statements of the Bible—that man is called to control and investigate nature, and to make inventions and discoveries—agree with his royal dignity. In the same way, the general outline of the history of salvation in Scripture—that man through his kingship on earth is an instrument in the hand of the Creator for the liberation and perfecting of the earth—bear witness to this high position of honour. What shall we say then of the *moral* teaching of the Bible? How far does this, in spite of its apparent disagreement, harmonize with the high dignity of the human race, that is, with the kingship and nobility of man?

I. HONOUR AND HUMILITY

Biblical humility is not infamy of character. It is the courageous result of a sober sense of reality. For, while making due recognition of all that is good and noble, it is right to see things, and also men, as they really are.

In his setting in the universe man is already small. Let us visualize of a number of pinheads, each a twenty-fifth of an inch in diameter and separated from the nearest by anything from 20 to 60 miles; if this represents the distribution of the stars in the universe, the 1,300,000th part of one of these pinheads, would represent the earth. One fiftieth of the surface of this microscopic speck of dust would be Europe, Europe from the south of Italy to the north of Scandinavia, from the Straits of Gibraltar to the Urals!

The bodily weight of man is also negligible. It is the 78 sextillionth part of this speck of dust we have pictured as representing the earth (a sextillion is a 1 followed by 36 noughts)! All the buildings in the world, all its ships, cities and villages, everything that its 2,700 million inhabitants live in and use put together, would not occupy even two and a half cubic miles. That is barely a thousand millionth part of this speck of cosmic dust we call "earth." How senseless then is all self-deification, how foreign to reality, how retrograde and childish, how naïve and primitive! It is as though Copernicus, modern astronomy, and a modern scientific picture of the universe had never existed.

But from the intellectual standpoint also man is small, in spite of all his progress in science and art. We are far from belittling the attainments of the human mind. Indeed, in the realms of technical science and organization its achievements are almost incredible. His urge for knowledge has even soared to the stars, and he has been able to discern the laws governing worlds thousands of millions of miles distant from our solar system. But it is equally true that he has never grasped the real fundamentals of existence. Even today, in the age of atomic research, we must admit that we do not know what "matter," or "life," or "death" is. Apart from Divine revelation we do not know the origin of the universe, and just as little its goal. "We swim in wonders like a fish in water" and daily explain things of which we know little by things of which we know nothing. As Goethe said, "We are eternally dealing with problems. Man is a mysterious being. He knows little about the world and least of all about himself." Even the triumphant achievements of modern science have in essentials been unable to change this fact.

True enough we can now see deeper into the nature of matter, and know that it is merely a swarm of many small and even smaller particles which revolve around and between one another with amazing speed, according to mathematical laws. But what these tiny basic particles, these electrons, protons and neutrons, actually are, no one can say.

How far are they solid and substantial? How far are they perhaps only small units of electricity, only phenomena of energy, bound to certain circumstances in the space-time continuum? Does our optical impression of something solid and firm arise perhaps only through their speed of motion?[1]

Is there in fact such a thing at all as "matter" in our customary use of the term? Can one still say that matter exists? Is it not perhaps better to say that matter happens? Is not all that seems at rest around us in fact a never-ceasing action, a continuous stream of events?

No one—not even the greatest physicists of our day—can completely answer all these questions. No one knows what really takes place in nature. We observe only the effects of events within nature, but not the nature of its forces. "The Creator has clearly taken care that we men should not satisfy our curiosity by looking into His workshop" (Heim, II, p. 166).

Dr. Wernher von Braun, the successful German-American scientist and director of the American army's rocket research, who on February 1, 1958 succeeded in launching the first American earth-satellite, has said, "The more we penetrate into science the more clearly we see that the terms which sound so profound are merely bad camouflage for human ignorance."

Thus the mysteries of the natural world have only increased the deeper we have penetrated into it. The more we look into these depths the more we realize the limits of our reason. Only the half-educated and ignorant can dispute this. Pascal said, "The last step of reason is to recognize that there are infinitely many things which go beyond it. And if reason does not come to recognize this, then it is very weak!"

"We must widen our minds to embrace the Divine mysteries, and not narrow these mysteries to the measure of our minds," wrote Bacon, the great English scholar. Hamann, the "Magus of the North," one of the greatest thinkers in the late eighteenth century, said similarly, "Once one has discovered what reason is, all discrepancy between it and faith ends."

Thus the natural sciences educate us in modesty and humility. "It is a well-known fact," says Professor D. Luthardt, "that the more thorough an investigator is, the humbler and more modest he becomes, for he realizes his limitations the more. On the other hand, the more superficial he is, the prouder he tends to be."

It should be obvious that we are not recommending our readers to be as ignorant as possible. How easily and thoughtlessly the wise maxim of Socrates is sometimes repeated—but without Socrates' wisdom—"I know that I know nothing." When we meet such irrational intellectual laziness or, at least, weakness, we should do well to quote the maxim of another

[1] See the note to Chapter 10, p. 159.

wise man, "Few know how much one has to know to know how little one knows!" In any case it remains true that worth-while knowledge promotes true modesty.

All this proves that true humility is no contradiction of human honour. It is the ethical conclusion drawn by the king of the earth, when he stands before the majesty of the King of the universe. It is the necessary and only realistic attitude which a thoughtful and honourable man can take up, when he looks into the wonders of nature and into the mystery of infinity and thereby becomes conscious of his limitations and finiteness as a creature. Modesty is true wisdom. Pride is always stupidity.

II. THE POWER OF RESISTANCE AND PATIENCE

Even if in the light of the above, a Christian's humility is not to be interpreted as lack of self-respect, what about the patience the Bible so often speaks of? Is not this at least a proof of weakness in personality? Does not submissiveness signify lack of character? Do not unwillingness to resist and to defend oneself show "slave morality" and lack of honour?

Christian patience is in fact something quite different from an unheroic passivity. It is "remaining under" an obligation or burden, even if suffering is involved. This is already implied by the etymology of the Greek word *hypomone*, used for it in the New Testament, which comes from *hypo*, under, and *menein*, to remain. Christian patience is strength supporting a situation, active loyalty remaining at its post, tenacity straining to its goal, even if victory seems delayed. Thus it involves steadfastness, bravery, confidence, "a living energy of faith." In its New Testament sense, "be patient" means, "Persevere! Do not play truant! Stick it to the end!"

That is why Scripture says, "Let us run with *patience* the race that is set before us" (Heb. 12: 1). "But he that *endureth* (*hypomeinas*) to the end, the same shall be saved," (Matt. 24: 13). "Behold, we call them blessed which *endured* (*hypomeinantas*)" (Jas. 5: 11). Just as faithfulness at one's post does not contradict military honour, so Christian steadfastness does not contradict the nobility of man. "In this sense to remain under is to stand above. Sometimes patience stands the test by 'standing at ease' when everything urges attack, by refusing to act, however necessary it may seem, until a clear command comes from above." Premature action and uncontrolled retaliation are in any case signs of weakness of character. Thus elements of Christian patience are a self-control strong in faith, inner discipline, spiritual strength, which in special situations may issue in the highest heroism.

This is how we are to understand Christian *self-denial* also (Matt. 16: 24; Luke 9: 23). Here again we are not asked for self-surrender, for self-torture, for fear of the world or for asceticism. The Christian is not required to burden himself with all kinds of suffering and to undertake voluntary penances and mortifications. What is meant is that "The disciples of Jesus are no longer to acknowledge their own selves as authoritative. They are to risk everything for their Master, cost what it may. They must cease to run their own lives. They should be unreservedly mobile at the disposal of one higher than they. If such service brings with it sacrifice and self-denial, then let them shoulder these manfully. The fundamental presupposition is, of course, their relationship to the one higher, from whom they receive their commands" (Ralph Luther).

Thus Biblical Christianity refuses to have its teaching about patience, self-denial and goodness understood as meaning weak-kneed suffering and feeble lack of drive. We see this especially in the fact that Paul, the leading apostle of early Christianity, in his teaching about Christian morals so often drew his comparisons from war and sport. Indeed, together with those drawn from the law courts, his favourite references are to the barracks and to the sports-stadium. He had profoundly realized that the Christian life is no pleasant afternoon stroll but a serious battle. It is a wrestling or boxing contest (Eph. 6: 12; I Cor. 9: 26, 27, R.V. mg), a race in the arena (Phil. 3: 14; II Tim. 2: 5), a holy war (Eph. 6: 10–20; I Thess. 5: 8). It is a wrestling with mighty world-rulers (Eph. 6: 12). At one time it is like hand to hand fighting with the sword (Eph. 6: 17), at another fighting at a distance with arrows and javelins (Eph. 6: 16), at another besieging the citadel of "Mansoul" (Rom. 7: 23), at another tearing down demonic strongholds (II Cor. 10: 4, 5). It is a struggle in which we have to attack the powers of darkness at the call of the heavenly general (II Tim. 2: 3, 4), it is a battle in which we can conquer through the power of God (Rom. 8: 37) and gain crowns of glory and awards of honour (II Tim. 4: 7, 8), and take part in triumphant victory processions (II Cor. 2: 14; cf. Col. 2: 15). And at the last Christ, the Lord of hosts, accompanied by His armies of angels, with His all-commanding shout and the sounding of God's trumpet, will lead His victorious hosts into glory (I Thess. 4: 16). Therefore, "Finally, be strong in the Lord, and in the strength of his might. Put on the whole armour of God" (Eph. 6: 10, 11). "Quit you like men, be strong" (I Cor. 16: 13). "Suffer hardship with me, as a good soldier of Christ Jesus . . . And if a man contend in the games, he is not crowned, except he have contended lawfully" (II Tim. 2: 3, 5).

III. LOVE OF ONE'S NEIGHBOUR AND SELF-ASSERTION

Christian love also, if it is to be lived out, demands power and strength of character. It is no mere sentimental love, no mere lovely but empty words, no inactive bemoaning of another's distress; it shows itself by will and act. It stands firm and has a backbone; it is both productive and active in itself (cf. Jas. 2: 17). True enough, the New Testament fights against the erroneous idea that one can merit heaven by one's own self-righteous works. "By the works of the law shall no flesh be justified in His sight" (Rom. 3: 20). But nowhere it is said that the justified are to remain without works! Grace is no pillow for inner weakness to rest on. On the contrary, it spurs on the whole man to a life of joyful activity. Paul wrote, "Let our people also learn to maintain good works for necessary uses, that they be not unfruitful" (Titus 3 : 14). Christians should be a people for God's own possession, "zealous in good works" (Titus 2 : 14). For only the faith which *works* through love (Gal. 5: 6) has value in God's sight.

Genuine Christianity is active Christianity. It works to a goal, it is a strong "muscular Christianity" (Charles Kingsley). It reveals itself as such in the organism of the Church, in the local community life of true Christians (Gal. 6: 10), in practical co-operation in the work of God far and near (Gal. 6: 6; Phil. 1: 5 ff.; II Cor. 9: 6–15). It shows its vitality also in helping one's fellow-men, in standing up for one's neighbour. A true Christian does not neglect his social duties. "Let us work that which is good toward *all men*" (Gal. 6: 10). Already in the Old Testament God said, "Is not this the fast that I have chosen. . . . Is it not to deal thy bread to the hungry, and that thou bring the poor that are cast out to thy house? when thou seest the naked that thou cover him; and that thou hide not thyself from thine own flesh?" (Isa. 58: 6, 7).

Thus love is at one and the same time servant and mistress. As Martin Luther said: "The Christian is lord over all things and subject to no man. The Christian is a willing servant of all things and subject to every man."

Love is a queen who serves. It is free and nevertheless feels itself bound. It even wants to say, "I must." Just because it is free it wants to feel constrained. By its very nature it fits itself in with others without constraint.

Love makes us see. It has keen eyes for opportunities for serving those around us. It has a sympathetic heart for the distress that surrounds it. It has a sure hand when it seizes opportunities and helps.

We must not forget, however, that it is never given us once and for all, and it must ever and again battle its way through in us afresh. In the Christian also it is involved in a continual struggle for supremacy in his everyday life. Everyone is only as strong as his love. "He who loves not lives not. He who lives through love cannot die" (Raymond Lull, missionary to the Muslims of North Africa and martyr, 1315).

In all this we cannot equate Christian love with self-surrender. It never throws itself away. It does not force itself on those that reject it. It guards its honour. "And whosoever shall not receive you, nor hear your words, as ye go forth out of that house or that city, shake off the dust of your feet. Verily I say unto you, it shall be more tolerable for the land of Sodom and Gomorrah in the day of judgment, than for that city" (Matt. 10: 14, 15; Acts 13: 51). Love seeks to win everyone. But even in wooing another it preserves its own dignity. "Give not that which is holy (i.e. your personal experiences of faith) unto the dogs, neither cast your pearls before the swine" (Matt. 7: 6).

Thus love is purposeful living, indeed it is the basis of the life of all true humanity that conforms to God's purpose. It is both the ideal and the highest fulfilment of true human dignity. It is the one true value in life. It is a piece of heaven upon earth, a ray of eternity within time, the splendour of God in the life of man.

He who loves makes his human nobility real, for love is God's nature. Since God is the great King, true love is a queen. Indeed, it is the real greatness in the realm of human life, the victorious power which is able to deal with all situations of everyday life, the fulfilment of all God's commandments, the "royal" law. "Thou shalt love the Lord thy God with all thy heart . . . and thy neighbour as thyself."

"But now abideth faith, hope, love, these three; and the greatest of these is love" (I Cor. 13: 13).

IV. BIBLICAL FAITH AND THE AFFIRMATION OF NATURE

Surely all that has been just said is for the most part a dream and ideal. These goals, despite all the emphasis upon practical everyday life, are surely mere figments of the imagination. What is the attitude of Christianity to the visible, tangible world of nature? Does it not amount to a denial of nature?

Surely the New Testament, and Paul in particular, teaches a fight of the "spirit" against the "flesh," and so of the spiritual against the material. This surely means that Christianity is asceticism, flight from the world and a despising of nature. It flees from the reality of the visible into the invisible, and thus into the unreality of a shadowy unsubstantiality.

We on the other hand live in a world of form and colour, in an ordered world of shape and matter and body! When the New Testament denies this, it shows the uselessness of Christianity, especially in its Pauline form, for the man of today. Such is the attitude of many a modern man.

In fact the New Testament nowhere teaches that we should deny the material. Only one who is totally ignorant of its doctrine of the triumphant perfecting of the world in its psycho-somatic unity can make such an assertion. Though it speaks of a conflict between "flesh" and "spirit" (Rom. 8: 4–9; Gal. 5: 17) this must not be understood in a heathen, Hellenistic sense, as if the body were the "prison" of the soul, and matter were to be completely denied. We are not here concerned with the difference between visible and invisible, bodily and spiritual, realism and idealism, but with the conflict between fallen human nature as a whole and a life lived in true holiness, between the "old" and the "new" man, between the "self" of the past life and the new principle of life planted in the believer by the Holy Spirit at his new birth (Col. 3: 9, 10; Eph. 4: 22–24).

Indeed, when "flesh" is used in this ethical sense in the New Testament, it is not based in any way on a distinction between soul and body in the individual, but on a concrete concept of the unitary man. Its starting point is rather the consideration of man as visible here on earth in contrast to the invisible world, to the angels and especially to the Creator, who is the Lord, the Spirit.

In the Old Testament the word "flesh" in this general sense means first of all human life within a body of flesh, i.e. the whole of the earthly and finite nature of man.[1] In this sense "all flesh" simply means "all mankind" (Gen. 6: 12). "The glory of the Lord shall be revealed, and all flesh (i.e. all mankind) shall see it together" (Isa. 40: 5). "I will pour out my Spirit upon all flesh" (Joel 2: 28).

But already in the Old Testament there is at times associated with "flesh" the consciousness of the weakness, transitoriness and frailty of our human nature which fell so deeply at the very beginning of its history. It is in fact just in the bodily sphere that "all flesh," the whole of humanity, experiences repeatedly and obviously its weakness and frailty, through its physical finiteness, sickness and finally death. It is therefore fully understandable that the word "flesh" is all the more readily used to connote this side of the weakness and transitoriness of human nature. "Cursed is the man that trusteth in man, and maketh flesh (human power in its weakness) his arm" (Jer. 17: 5). "With him (Sennacherib, the hostile, heathen king) is an arm of flesh (inadequate, human power); but with us is the Lord our God" (II Chron. 32: 8). "Now the Egyptians are men, and not God; and their horses flesh (hence, weak creatures), and not spirit" (Isa. 31: 3). "He remembered that they were but flesh (i.e. frail and weak); a wind that passeth away, and cometh not again" (Psa. 78: 39).[2]

This is the starting point for a substantial broadening and deepening of the meaning of "flesh." This occurs especially in the New Testament, particularly in Paul. Because "all flesh," i.e. all mankind, has through sin become hostile to God, the word flesh acquires in addition the sense of *fallen human nature as a whole as the captive of sin*, the state of sin which rules in the whole, human world, the whole "old man," the whole of his inherited, sinful nature. It is in this sense that Paul confesses "I know that in me, that is, in my flesh, dwelleth no good thing" (Rom. 7: 18). "They that are in the flesh cannot please God" (Rom. 8: 8). "The mind of the flesh is enmity against God" (Rom. 7: 7).

Only from this standpoint can we do justice to the range of the concept of "flesh" in Paul's writings. "Flesh," in the Pauline sense, is more than the sinful impulses of a carnality that has broken its fetters and is in conflict with God. More than half of the "works of the flesh" which Paul enumerates in *Galatians* belong to the sphere of man's spiritual life. Not only

---

[1] In its literal sense the word "flesh" in the Bible has normally one of two meanings. (1) Flesh as a constituent part of the earthly body, e.g. Gen. 41: 3; also in the expression "flesh and bone" (Psa. 102: 5). (2) Deriving from this, but with an enlarged connotation it denotes the whole body as clothed with flesh (II Cor. 4: 11; Col. 2: 5).

[2] This use of 'flesh' is found also in numerous New Testament passages, e.g. Rom. 6: 19; Matt. 26: 41.

adultery, unchastity, drunkenness, i.e. *sensuality*, are works of the flesh, but
also enmity, jealousy and strife, i.e. lovelessness, together with sorcery and
idolatry (Gal. 5: 19–21). Indeed, Paul even reckons legalism and bodily
asceticism (Col. 2: 18–23, cf. vv. 16, 17) as belonging to the flesh, i.e. just
the avowed *opposite* to sensuality, namely self-sanctification. He ascribes
them to the pious "flesh" with its mask of religion, i.e. to "flesh" in its
self-glorifying strength which it thinks it has. It was indeed just to the
Galatians, who thought that they must bring about their own perfection
through legal self-sanctification that Paul wrote with reference to their
religious self-ennobling efforts, "Having begun in the Spirit, are ye now
perfected in the flesh?" (Gal. 3: 3).

We see then that in the Old Testament the word "flesh" means principally the God-appointed natural distinction between man and the invisible world. It affirms that man, in contrast to God and the angels,
possesses a visible, material body of flesh. It implies that he is bounded not
merely in body and space, but also in spirit and in his personality, and
therefore that he is a finite being.

In the majority of passages in the New Testament the meaning of the
word "flesh" goes beyond this and signifies the unnatural conflict caused
by sin, between the sinner and a holy God. "The mind of the flesh is
enmity against God" (Rom. 8: 7). "He that soweth to his own flesh shall
of the flesh reap corruption" (Gal. 6: 8). At the same time the word "flesh"
denotes also the sinner in his utter inability to redeem himself. "By the
works of the law shall no flesh be justified in his sight" (Rom. 3: 20). It
follows then, that all legalism and self-sanctification is from the very
outset "flesh" (Gal. 3: 3; Col. 2: 16–23).[1]

It cannot possibly be affirmed, therefore, that in Paul's picture of the
conflict between "flesh" and "spirit" any repudiation of the body or
enmity against nature is meant. On the contrary, it is precisely in the Bible
that we find that the body is an instrument for righteousness, a means for
the glorification of God, the seed-corn of a transfigured, spiritual body
(I Cor. 15: 43–47). "Present . . . your members as instruments of righteousness unto God" (Rom. 6: 13), in order that "the life also of Jesus may be
manifested in our body" (II Cor. 4: 10). "Glorify God therefore in your
body" (I Cor. 6: 20)! God shall "quicken your mortal bodies" (Rom. 8:
11). "This corruptible must put on incorruption" (I Cor. 15: 53). And
when Christ, our Lord, appears from heaven, "the body of our humiliation" shall be fashioned anew that it may "be conformed to the body of
His (Christ's) glory" (Phil. 3: 21). Thus the drawing out of the body's
highest activities is part of the life of the spirit and not its being put to
death. We repudiate the "flesh" but affirm the "body" in its sacredness.

---

[1] We might say that in the Old Testament usage of the word 'flesh' the *metaphysical*
contrast to God and the invisible world appears in the foreground; in that of the New
Testament more the *ethical* contrast.

The triumph of the "spirit" is perfected in the resurrection and eternal transfiguration of the "body."

We grant that within Christendom there have been examples of fear of the world, of monasticism, of despising of the body and of despair of nature, but these have always been caricatures of a life lived in Biblical faith. Normally they arose under the influence of a completely different manner of thought, especially as a result of the concepts of the Hellenistic and even of the Middle-Eastern outlook on life. As these heathen influences gradually spread they affected many simple men, who were ignorant of the history of philosophy and hence could have no clear idea of where the roots of their conduct were to be sought; they thought it was Biblical, but for all that it sometimes deviated from a healthy, Biblical life of holiness.

It is possible to be influenced by Platonic thought, without ever having heard the name of Plato. One can be affected by the outworking of the late Greek or Oriental repudiation of the body, even if one has never directly heard or read anything about the pessimistic dualism of the late classical period.

Even today there are here and there not a few Christians, who though basing themselves on the Bible, suffer from these narrow ideas, as if pleasure in God's creation, the singing of songs about the beauties of nature, the enjoyment of noble art (music and painting) and the sound care of the body were unholy and unchristian and hence unworthy of a true Christian, at the best to be looked on with disdain. Are we really to imagine that this is the meaning of the apostle's words: "Love not the world, neither the things that are in the world" (I John 2: 15)?

With all our emphasis upon the work of *redemption* we must learn not to forget the glory of God in *creation*. With all the attention we pay to the second article of the Apostles' Creed, "I believe in Jesus Christ, his only Son . . . ," the Redeemer, the first article must not be overlooked, "I believe in God, the Father Almighty, Maker of heaven and earth."

Today, in fact, we need to be released from Hellenistic thought. We must learn to become more Biblical again, and therefore truer to nature. Professor Spörri has rightly said, "We reach the supernatural only through the natural, never through the unnatural."

That the body is merely the prison of the soul and therefore has no future was taught by Greek and Hellenistic thought and not by Christianity. It was not the prophets and apostles but the heathen philosophers who declared that the final goal of the world and of man consists in a state of pure spirit; that consequently there could be no resurrection of the dead and hence no redemption of the body but only a redemption from the body (Acts 17: 32).

Biblical revelation knows nothing of such a degradation of the human body and of the world of nature in general. It was Paul, whom so many accuse of despising the world, who spoke the profoundest word about the human body that any has yet uttered, "Know ye not that your body is a temple of the Holy Spirit?" (I Cor. 6: 19). It is precisely Christianity, rejected today by so many modern men because of its alleged alienation from Nature, which teaches the resurrection of the body! It is just the revelation given by the Scriptures which tells us that the body and, with it, matter in general have an eternal future! It is just the Bible, regarded by so many as repudiating Nature, which sees in the *incarnation* of the Son of God the foundation of world redemption. "Every spirit which confesseth that Jesus Christ is come in the *flesh* is of God: and every spirit which confesseth not Jesus is not of God" (I John 4: 2, 3; II John 7). This incarnation of the highest Spirit of all, which is emphasized in the Bible as pivotal in God's plan, proves irrefutably, that God takes the world of matter and body most seriously.

Many Old Testament psalms are filled with joy in nature. One need only read those that deal with nature and creation, the evening and morning psalms, the psalms which speak of the sun (Psa. 19) and of the stars (Pss. 8, 148), of the clouds and thunder-storm (Psa. 29), of the countryside and fields, animals and plants (Psa. 104). It has been fitly said that Old Testament poetry has an "earthy fragrance."

When we come to the New Testament, this contemplation of nature is further ennobled and lifted even higher into the realm of the spiritual. In the metaphors and similes of the Gospels and in the colourful parables of Jesus, nature is used as a picture book of revelation. To the Old Testament's religious and aesthetic view of nature the New Testament adds a moral and spiritually symbolic meaning. Everything visible becomes a proclamation of the invisible, everything material a garment for the spiritual; everything earthly is ennobled by becoming a reflection of the heavenly. Just as the Bible has ennobled man so it now also ennobles his kingdom.

Nature awakens involuntarily an intimation of the infinite. The believer in God finds nature speaking to him. Everywhere we feel the breath of God in it. "The heavens declare the glory of God; and the firmament sheweth his handywork. Day unto day uttereth speech, and night unto night sheweth knowledge. There is no speech nor language; their voice cannot be heard. . . . Their words (are gone out) to the end of the world" (Psa. 19: 1–4).

"Just as man's soul, though invisible, expresses itself in his face, even so nature, as it were the created face of God, reveals to us the hidden Spirit, immanent and transcendent."

How poor in contrast is the attitude of unbelief! It entangles itself— precisely, when it has to deal with nature—in a meaningless contradiction.

As long as it is concerned with the *present* it often idolizes the body. This shows itself in sensuality and the lusts of the flesh, in rapacity and the coveting of earthly goods, and speaking generally, in every over-emphasis on bodily things, in some exaggerations in fashion and in frequent excesses

H

in sport. The last was exemplified in the ancient Roman amphitheatres, e.g. gladiatorial combats, fights with animals, etc.

When it looks to the *future* the same unbelief asserts that there will be no resurrection of the body. In other words it declares that the human body, which at times it serves as if it were its god, finally, in fact, becomes meaningless.

That which applies to the body in particular applies to nature in general. So the non-Christian oscillates between glorifying nature and despising it, between happiness in nature and despair about it, between deifying nature and denying it.

Surely the Biblical revelation is much more logical. It teaches the sanctification of the body in the present (Rom. 6: 13; 12: 1) and its transfiguration in the future (Rom. 8: 11; Phil. 3: 21; I Cor. 15: 43–57); not, as does unbelief, its deification in the present and its denial in the future. Thus faith knows a harmonious completion, unbelief, on the other hand, only a disharmonious contradiction. Faith looks for organic development, unbelief sinks into chaos. Here again we see how infinitely high Biblical thought towers above the erroneous ideas of those that despise it and how far superior it is to them.

We grant that also the Christian is aware of the duality in natural life. Indeed, it is just he who understands this more deeply and truly than the non-Christian. But he knows that one day these tensions will be resolved.

This will be brought about by the triumph of the kingdom of God and the transformation of nature bound up with it, by the perfecting of the world and the coming of the spirit's domination of the body. When we think of these things, we find that faith speaks of the royal appointment of man to be a blessing to the earth, of the victory of his spirit, which is linked to a transformation of nature, of a royal nobility of man and of an ennobled kingdom of humanity. What is more, this king of Paradise will one day make a paradise of his realm. "The earnest expectation of the creation waiteth for the revealing of the sons of God . . . in hope that the creation itself also shall be delivered from the bondage of corruption into the liberty of the glory of the children of God" (Rom. 8: 19, 21). "According to his promise, we look for new heavens and a new earth, wherein dwelleth righteousness" (II Pet. 3: 13).

CHAPTER IX

THE DIVINE WORK OF REDEMPTION: ITS GREATNESS AND POWER

"CHRIST is risen!" With this message the Gospel has spread round the world. Biblical Christianity is both acceptance of life and joy in life in the highest and noblest sense of the word. Christ, the Living One, is the source of a Divine, perennial river of life, creating and maintaining life.

I. Hero (Lion) and Lamb

Non-Christians have reproached the apostles, especially Paul, for placing the cross unduly in the foreground. The message of the cross is said to be a message of death. But since death is something negative, indeed, of all negatives the most negative, Pauline Christianity is really negative Christianity. We, however, they say, need something positive; not a "No" but a triumphant "Yes" to life.

This reproach rests upon a complete misunderstanding of the message of the New Testament. For Paul also, the death of Jesus is not *in itself* a means of redemption, but only His death annulled by His resurrection. "If Christ hath not been raised, then is our preaching vain, your faith also is vain" (I Cor. 15: 14). Especially for Paul, as for the whole New Testament, true faith in Christ is faith in the resurrection. Not death but the triumph of life is the last word.

Opposition has been focused especially on the message of the "Lamb" of God. This expression is met more than thirty-five times in the New Testament. "Behold, the Lamb of God, which taketh away the sin of the world!" (John 1:29, 36). "Knowing that ye were redeemed, not with corruptible things, with silver or gold, from your vain manner of life handed down from your fathers; but with precious blood, as of a lamb without blemish and without spot, even the blood of Christ" (I Pet. 1: 18, 19).

This expression is found especially in the Johannine writings, particularly in the Revelation, where it occurs no less than twenty-nine times. The Greek word used (*arnion*) is really a diminutive ("little lamb"). This book, which deals with the coming, final perfection of the world, most forcibly contrasts the apparent weakness of the Crucified with His glorious, final triumph. Although the expression, "Lamb of God," is not found in Paul's writings, he does call Christ, who gave His life for us, "our passover." "For our passover also hath been sacrificed, even Christ" (I Cor. 5: 7). This title was the more appropriate as Paul wrote the first letter to the Corinthians before Pentecost, that is, about the time of the Jewish Passover (I Cor. 16: 8).

In many countries unbelief has launched a mighty assault on the New Testament message of the Lamb of God, and still does so. Such a message is said to be unbearable for modern man. This effeminate mysticism of suffering, this contradictory idea of the blessedness of pain, this weak endurance, this sentimental melancholy is opposed to every healthy impulse of life. Such a picture of a suffering, dying, weakly expiring redeemer is irreconcilable with the dignity, the consciousness of power and the strength of character of a healthy-minded man. How much less, then, can the crucified be in addition the saviour of the world?

There is no contradiction between the New Testament message of the Cross and a manly ideal of heroism; they belong together. After all what are the essentials of heroism? Strong muscles do not make a hero, otherwise all the beasts of prey would be heroes. Mere brutality and the callous strength that smash the antagonist do not make a hero, otherwise all barbarians and criminals would be heroes. Brutality is certainly not heroism; it is sub-human. The essentials of heroism are in the spiritual and moral realm, not in the physical, in a positive, moral, idealistic attitude, always true to its character.

A soldier is a hero, if he willingly risks death, when by his so doing victory can be gained. A prisoner of war is a hero, if, rather than betray a military secret, he allows the enemy to shoot him, although he could save his life by treachery. The hero, therefore, is one who, though he can avoid danger and even loss of life, exposes himself to it for the sake of an ideal. There are five factors which belong to the essence of heroism: Freedom of will, single-mindedness in pursuit of an ideal, readiness to act, self-sacrifice, devotion even to death.

In self-sacrifice heroism reaches its peak. That is why the sacrifice of Calvary is so tremendous. Here all the elements of heroism are united. Here we see one acting who could have avoided the whole problem. Here we see one remaining on the cross, though He could at any moment have freed Himself and come down from it (Mark 15: 30). Here we see one who surrenders Himself to death, although it would have been but a small matter for Him to have shattered His foes with legions of the heavenly hosts. "Or thinkest thou that I cannot beseech my Father, and he shall even now send me more than twelve legions of angels?" (Matt. 26: 53).

He knew, however, that if He saved Himself, He could not save others. The redemption of the world could be made possible only through a substitutionary death. If, therefore, the Redeemer of the world had evaded death, this supreme, ideal goal would never have been reached, and humanity would have remained unredeemed. Where else can we find such a marvellous mastery of self, such discipline of the spirit, such concentration of will-power, when He was *able* to descend from the Cross and did not do so (Matt. 27: 40), when He was *able* to destroy His foes and yet forbore to do so (John 18: 6), when He needed not to die and yet died, merely to win life for others?

Who will deny that this is highest and most perfect heroism? Even as other lights before the sun, so all heroism recorded in human history pales before His. All the elements of heroism already mentioned, freedom of will, single-mindedness in the pursuit of an ideal, readiness to act, self-sacrifice and devotion even to death, find their perfect and unique combination in Jesus Christ.

Christ was the only man who was active in His death, who died. All other men have been *passive* in their death, they had to die. But Christ had full authority over death and likewise He had full authority over His return to life, over His resurrection. He did not die because His enemies killed Him, nor did He die of a broken heart; He died because He *wanted* to die. He said Himself: "No one taketh it (my life) away from me, but *I lay it down of myself.* I have power (authority) to lay it down, and I have power to take it again" (John 10: 18).

Thus Christianity offers the very reverse of something effeminate in its message of the cross. The cross is the sign of victory. He who did not resist the might of man has broken all resistance. He who apparently collapsed in weakness is seen as the one who rises again in power, the Divine Hero.

This self-surrender, this readiness for suffering which never complained and this one true sacrifice were preached symbolically in advance in the Old Testament, in its centuries of teaching about the way of salvation. This was done in the sacrifice of lambs, above all on the altar of burnt offering in the Jerusalem temple. In addition, the fact that the sacrificial animals were without blemish, was a prophetic indication of the purity and perfection of the true sacrifice, Jesus Christ (Exod. 12: 3 f.; Lev. 9: 3; 23: 18; etc.). Especially for a pastoral people like Israel there could have been no more suitable picture. We know, however, that no single picture or comparison can express the whole truth at one time. The figure of the lamb also does not express the whole of this truth.

The fact is that the outwardly quiet ("dumb") surrender of the Redeemer (Isa. 53: 7) was inwardly a mighty conflict, and precisely in this conflict Christ victoriously proved Himself a hero. That this side of the work of salvation might also find expression, the lion is added to the picture of the lamb in the Biblical revelation. Both pictures belong together. For the final goal of the self-sacrifice of the "Lamb of God" was from the very outset the royal triumph at the end.

Hence John in his prophetic vision in Rev. 5 heard the proclamation of victory from heaven. "Behold, the Lion . . . hath overcome" (v. 5). But as he turned to see the "lion" he saw—a *lamb*. "And I saw in the midst of the throne . . . a lamb standing, as though it had been slain" (v. 6). The lamb is also the lion. The outward apparent defencelessness was derived from an inward, gigantic strength of will.

The world could be saved only by sin's being overcome, for sin is the root of all trouble. Sin, however, is separation from God, the Ever-living, and therefore a separation from life, in other words death. But since it worked itself out in reality and history, it could therefore be validly countered and eliminated only within the framework of real history. So God's triumph in the world could be won only as He faced sin in history and as a holy Judge. There had to be a real expiation corresponding to the nature of sin.

The wages of sin, however, is death (Rom. 6: 23). Therefore sin and death could be overcome only by a substitutionary death. "Apart from shedding of blood there is no remission" (Heb. 9: 22). So the Mediator, to reach His goal, had voluntarily to dispense with all the powers at His disposal by which He could have delivered Himself. To have delivered Himself would have been to abandon the whole work of salvation. Any external "victory" would have under these circumstances been real defeat. Therefore the external, apparent allowing of Himself to be conquered was but the outworking of a mighty, inner victory. His death as a "lamb" was possible only because of His life-force as "lion." Christ's deepest suffering was in its essence the highest possible action. Only because He was the "lion" could He be the "lamb."

The day is coming, when all this will be universally revealed. Then everyone will recognize that the Hero who died is also God who rose from the dead. All will see, that the Crucified is now crowned. The Lamb is the Hero, and *more* than hero, the Son of God and Redeemer of the world, Conqueror of death and Victor, Lord of the universe and therefore Judge of the world (John 5: 27; Acts 17: 31). Then an unbelieving world will experience with awful terror that there is such a thing as the "wrath" of the lamb. "And they say to the mountains and to the rocks, Fall on us, and hide us from the face of him that sitteth on the throne, and from the *wrath of the Lamb*: for the great day of their wrath is come; and who is able to stand?" (Rev. 6: 16, 17). May all those who despise the message of the cross ask themselves this question.

There is another aspect to be considered. The Bible often calls Christ the "Shepherd" and His followers His "sheep." We find this especially in the shepherd parables in John 10, but also in Paul, Peter and the Epistle to the Hebrews (Acts 20: 28; I Pet. 5: 2-4; Heb. 13: 20). It has its roots in the Old Testament, being found both in the Psalms and the Prophets (Psa. 23; Ezek. 34).

"I am the good shepherd" (John 10: 11); "My sheep hear my voice" (John 10: 27). Many have laughed at these words. In reality, however, nothing trifling is here being said. On the contrary, nothing less than the *principle of spiritual leadership* is being expressed. What a shepherd is to his flock, Christ is to His own. He goes before them; He determines their path; He knows them and leads them; He has the responsibility of being their Leader. But they must follow Him, they must do what He commands, they must submit, take their due place and obey. "I know them, and they follow Me."

Anyone speaking in the country to peasants and wanting to make the principle of leading and following clear would choose as illustration the event the countryman might see any day, *viz.* a shepherd teaching his sheep.

Anyone familiar with rural conditions in the Near East would know at once that nothing trifling was intended. In those lands, when these parables were spoken, a shepherd's life was far from being without danger. Often he had to fight for his flock with wild beasts and to risk his life. How bravely David defended his flock against lion and bear (I Sam. 17: 34, 35)! Jesus Himself speaks of the true shepherd's fight against the savage wolf which comes to destroy his flock (John 10: 12). "The oriental shepherd shares everything with his flock. He is with it night and day. He endures hunger, thirst and the inclemency of the weather together with it. He knows himself to be the responsible leader of the whole flock, but also the protector of each single one. He it is who takes the lead, who always stands in the breach and faces every threatening attack."

It is also worth noticing that the main chapter in the New Testament about the "Good Shepherd" (John 10) does not record a tranquil conversation between Jesus and His disciples but a polemic against His enemies. The conflict was caused by the hostile attitude of unbelieving Jews to one of the Lord's followers. They had excluded the man born blind, whom Jesus had healed, and "cast him out" from their synagogue (John 9: 34, 35). In John 10 we have Jesus' answer to His enemies, and in it are His parables of the Shepherd. His answer is thus firstly directed against the Pharisees and their associates. Just here in His shepherd parables Jesus turns against the false shepherds and seducers, against the "wolf" (v. 12), the "hirelings" (v. 12, 13), the "thieves" and the "robbers" (v. 1, 8, 12). Thus the parables of the shepherd are the fruit of a bitter conflict. Indeed, the atmosphere became so tense through attack and counter-attack, that at the end many hearers declared Jesus to be possessed by a demon, and would gladly have stoned Him (v. 20, 31). To speak here of effeminacy and feebleness is clearly a misjudgment derived from obvious thoughtlessness and superficiality.

II. Sin and Grace

The chief cause of offence, however, is found in the Biblical doctrine of sin and grace. The Bible, especially Paul in the New Testament, declares that man is a lost sinner, radically, essentially, and totally corrupt; he cannot redeem himself by all his best endeavours, aspirations and self-improvement. To hundreds of thousands of modern men this doctrine comes as a shocking presumption, an insult to their honour, an unbearable slight on and denial of their dignity as men.

"Sin" in an absolute sense can be used only of man's relationship to God. "Against thee, thee *only* have I sinned" (Psa. 51: 4). It follows that anyone who denies the existence of a personal God and of a Divinely appointed moral order for the world must also deny the reality of sin. For him there can be only "imperfection," "defectiveness," "discord," "in-adequacy," but not "sin." At this point we are not arguing with such atheists or pantheists but we would refer them to Part IV of this book. Here we are concerned only with those who do not deny the existence of a personal, transcendent God but who as idealists believe in the possibility of self-redemption.

If there is a personal God—and the world around and within us is full of testimonies we cannot avoid hearing to His unconditioned, eternal and living existence—He must be the fountain of all life and the embodiment of all perfection. Nature then can also really have "life" only in so far as it is united with this fountain and shares His life, *i.e.* has communion with God.

Now here is precisely the disastrous fact in man's life; he no longer possesses this union with God. God no longer plays any decisive part in his life. Most could imagine that God does not exist, and it would not make any essential difference to their lives. So many live in practice as if God did not exist, although they may acknowledge His existence in theory and on occasion honour Him by attending a religious service. Precisely this is the essence of what the Bible calls "sin." We are not concerned here with terminology but with facts. "To sin" means to have detached oneself from God, to have dissociated oneself from Him, to live far from Him. "Sin" is the creature's deliberate becoming a law to himself. It is eliminating the Divine claim to rule, the ignoring of the supreme authority, the disregarding of the supreme majesty; the freeing of the creature from the Creator. We must not explain it as an inner feeling of inferiority, but as an inherent condition, shared by both superior and inferior characters (Rom. 3: 23). It characterizes the whole of man's existence, not only his individual actions. Through sin the creature makes himself independent, flees from the reality of his creaturely subjection, and lives in an illusion about his actual finiteness.

According to God's plan man belongs to a spiritual *Copernican* system, in which he is a point on the circumference, dependent upon God as sun and centre. Instead of accepting this, he has fallen into the error of the *Ptolemaic* system; he has made himself the centre of all, around which God and the world must revolve. This means that sin is rebellion against God, a revolution in the spirit-realm, the aim of which is to usurp the Divine government of the world.

In this context even the "smallest" sin proves to be of catastrophic significance. For if God is the Absolute and Unconditioned—and hence the one creator and consequently sole possessor and ruler of the whole world—every act, however small, in any way directed against His will, questions His absolute omnipotence, and in so doing His deity as a whole. Every sin, even the tiniest, poses the vital question, whether God is still absolute king, and so lord of the universe and sole God. "Even the smallest sin always means an attack upon the reality of God Himself, a revolution against the majesty of God which must proceed from another power and is an attempt of this revolutionary power to thrust God from His throne and to set itself in His place. In other words, every sin against God, even the smallest, has a satanic character" (Heim, II, pp. 141, 142).[1]

By his actions, therefore, man plunges into the greatest conceivable guilt. For is it not reasonable and logical that the Lord of the universe, the Most High, must occupy the highest place throughout His universe? Is it not right and proper that the Creator has the first claim upon His own creation, which after all He brought into existence? Is it not logical that He who stands at the summit of the universe must have the pre-eminence in each individual member of this mighty world organism, which, as His work, has belonged to Him from the first as His own private possession, not only in theory but also in practice? It must be so, and therefore it is both rational and logical, when the New Testament declares that love towards God is the greatest of all commandments; "Thou shalt love the Lord thy God with all thy heart, and with all thy soul, and with all thy mind. This is the first and great commandment" (Matt. 22: 37, 38).

Failure to obey this greatest of all commandments, if we do not truly love God before all else, must, therefore, be the greatest of all offences. Every man, therefore, even if he is moral and noble, is under condemnation for the greatest of all sins. No hair-splitting or sophistry can evade this shocking fact. Truth is hard; but only "the truth" can make us free (John 8: 32). Sin is not only outward behaviour but also inward attitude; and this attitude consists in not maintaining man's relationship to God.

So sin is the rejection of authority. Man concentrates on himself staggering feverishly round his own axis. It reaches its peak in self-deification. It rejects God's leadership and makes an idol of man's vital instincts while ignoring the true God. Hence it also ignores the fountain of life. This means that in its real essence it is denial of life, disintegration and des-

---

[1] Anselm, Archbishop of Canterbury (eleventh century), expressed a similar view in his work *Cur Deus Homo?*.

truction, spiritual and psychic "death." No wonder that it leads to bodily death as well. "The wages of sin is death" (Rom. 6: 23).

The death of the body is thus not merely a natural event, but has to be understood ethically. The sinless man need not die. Death is judgment. It is both the *essence* of sin and its necessary *consequence*.

A wrong attitude leads to wrong acts; on the tree of sin grow the fruits of sin; from sin come sins: lying, hatred, presumption, self-conceit, pride and immorality. Man is "dead in trespasses and sins" (Eph. 2: 1).

By its fruits, however, sin dishonours man's personality, lowers his behaviour and squanders his hereditary dignity; in other words it mars the image of God and debases man's nobility. Sin is our misfortune. "Sin is a reproach to any people" (Prov. 14: 34).

In this situation self-redemption is *powerless*. Even should a man, by working at himself, by education and self-refinement, attain an absolutely faultless and perfect life (which, however, no one does), the old debts would still be there. Nothing could ever make these as though they had not been. It would be a foolish delusion to hope to make reparation for this old debt by works done in one's own strength and in so doing to pay it. The essence of self-redemption through noble acts would still consist in these new good works, separately and externally, being meritorious in themselves and in isolation. They would have to be dissociated from the organic whole of the character and to be regarded as isolated actions, with which as it were "payment" would be made. But if the works are to have any value at all, the dominating attitude of the character must be love towards God. This is the greatest commandment of all. But it is precisely here that man is a helpless captive, even if we ignore all his individual immoral actions. But where self-redemption is attempted, works would be done not from love to God but from love to himself. He would want to help *himself*, to acquire redemption for *himself*! Therefore his works would no longer be truly perfect actions. They would have been of value only if they had been the expression of a pure, holy and selfless love to God.

But it is precisely this love that is lacking in the sinner. In order therefore, to reach a right relationship to God, man would already have to possess it. He would already have to *be* at the goal before he could *begin* the course which leads to the goal. He would have first to *possess* redemption in order to *acquire* redemption with the powers it gives. But this is moving in a circle, as if a mathematical theorem had first to prove its own axioms. So self-redemption can never create a new man because its efforts are based on the powers of the old man. Old debts are never paid by incurring new ones. "What can a man give in exchange for his soul?" (Matt. 16: 26). So the works of the old man are powerless to achieve self-redemption. They "fall short of the glory of God" (Rom. 3: 23).

But this is not all. The path of self-redemption is downright *dangerous*. The man who is following it does his "good works" to gain a legal right to reward from God, as it were paying an instalment on his debt. Thus he regards something worthless, the product of a false attitude, as something worthy of supreme, Divine recognition. In so doing he plunges into foolish pride, and instead of saving himself achieves the opposite. Experience has shown that the self-righteous, whether they are heathen, modern idealists or "Christians," are the hardest of all to win for Christ. The fact is that man owes God not only isolated good works but his whole being, his whole self, his whole life. If, therefore, he would really pay off his debt, he would have to be able to begin his life anew, the whole of which is pervaded by sin.

Naturally this is equally impossible. But even if it were possible, man would still have no prospect of acquiring any kind of merit before God. In no form of existence, either present or future, could a *plus*, a surplus of good works be attained, by which the *minus* of his former life could be made up. None can be more than holy. And holiness can never become a "merit" going beyond the law of God and therefore balancing an earlier debit. No; *to be holy is simply our duty*. So even if it were possible to live our life over again, there would not be the slightest prospect of compensating for the debts of our former life. "When ye shall have done all the things that are commanded you, say, We are unprofitable servants; we have done that which it was our duty to do" (Luke 17: 10). We cannot escape from the fact that "by the works of the law shall no flesh be justified in his sight" (Rom. 3: 20; Gal. 3: 10). Revolt as we may against it, struggle as we may, look on it as we may in our infatuation as a slander on our dignity as men; we cannot get round this truth: if there is to be any redemption at all, it must be the work of *God*. It must be a free gift from above; it must be GRACE.

Grace does not degrade, it exalts; it does not debase, but ennobles; it does not dishonour, but crowns. "Who crowneth thee with loving kindness and tender mercies" (Psa. 103: 4). True enough, it does humiliate us deeply that we can contribute nothing to our salvation; it humbles us that it must be not by merit but by gift, not by achievement but by a present. But that a dust-born creature should accept a gift from the eternal God surely does not destroy our human dignity. If it were so, it would mean that every present in everyday life would be an injury to our honour.

What does contradict our nobility as men is *sin*, not redemption. Man should be ashamed of *sin*, not of repentance or of a change of heart.

In its scriptural sense repentance is not a pessimistic looking at oneself in a mirror, not a hopeless state of contrition or a morbid sense of fear, but an inward, new attitude of life to God. The literal meaning of the New Testament word (Gk. *metanoia*) shows this quite clearly. It is "a change of mind".[1] It carries the thought of a re-thinking, a change of the whole, inward man and, with this, a re-ordering of his outward behaviour.

[1] So Arndt and Gingrich: *A Greek-English Lexicon of the New Testament.*

To repent does not mean to enter a monastery, to torture oneself, to get bogged down moaning and lamenting over one's guilt. It does mean *to return to God* both in humility and grief for one's own sin, and in faith in the salvation brought by Christ. "Repent" means, "Change your mind! Be renewed! Change completely! Turn right round!"

Repentance is thus the active experience of a moral and spiritual revolution. It is the entrance into a new attitude to life. It is a personal act of will for which man is responsible and which is, therefore, *commanded* him by God. "He commandeth men that they should all everywhere repent" (Acts 17: 30).

The goal of all this is the *exaltation* of man. Grace does not throw down but lifts up. It is the concentrated power of God, which lifts man to true, eternal nobility. It gives him genuine freedom as lord of a God-willed personality. To be pardoned is to be crowned.

Let us not forget that God can show His grace only in ways consonant with His holy nature. He cannot simply cancel sin, but must deal with it as judge. Two men with mutual grievances may decide to say, "We will forgive one another; we will forget and bury the past." But God is not a sinner. He must act as protector of His holy law; the law of His own being confines Him to showing grace only in a way that expresses His own holy nature. "If God is God, He cannot treat the sin of the creature as a trifle, which means nothing in His sight. He cannot eternally ignore sin, as if it were a mere irrelevancy, which need excite no one." The holiness of God demands that He say an emphatic "No!" to it. He can reveal His grace to the sinner only in a way that does not make His holiness and righteousness inoperative but includes them. They cannot be denied but must be maintained. Therefore expiation is a demand of a loving, redemptive holiness within God Himself. Grace and justice belong together in redemption. On Golgotha the two are perfectly united. "Righteousness and judgment are the foundation of Thy throne: Mercy and truth go before Thy face" (Psa. 89: 14).

The New Testament word for grace (Gk. *charis*) has the same root as the word for joy (Gk. *chara*). It meant first of all "something which gives joy." As, however, hardly anything gave the Greeks more delight than loveliness and beauty, the word came to mean charm, loveliness or gracefulness. There are several passages in the New Testament where it is so used, e.g. Jesus spoke "words of grace" (Luke 4: 22) in the synagogue in Nazareth. Similarly the Ephesian Christians were exhorted so to speak that they "may give grace to them that hear" (Eph. 4: 29).

But every token of favour, especially from one highly placed, gives joy, and so the word came to include the meaning of good will, or favour. Some New Testament passages are so to be understood, e.g. the early Church in Jerusalem had "favour" (Gk. *charis*) with all the people (Acts 2: 47; cf. also Acts 25: 3; II Cor. 8: 19).

Finally, since oriental rulers were absolute monarchs, acts of favour by a king, by which he conferred riches, titles and a position of honour, depended solely upon his own free decision. It was, therefore, an unearned gift, i.e. "grace," and, indeed, "grace" that meant riches, splendour, joy and advancement for the receiver.

This is the starting point for the Biblical revelation's further ennobling and glorifying of the word "grace." It was lifted from the description of an *earthly* boon to that of a *heavenly* one. It describes a token of favour from *God* to men, and therefore of necessity from the All-Worthy to the unworthy, from the Holy One to the sinner. Thereby the word *charis* attained its full Biblical sense of "grace." It means a manifestation of the love of God which unfolds itself in complete freedom, an undeserved present, a free gift of God and also the inner attitude of the Divine love which makes this possible. God does not only "give" grace, but He "has" grace and mercy.

Thus "grace" in the New Testament always means a gift that gives joy. This root connexion with joy is found in all the passages where "grace" is used. Paul speaks repeatedly of the *riches* brought by grace (Eph. 1: 7; I Tim. 1: 14). Where grace is, we can draw on the Source of all riches. He also speaks of the glory of grace (Eph. 1: 6), for it gives man something radiant. Grace never means merely forgiveness, but always also a giving by God beyond description, not merely a cancellation of debts, but also a gift of the eternal riches of heaven.

Thus grace brings us close to God, into His family. Grace is a queen (Rom. 5: 21). It makes those to whom it grants gifts partakers of its own nature. Those who have been pardoned it makes free men, an "elect race" (I Pet. 2: 9; Rev. 1: 6), sons of the Most High (Rom. 8: 14-17). Grace grants true nobility to man. Therefore those who have received it should walk "worthily" of it (Phil. 1: 27; Eph. 4: 1).

Sin is Satan's dark denial of all true life. It desires the destruction and annihilation of all lasting values. It ensures that the man who surrenders himself to it will pass away and subjects him to bodily, spiritual and eternal death. It seeks to cause his downfall, and to make him sink for ever into slavery, night and destruction.

Man is born in a dungeon. A member of a royal, but fallen and de-throned race, he finds himself from the very first under the power of the evil one. He indubitably has a certain amount of freedom. He need not fall to every single sin which approaches him. But although he has freedom *in* and *under* sin, yet he has no freedom *from* sin. He has a relative freedom of movement *within* his dungeon. To some extent He can choose the place *in* this dungeon where he will sit down. But to burst open the door of the prison, *that* is beyond his power.

Only one can do that, Jesus Christ, the Holy one, He, whose character and being remained outside the dungeon of sin, and who is now able to set free all those who live in sin's power and allow Him to save them. With this gift of freedom He unites that of eternal life. True Christianity gives imperishable riches. It is as if a rebel who had been sentenced to death were pardoned by the judge and adopted into the royal family.

Christ is never a disappointment, but He is always a surprise. He redeems the believing soul and brings it out of the miserable dungeon of death into the royal palace of heavenly life. His victory has brought life and immortality to light. This is true both for the individual who believes and for the perfecting of God's whole plan of salvation as foretold by Scripture.

In dealing with this gift of imperishable possessions we have touched upon the subject of Christian hope. Here again New Testament faith demonstrates its superiority over all unbelief.

III. The Transient and the Eternal

Truly to accept life, from the standpoint of absolute eternity, i.e. infinity is possible only on the basis of Biblical Christianity. Only if we believe in the transfiguration of the world at the end of time, can we believe in truly eternal, i.e. endlessly existing, values. For unless a miracle takes place, all things must end in destruction. At least this is the only possible end of the development of the universe seen from the standpoint of the modern picture of the world based on purely natural law. Only if Divine powers break into the general order of nature, as known to us, can this be prevented.

According to astronomy the universe is heading for death by cold or by heat, or rather by fire. The individual constituents of the universe (suns, planets and moons) are continually cooling down as they fly through the cold of inter-stellar space. It follows, therefore, that a state must finally be reached—and this applies inescapably to the earth—in which the warmth of the sun, and of the earth itself, will have so far decreased that all life will vanish. The last living being—the last man also—will take its last meal, be overcome by the cold and will die. With it all the efforts of millennia, the whole cultural progress of the human race, every masterpiece of art and science, all achievements in self-ennoblement and idealism will sink into a dark, cold, icy grave, and the earth, a round, icebound, mass cemetery, will race on through the even colder darkness of space, until, perhaps, further developments cause it to vanish completely.

This expectation becomes the stronger when we consider the inconceivably sparse distribution of matter in space. Our sun, together with a few hundred other bright stars, belongs to one particular star-cluster. In such a cluster the fixed stars are comparatively close to one another. But even in such a "concentrated" cluster as the "solar cluster," the fixed stars—if their total mass were to be evenly distributed over the total space occupied by the cluster—are so widely separated, and hence their mass so relatively small, that it would be like a dozen tiny specks of dust in each cubic mile of space. And inter-stellar space really only begins, when we pass beyond such a "concentrated" cluster of stars, inter-stellar space with its vast emptiness and its inconceivable distances. Hundreds, indeed, thousands of light-years would pass by before one met another such island star cluster. A light-year is the distance covered in a year by a ray of light travelling at 187,000 miles per second, or seven and a half times the length of the earth's equator. The presence of a star in space is really only an inconceivably rare exception.

These "specks of dust" radiate their heat into inter-stellar space, which surrounds them at a temperature of minus 273° Centigrade. This means a tremendous loss both of heat and energy.

"Thus our earth," wrote Johannes Riem, Professor of Astronomy in Hamburg, "receives only the two thousand millionth part of all the energy which the sun is continually radiating into space; and all the planets in the solar system together receive only the 225 millionth part. All the rest is radiated apparently uselessly into space and is irretrievably lost for matter and the bodies it builds. It is the same with all the stars."

Hence there is bound to come a point in time, which will be the final state, when all stars will have radiated all their heat into space, so that there will no longer be any temperature differences in the universe. Through the radiation of heat and energy mass will have been evenly distributed throughout space and as a result all the processes of the universe will have run down.

Another German scholar, Professor H. Rohrbach, expressed it as follows in 1954, "We must assume with high probability that in the distant future at some time a position will be reached in the cosmos, when everything will be in a state of equilibrium, when its whole mass will be evenly distributed throughout space, and then nothing more can take place. This is the 'thermo-dynamic equilibrium,' the universal heat or cold death of the universe. Yet we cannot calculate how many years will pass before then, since we cannot eliminate the possibility of unpredictable events taking place."

In view of the inconceivably sparse distribution of matter in space there is from a scientific standpoint nothing astonishing in the expectation of such a death of the universe through a cold-death. "We grant that the thought is most repulsive," wrote Professor Riem, "and much trouble has been taken to disprove it. But there has been no success in the search for an argument which could free us from this nightmare."

"Man has no possibility of finding a way out by himself. All attempts to escape this universal cold-death (= heat-death) are in vain. We are, so far as we ourselves are concerned, abandoned to this nihilism" (Heim, II, p. 151).

According to the conceptions of modern thought, all this may not take place until after many millions of years, so that men today do not need to take it into consideration for themselves or their descendants. The world still has time for development. But when we look on the situation as a whole, this is very poor comfort, which can in no way liberate us from this sad outlook and this nihilistic frame of mind. It is certain that the end of the world must come sooner or later. Science at least knows of no other possibility. The death of the universe is approaching. Its end is destruction.

"The length of the respite granted the cosmos does not blind us to the true situation of the universe. This resembles a man condemned to death with a long interval between the sentence and the morning of his execution. That, however, does not change its sad situation, if the prediction of the future of the world, pronounced by leading scientists, is correct" (Heim, II, p. 113).

There is only one way of escaping this gradual cold-death. According to modern science it is—if the great miracle does not take place—by heat-death, or rather fire death. This means a catastrophe caused by increased radiation from the sun or by the collision of two worlds—our earth, or our solar system, with some other body—causing a tremendous explosion, which would dissolve all the elements of the earth in flaming heat.

Astronomic theory recognizes another way by which the earth could become uninhabitable much earlier than by a cold death or fire death of the solar system or of the universe as a whole. It is perfectly possible for a process to take place, in its essence temporarily opposite to the ice-death, *viz.* a great *increase* in the intensity of solar radiation leading to a tremendous rise in temperature till it reaches unbearable heat.

Astronomy speaks of "novae" or new stars; these are stars which flare up and appear as new stars comparatively quickly. It has, however, become clear that most of these novae are not actually new but rather "variable" stars, whose luminosity rises temporarily to about 25,000 times, and in exceptional cases, that of the "supernovae," hundreds of millions of times that of the sun.

If our sun should one day prove to be such a "variable star" and then temporarily produce heat like that already indubitably observed in numerous fixed stars, "then all the water of the earth would evaporate and its cloudy envelope would resemble that of the planet Venus. Whether any form of life would be able to adapt itself to these conditions, we cannot say, but presumably man will not. This is a far more terrible prediction for man than the ice-death. What would then take place, when our last descendants have to fly from the tremendous heat into caves, in which all survivors will crowd together to keep themselves alive by creating artificial cold, would be so terrible, even if our imagination works on only a few details, that Dante's *Inferno,* in which the torments of the lost are described, would appear as a trifle in comparison" (Heim, II, pp. 114, 115).[1] So far as the history of the earth is concerned, however, this would only be a temporary development. The final and universal cooling down, the ice-death, would come later just the same. Destruction comes certainly in every case.

In view of the sparse distribution of stars in space, it may well be, purely astronomically, that the death of the universe through cold, through gradual cooling down, is more likely than death through heat. But from a purely scientific standpoint it remains incontestable, that such a death of the universe through fire, or rather heat, would be the only way in which in conformity with natural law, the death of the universe through cold could be avoided.

Professor Karl Heim makes no bones about it: "That the universe will remain protected from death by cold is as improbable as that a measure of water, placed over fire, would turn to ice. The possibility of the universe's escaping death by cold is equally out of the question" (II, p. 112).

The atheistic scientist Professor Dubois-Reymond also affirmed that there exists a "scientific eschatology," *viz.* the expectation of a point in time, which cannot be arrested, when in the world all mental life, and with it all knowledge, will be extinguished, and all ideals, all works of art and all cultural achievements will be destroyed.

"Like a dark thunder-storm, which will one day break, this concept of the death of the universe faces man. It remains a fact that not only men and all forms of animal life, but also the whole of the inorganic world, is approaching its fate of total destruction."

Unless the miracle takes place in which we Christians believe! The miracle that God Almighty should intervene in world affairs! The miracle that He should avert the catastrophe which the "laws of nature" make inevitable! The miracle that He, as Perfecter of the world, should transfigure it at the time of His determining.

"Our human attempts to penetrate the secret of the end of the world leads us therefore to two possibilities only, both of which embrace the whole entity of reality. The first possibility is the *nothingness* in which all earthly processes come to rest, the death of the universe, which is science's last word about the future of the world. A second possibility exists only

---

[1] Even if such a comparatively *quick* burst of heat from the sun, as in the case of the variable stars, were not to occur, we should still, according to astronomy, have to reckon with the possibility of a heat-death for man. According to the astronomer Gamow (1948) a *slower* rise of temperature is to be expected for the sun and for the majority of the stars. "This comes from the fact that the helium formed from their hydrogen is more opaque and holds the heat together more, until the temperature finally forces its way through, whereby the radiation of the surface in about ten million years will be a hundred times that of to-day." This would also cause death by heat of all earthly life. Of course universal ice-death would in any case come at the last.

I

if the universal Easter message, which the messengers of the risen Lord have carried throughout the world, is in fact true. According to this message the world does not await nothingness, but the great transformation of the world" (Karl Heim).

Apart from faith in this great miracle it is impossible to have any faith in an endlessly existing, universal purpose in the order of nature in which we live. Whoever therefore denies this miracle denies any and every spiritual and moral value valid for all time. For him there can also be no absolute, endless, triumphant nobility of man.

We deliberately say "endless" and not "eternal," for people often speak of eternal values without reference to this belief. The word "eternal" is often used in the sense of inconceivably long, ancient, lasting through the ages, or continuing uninterruptedly. But with these the idea of absolute unendingness and endlessness is not necessarily associated. What is more, this is true not only in ordinary, human usage, but also occasionally in the Bible itself, at least in our standard translations.

Thus the Old Testament speaks of "everlasting hills" (Gen. 49: 26; Deut. 33: 15), "everlasting doors" (Psa. 24: 7, 9) and "eternal statutes." But these last had validity only as long as the Mosaic law continued, with its priesthood, sacrifices and festivals, i.e. for the less than 1,500 years from Moses to Christ. The Passover (Exod. 12: 14), the offering of first-fruits (Lev. 23: 14), the feast of Weeks (Pentecost, Lev. 23: 21), the meal offering (Lev. 6: 22) and the law concerning the lighting of lamps in the Tabernacle and the Temple (Exod. 27: 21) are all described as "statutes for ever." If a servant never wanted to receive his freedom again he became a "servant for ever" (Deut. 15: 17; Exod. 21: 6; cf. I Sam. 27: 12). Here "for ever" means "for the length of his life." In the same way Samuel's life-long service in the Temple is described as "for ever" (I Sam. 1: 22).

Thus, if the Christian or non-Christian, *without* reference to the transfiguration of the world foretold by the Bible, speaks in everyday life of eternal values and eternal powers, this is quite justifiable and, indeed, Biblical. The word "eternal" then means, as in the above passages of Scripture, age-long, inconceivably long, continuing without intermission through immense periods of time.

But of "eternal life" and "eternal values," with the meaning of *absolute endlessness*, only he can speak who believes in the transfiguration of the world prophesied by the Bible. Everything else, even if it lasted millions and billions of millennia, is nevertheless limited in time and so is finite. It is the laws of nature known to us and of the modern, scientific picture of the universe that guarantee this.

It has been suggested that after this universe has run its course and ended with its cold- or heat-death, a new and fresh world system will begin, following on a collision of our old dead or dying solar system with another. This would begin as a flaming, nebular mass, but finally, after protracted development and millions of ages, it would meet a similar fate to ours. In the same or in a similar manner another one would follow it, giving us an endless line of new universes.

There is an all-sufficient answer to this. If it were true, the whole development of the universe would be only an endless coming and going of worlds, a continuous cosmic birth, death, resurrection and dying again, and its history would be nothing more than an eternal cycle of becoming and disappearing, lacking in the final analysis any meaningful goal or purpose.

Then the universe would be an "all-devouring grave," an "eternal monster chewing its cud" (Goethe), a Saturn devouring his own children. It would be a giant organism inconceivably exactly and purposefully built up, right down to its minutest details, but which taken as a whole proclaims itself completely without goal or purpose. Then all earthly values from the standpoint of the infinite, would be in the last analysis only shadowy imagination, and the purposeless would be eternally the origin of all that is purposeful. Non-Christian thinking based on purely earthly and natural law and rejecting the possibility of miracle, must affirm that there exist no real, truly eternal values. The end of all hope is complete hopelessness. Eternal, in the sense of endless, is only death for us.

Surely Biblical revelation is far more reasonable. It is more reasonable to believe in an almighty God's miracle than in the meaninglessness of a meaningfully ordered cosmos. It is more reasonable to believe in the renewal and the transfiguration of the world than in the endless victory of destruction and chaos. It is more reasonable to believe in the triumph of the spirit than in the dominance of the brutal, murdering, destructive power of matter.

So here too faith demonstrates its superiority. Unbelief denies life; faith affirms it. Unbelief sinks into the night of death; faith rises to the triumph of life. The end of unbelief is destruction; the perfecting of faith is world transfiguration. The end of the one is death by fire or cold, but the goal of the other is life and an endlessly glorified nobility of man. So Scripture says, "The world passeth away, and the lust thereof: but he that doeth the will of God abideth for ever" (I John 2: 17).

"Thanks be to God, which giveth us the victory through our Lord Jesus Christ!" (I Cor. 15: 57).

IV. CHRIST, THE SAVIOUR

The redeeming work of Christ is valid for all eternity, brings blessing to man in body, soul and spirit, and spiritually transfigures physical nature. Hence Christ is the "Saviour," i.e. the Bringer of salvation. Here again we have a vigorous, "royal" term, a ruler's title of highest honour.

Through ignorance it has, however, often been misunderstood, especially when used by a sloppy, weak, emotional mysticism, as if Christians always prayed only to the "dear Saviour," like children in the nursery before going to bed, or like the "tinies" in Sunday school or children's service.

In the first century A.D. the term "saviour" (Gk. *sōtēr*) was much used in the worship of the mystery religions to mean a saviour-god, who died and came back to life again, who in conformity with the ideas of nature deification appeared upon the earth, liberated man's soul from the prison of its material body and thereby led it to full "salvation" (Gk. *sōtēria*).

The idea of a nature-god, who died and returned to life, came from the deification of vegetation withering and then springing to life again and from the rising and setting of the sun, moon and stars. The great, basic principle of "die and live" in nature was here expressed in heathen mythology. Man in his search for help is, however, a part of this totality of nature. Therefore through mystical union with this dying nature-deity who returns to life he also shares in his experience. Since, however, these gods were not only the personified, mythological representations of death and destruction in nature, but also the deification of the victorious vanquishing of death and of life arising from death again, therefore participation in their experience meant victory and deliverance for man. Hence these oriental deities were called "saviours," or "bringers of salvation."

Thus the Egyptian-Hellenistic mystery deities Isis and Seraphis were worshipped under the title of "Saviour." In Pergamum in Asia Minor it was the Greek god of healing, Aesculapius, who bore this title. This title meant then deliverer, upholder, protector and liberator.

In spite of all this the New Testament usage of the word "Saviour," when applying it to Christ, is not to be traced back to the heathen mystery religions. Neither was it a conscious and deliberate adaptation by early Christian missionary preaching to this heathen, religious usage, so that the hearers might understand the message the better. It was entirely rooted in the Divine revelation of the Old Testament, which in its Greek form (the Septuagint) was the Bible of early Christianity.

When the apostles called Jesus Christ, their Redeemer and Lord, "Saviour" (Gk. *sōtēr*), they were using the same term as that employed at times by the Old Testament to denote *God Himself*, e.g. Psa. 25: 5; Psa. 27: 9; Mic. 7: 7. Like the word *ecclesia* (church), the New Testament word *sōtēr*, although it was used in the surrounding heathen world superficially at least in the same way, was not borrowed from Hellenism but from the Greek Old Testament.

Already by 400 B.C. the term *sōtēr*, "saviour," became a title of honour for men in high positions; in inscriptions and papyri it is often used as a title of honour for high public officials and influential private persons. But in ever increasing measure it was used above all, and often openly as a mark

THE DIVINE WORK OF REDEMPTION

of religious worship, for powerful rulers, kings and emperors. Antiochus I (281–261 B.C.), the second ruler of the Seleucid empire, comprising Syria and Babylonia, bore the title Saviour for his victory over the Gauls in Asia Minor. So too Ptolemy I, the founder of the Ptolemaic empire (i.e. Hellenistic Egypt), was honoured with the epithet Saviour by the inhabitants of Rhodes because he had given them effective military aid in 305 B.C., when they were involved in military difficulties. His descendant Ptolemy VIII (116–80 B.C.) also bore this title.

In 48 B.C. Julius Caesar, then Dictator of the Roman empire, was hailed by the town council of Ephesus in conjunction with other Greek cities of Asia as "the God made manifest . . . and common Saviour of human life." The emperors Augustus to Domitian (A.D. 96) and for a long time afterwards bore religious titles like "Lord," "God of God," "Son of God," "our Lord and God" and also "High Priest," "Saviour of the world." This last was applied to Julius Caesar, Augustus, Claudius, Nero, Vespasian, Titus, Trajan and Hadrian.

An inscription found in Priene, south of Ephesus, gives the Emperor Augustus the titles "Saviour" and "God." Another inscription from Halicarnassus in Asia Minor, south of Miletus, even calls him "Saviour of the whole human race." For the worship of himself as emperor and world-saviour Nero even coined a new adjective, "world-saving." Visits by the emperor to the cities of the Roman empire were called his *parousia* (Lat. *adventus*) or his *epiphaneia*, that is, his "coming" and "appearance." His letters were "holy writings" and his decrees were "gospels."[1]

Thus for these mightiest of men of that civilization the title Saviour meant the triumph of their victories, the greatness of their kingdoms and the glory of their rule. Even more then in the case of Christ it denotes His royal power and the glory of His work as Deliverer, which makes Him World-Ruler. It is an expression of the greatness of the Divine Mediator, of the nobility of the Redeemer of mankind.

To try to find mawkish mysticism, emotional ecstasy or childish naïvety in the use of this term, when applied to Christ and in Christianity, though it was applied by the contemporaries of primitive Christianity to their mightiest and greatest personalities, is possible only where there is utter ignorance of the general cultural and religious situation of the first century. But we Christians also have to learn to think and speak of Christ and His redemptive work in a manlier way, to bear a more virile testimony and to exhibit really practical Christianity.[2]

[1] For further details see Deissmann, pp. 338–378, also Moulton's and Milligan's *Vocabulary of the New Testament*.

[2] We have confined ourselves here to the New Testament use of "saviour". The Septuagint occasionally uses the same Greek word (*sōtēr*) for certain judges that God raised up to save Israel from national distress, e.g. Judges 3: 9; II Kings 13: 5 (see also footnote on p. 92).

We must therefore distinguish a double Biblical use of the word "saviour": (a) Men

It is not enough, therefore, when explaining the title "Saviour" (*sōtēr*), to take into account only its linguistic derivation from *sōzein*, to heal, or make whole (cf. Matt. 9: 21; Mark 5: 23; 6: 56). The linguistic derivation of a word, its etymology, is never immediately decisive for its idiomatic use and range of meaning. When the New Testament speaks of healing the sick, as a rule quite another word (*therapeuein*, as in Matt. 4: 24; Mark 3: 10 and some thirty-five other passages) is used.

As "Saviour" Christ is much more than Healer, much more than physician of soul and body, much more than merely overcomer of all hindrances and inhibitions in spirit, soul and body in both individual and community. As "Saviour" and "Deliverer" He not only brings the minus up to zero, not only removes the negative, not only causes all sickness to disappear, but also gives with this something overwhelmingly *positive*, riches that exceed zero a millionfold (Eph. 1: 18). As "Saviour" He gives overflowing enjoyment of life (John 10: 10), inexhaustible happiness (Phil. 4: 4), strength for a victorious life (Rom. 8: 37), true dignity of personality (I Pet. 2: 9; Eph. 4: 1), in short, the eternal realization of man's true nobility.

Spiritual salvation in the New Testament sense is therefore "the unsearchable riches of Christ" (Eph. 3: 8), "the sphere of activity of the risen Christ, the sum of His working in power here below."

As "Saviour" Christ is the Bringer of salvation, the Victor over all the powers of darkness, the Sun radiating all the powers of the new life, the Fulfiller of true human nobility, the Bringer in of the kingdom of God, the Triumpher of world stature (John 4: 42; 3: 16; I John 4: 14).

Therefore our testimony may be given in the words of the German poet Ernst Moritz Arndt:

> I know on whom I've trusted,
> I know what standeth fast,
> Though all things here, when tested,
> Like smoke and dust depart;
> This is the Light supernal,
> My Saviour Christ the Lord;
> This is the rock eternal
> On which I stand assured.

are "saviours", when they lead their people out of tribulations to a state of earthly and national welfare (salvation); (b) God and Christ are "Saviour"; starting with redemption they lead the individual to a personal, universal, spiritual and eternal salvation. Only God and Jesus Christ are "Saviour" in this sense. "In none other is there salvation" (Acts 4: 12); cf. also the repeated expression "God our Saviour" in the Epistle to Titus (1: 3; 2: 10, 13; 3: 4).

CHAPTER X

HOLINESS AND GLORY IN THE ETERNAL PERFECTION OF THE HIGH CALLING OF MAN

WE have seen that the creation of man was great and wonderful and the goal to which he was called was high and holy. All that lives and exists here below was to be liberated from the rule of Satan and led into a state of harmony with the Eternal God through him as king of the earthly creation. Through him the redeeming powers of the Most High were to be morally revealed. The end of an undeviating, upward development was to be nothing less than glory to God in the highest, peace on earth, and good will towards men.

Yet great and glorious as man's gracious appointment might be, it could not be the whole or even the chief part of God's purpose. For if this were the sole purpose for which God had created man, then man's significance in the cosmic plan of salvation would not have been personal and direct but only indirect and derivative. Fundamentally he would have been a mere means to an end. The chief stress of his existence would not have been, so far as his position as creature was concerned, on him but on his earthly surroundings. Besides, his task would then have been limited in time. His further existence in eternity would have been irrelevant and without any continually new, significant values. At the coming of the new heaven and the new earth everything capable of redemption will have been redeemed. From the moment this goal had been reached, were the mediating of this redemption to be man's sole work, he would remain without real positive content in life and purpose in existence.

But according to Scripture he occupies to all eternity an important, even a central position in the cosmos. It follows that from eternity in God's plan there must have been linked with this purely temporal vocation to the work of redemption a still higher, endless, eternal vocation. We can discover the details of this only from the main purpose of creation as a whole. Earlier we saw that this purpose is the establishment of a fellowship of life and love between the Creator and his creation. Hence love and communion in love are the supreme moral principle of all existence, temporal and eternal. We must, therefore, deduce from these concepts the will of God in all individual details.

I. Man's Eternal Vocation to Worship

1. THE NATURE OF LOVE

Love is the will to fellowship. In human life as a whole it shows itself as a feeling of being attracted to and as a striving towards a person or object which appears to us of value in its own right and which we think will bring happiness to our sensual or spiritual ego. It evidences itself by a continual delight and pleasure in the possession and presence of this person, and the complete union of the whole life with him. Thus two things find their expression in love:

(a) a striving after the *completion* and *extension* of one's own self;

(b) a striving after a constant *merging* in the self of the other.

From this point of view then it expresses itself in two chief ways. These are always there and they show themselves, whenever true, ideal love is present. The one is love's sharing of the other's inner and outer experiences; the second is the communication and surrender of one's own being and experiences to the other. The former works *inwardly* on the lover himself, the latter *outwardly* on the beloved. In the first we see the receptivity of love, in the second, its active spontaneity.

The communication of love is here a freely chosen compulsion to share with the beloved not only one's worldly goods but also one's innermost experiences. True love draws the other unselfishly into the world of one's own thoughts and feelings with its desires and efforts. In so doing it offers to the beloved the lover's true inner self and personality.

It follows that when the term love is used in this perfect and ideal sense, it can be used only of persons. In the same way it can, in this its highest and truest sense, reach out only to another person. Thus the foundation of all true intercourse of love must be the existence of an unimpaired personality on both sides. Only a self-conscious personality can love, and the more real and rich this personality is inwardly and outwardly the greater is the blessing that passes to the other from its life and love. Therefore it is of the greatest importance for love that this independence of personality, which is the foundation of its existence, should be preserved perfect and intact. "However much surrender of self is involved in love, it must never cause much abandonment of self, i.e. loss of oneself in the other. Every injury to my own nature involves also loss for the one I love. So love may renounce *outward* possessions and may limit itself in its outward activity for the sake of the beloved. It is just here in fact that it proves its strength and purity. But it must hold fast and guard all those *inner* things that form its essential self, not only for its own sake, but also for the sake of the one loved" (Dr. L. Schoeberlein).

2. GOD'S LOVING CONDESCENSION AND MAJESTY

This means, however, in the intercourse of love between Creator and creation that "in all His manifestations of love, however great and sacrificial they may be, God must unwaveringly maintain the absoluteness and holiness of His eternal personality. However much He gives Himself to His creation, God can never waive the fact that He is absolute Spirit and absolute Love. However deeply God may condescend to man, it will never cease to be true that man must draw the whole strength of his inward and outward existence from God alone. *His* will must remain the eternal law over *man's* will. In all eternity He will unwaveringly assert this His authority with holy power. Briefly, God remains absolute monarch for man, who remains always in a state of absolute dependence. Only so can God reach the goal that He has set Himself in His absolute love. Only so can He make His creature a partaker of the fullness of love that dwells in Himself."

3. WORSHIP THE SUPREME DEVELOPMENT OF THE CREATURE'S LOVE RESPONDING TO GOD

It follows that both man's sharing and communicating of his responsive love as creature must, in its intercourse with the supreme Monarch, assume forms which man's love for man does not and indeed cannot possess in this way.

The sharing of the life and being of the beloved, which works inwardly on the lover, must here become an adoring disappearance of the creature in the greatness and glory of the eternal personality of the Creator.

The giving and communicating of this love, directed towards the Beloved, looking outwards and upwards to God, must involve an expression of the feelings thus created through prayer, thanksgiving and praise.

This means, however, that the Creator's love of His moral creation, and the creature's responding love of Him, the All-loving and Eternal, interact spontaneously to produce the worship of the beauty and splendour of His holy being by the creature who lives in His love and is blessed by it. Thus love towards God finds an essential and necessary expression in worship. In it the active and passive sides of the creature's love to God are blended into a wonderfully elevating harmony. It unites admiration and praise of the person and of the glory of God. A sense of wonder that prostrates the soul is the mark of its passive side, the praise and glorification of God is its spontaneous, active side.

Thus worship, when it is the outcome of the fellowship of love between Creator and creature, is the highest point the latter can reach in response to the love of God. But in that man was from the first appointed to such a fellowship of love with God, he was also ordained by the very fact of his creation to worship. It is the first and principal purpose of his eternal calling. Through all the ages of the ages he will have the right, together with the heavenly host, to praise the Lord of Lords with exulting heart and to say, "Salvation unto our God which sitteth on the throne, and unto the

Lamb. Blessing, and glory, and wisdom, and thanksgiving, and honour, and power, and might, be unto our God for ever and ever. Amen" (Rev. 7: 10, 12). "But the hour is coming, and now is, when the true worshippers will worship the Father in spirit and truth, for such the Father seeks to worship him. God is spirit, and those who worship him must worship in spirit and in truth" (John 4: 23, 24, R.S.V.).

II. MAN'S ETERNAL APPOINTMENT TO THE IMAGE OF GOD

1. MAN'S BEING IN THE IMAGE OF GOD AN EXPRESSION OF THE DIVINE LOVE

We have shown that worship is the highest development of the love of a moral creature responding to his all-loving Creator. But it can exist and be perfected only where this mutual relationship is built on a foundation of fellowship. For love, in its true and ideal sense, is nothing other than the highest form of fellowship between free personalities. Its nature consists in "I want my ego to exist not for myself but for the other, in and with him. True love exists only where my whole being and possessions find their value for me in my being able through them to live for the *other* and to dedicate all that I have and am to his service. Love enables his life to be completed and fulfilled through mine; similarly mine finds its completion and fulfilment, its peace and happiness, in my living for the other."

Thus the claim and basic law of all love is responsive love, involving a perfect exchange in giving and taking, a fullest mutuality in life and experience. "Mine is yours, and yours is mine" is its essential and fundamental principle. In love the individual no longer stands alone and for himself, but "love makes all things common. Each supports the other and individual possession becomes common riches. Its goal is that there should be nothing in the life of the other which it does not appropriate for itself, and nothing in its own life which it does not offer for the enjoyment of the beloved. But this involves that life *for* the other becomes life *in* the other. Lover and beloved, though distinct in personality and individuality, become completely one by deepest and most intimate interpenetration. This begins at the innermost centre of personality and embraces the whole natural and personal life, so that love can say in truth 'I in you, and you in me.'"

It is obvious that such a fellowship, with such an intimate, and all-embracing intermingling of lives can exist only between spiritually related persons. Only if I recognize in another an equality of birth and a certain similarity of nature can I really yield my personality to him. Only if the other possesses and manifests the ability and capacity for true, ideal, mutual love can there be actual *intercourse* in love. Love would be only throwing away its inner self, and therewith its true foundation, if it sought to maintain unimpeded communication and sympathy with a being with whom it had no spiritual or moral links.

Therefore, if there is to be a relation of mutual love between the Creator and His creature, between God and man, then His finite creature, in spite of his ever remaining different from the infinite Creator, so far as philosophical thought is concerned, must nevertheless be united with him in a *morally based spiritual relationship*.

But God's moral nature is holy love. Hence man must also have been so made that holy love is his vocation and ideally the basic power of his personality. Therefore he must be a created likeness of his eternal Creator, and, since God's moral creation is called to have fellowship in love with God, he must also of necessity be in the image of God. Therefore Scripture says of the creation of Adam and Eve: "God created man in his own image, in the image of God created he him; male and female created he them" (Gen. 1: 27).

2. THE NATURE OF THE IMAGE OF GOD

The image of God has two aspects, an outer and an inner. The outer is not the essential one, but for all that it must not be overlooked. It concerns man's bodily nature.

Obviously this has not the meaning it had in Babylonian mythology, according to which the *essence* of man's being in the image of God would lie in man's body being similar to the form adopted by the Deity in His earthly theophanies. This is far too materialistic and superficial. Nevertheless an element of truth is to be found even here.

Man's body itself expresses certain characteristics of his inner, spiritual being and shows his superiority over the rest of the earthly creation. In particular his upright posture and his look directed upwards express the upward-look of his spirit, its superiority over all earthly things and its being turned to God. The soul in man's body is "not only like the sailor in the boat he steers, but it also shapes man's physical side."

The body is the necessary instrument through which the human spirit manifests itself. The activity of the human spirit does not exist for itself, but only in and through the body. Its every expression is bound to it. The body is like a musical instrument, on whose strings the spirit, as a master-player, forms and produces its harmonies. With this is linked also man's ability to reflect his inner feelings in the play of his features, in blushing, laughing and weeping.

It is also obvious that God could not have appeared in Paradise in the form of a man, if that which is *common* to Him and man had not found some expression in this way (Gen. 3: 8). Above all, there could have been no incarnation of the Son of God, indeed, no bodily resurrection and transfiguration of the body of Jesus, if the body of man had not in some way been a fitting house and vessel for the human spirit created in the image of God. Christ, however, is risen with a transfigured *body* and waits in heaven as a glorified *man*. Linked with this the Bible states that perfected man will have a body in his glorification which will be like the body of the glorified Son of Man.

In addition both the transfigured body of Jesus and of the saved proceed from the earthly body of our present humanity and are linked with it. The fact of bodily resurrection proves this. For if there were no link between the heavenly and the present body, why should there be an opening of the graves and the raising of the earthly body? What would be the point of Easter in the story of Jesus? In addition, Scripture says of the dead in Christ, of those who must pass through death before the return of the Lord, "This corruptible must put on incorruption, and this mortal must put on immortality" (I Cor. 15: 53).

Thus man's body—both at its beginning in Paradise and later in the whole setting of the history of salvation—is linked with the image of God, and with the nobility of man. During the course of history sin has succeeded in marring it, but not in fundamentally destroying it. Therefore there is hope also for the body of man.

Scripture bears clear witness to the eternal link between likeness to Christ and the transfiguration of the body. It teaches that also in the ages to come the image of God through Christ will shine out from their transfigured bodies. "For our citizenship is in heaven; from whence also we wait for a Saviour, the Lord Jesus Christ: who shall fashion anew the *body* of our humiliation, that it may be *conformed* to the *body* of His glory" (Phil. 3: 20). And in his classic teaching about the resurrection of the body (I Cor. 15) Paul, dealing with the coming transfiguration of the bodies of the saved, declares, "And as we have borne the image of the earthy (Adam), we shall also bear the image of the heavenly (Christ)" (I Cor. 15: 49). Here also the transfigured body and Christ are connected with one another.

For all that the real *essence* of the image of God in man lies much deeper. The body is only the instrument through which the spiritual manifests itself. It is the spirit that is decisive. Man's body reflects something of the image of God only because the body is the home of man's spirit, and because the spirit which lives in the human body was created in the image of God. Man's body derives its nobility from the nobility of the human spirit, and the nobility of the spirit is rooted in God in virtue of its creation and divine purpose.

Thus the essence of the image of God in man lies in the spiritual and the moral. It is based on the nature of his inner life, on the real substance of his spiritual personality.

In his thinking man is able to move in the world of idealistic concepts, in the world of the true, good and beautiful, whose origin is in God. This very fact shows that man's original home is not really this world below, but that which is above. Man conceives of eternity and God in his thoughts. God is the content of the highest thoughts of the human spirit.

Thus the capacity of his thought proves that he comes forth from eternity and is intended for eternity, that he exists for God.

In the same way too man conceives of his self. In his thinking he somehow becomes conscious of himself as a personality. "If I could convince myself," said Immanuel Kant, "that my horse could grasp the concept of 'self,' I would at once dismount and treat him as my friend." Thus man, in distinction from animals, possesses self-consciousness, understanding and reason, all these combined with his moral endowments.

His understanding enables him, by associating or separating concepts, to form positive or negative judgments, and to draw conclusions from them. His reason enables him, by a continuous chain of inferences, to reach the concept of the universe and to divine the idea of God. But since man is able at the same time to conceive both of God and of himself, he shows through this scope of his powers of thought the relation of his personality to God and thereby his possession of the image of God and the nobility of his existence as man.

This spiritual nature expresses itself chiefly in man's power of speech. Speech is the direct self-revelation of the human spirit. Word and spirit belong together in the structure of human personality. Thought is, as it were, the inward speech of the spirit, and the spoken or written word forms a body for thought. Through the word we make the inward "seeing" of our soul known to our fellow-men.

Classical writers tell how the Greek philosopher Socrates met a young man who devoted himself to ideological and moral problems and who had been hoping to be further stimulated by meeting Socrates. But contact with this intellectual "giant" so overawed him that he scarcely dared to open his mouth to speak, or to ask a question. So they walked side by side for a while without conversation. Then Socrates suddenly broke the silence and said kindly but briefly to his young companion, "Speak, that I may 'see' you."—In this short sentence lies the deep recognition of the connexion between spirit and word. Speech is the instrument for the manifestation of the human spirit.

Through speech, by naming the animals in Paradise, Adam began, according to Scripture, the exercise of his earthly sovereignty (Gen. 2: 19, 20). Speech is therefore the expression of man's kingship; it is his sceptre, the witness to human nobility.

With what restricted phonetic means this royal self-revelation of man's spirit is accomplished! A painter can develop the wonders of his art with only a few colours. Musicians like Johann Sebastian Bach, Ludwig van Beethoven, Mozart, Haydn, unfold their musical riches using the same series of twelve notes the child strums on the piano. Even so man has only about thirty sounds at his disposal when he speaks.[1] The child uses them in his first attempts at speech, and with the same thirty Goethe wrote his

[1] [This is a slight underestimate for English. (H.L.E.).]

Faust, Shakespeare his plays, and Tolstoy his novels. It follows that the art of the use of words is one of the highest of the arts. With most limited means the highest achievements are made possible.

Therefore man alone has the faculty of speech, for only he has "thoughts" in the true sense. The fact that he "speaks" proves that he thinks. Here also we see the crucial distinction between man and the animal world. Man thinks, the animal only feels. The animal has instincts, man a will. The animal makes sounds, man has language.

To produce sounds is by no means the same as to speak. When a child cries, we do not say it is speaking, for only when there is a conscious, systematic use of the vocal organs to produce sounds with a meaning, do we have speech. Therefore animals do not "speak," because they do not think. Indeed, animals cannot have a language, because they have no concepts. The apes have highly developed organs of speech—indeed, according to many natural scientists, even better than those of man—but they do not "speak," because they do not have any "words;" or, as the well-known philosopher Wilhelm Wundt once expressed it, "Animals do not 'speak,' because they have nothing to 'say.' "

This all shows that human speech is a testimony to man's superiority over all other earthly creatures. His power of speech, his position as king and his human nobility belong together.

Karl Ernst von Baer, the celebrated natural scientist,[1] recognized a fourfold ability which raises man above the level of the animal, viz. the religious, the moral, the intellectual and the aesthetic. "The gracious Creator put into the human breast a fourfold longing, which he denied to the animals: longing for the Holy, i.e. *faith*; the demands of duty, i.e. *conscience*; joy in understanding, i.e. the *desire for knowledge*; delight in beauty, i.e. the *aesthetic sense*. This fourfold longing bears witness that man is the image of God; it is the magnet, which draws man upwards."

To this we must add man's call to an eternally continued existence, i.e. his capability by nature for *immortality*. This is also a crucial difference between man and the animals. The characteristic of man which distinguishes him from all other creatures is that he is not created to disappear but to exist endlessly, and that God should be for ever glorified in him and he in God. The animal, however, is appointed only to propagate its kind, but to disappear as an individual creature.

All this proves that the dissimilarities between man and the animals in the realm of soul and spirit are incomparably weightier than all the similarities between them in the realm of the outward and material, so often overemphasized by unbelief.

In all this man's relation to the world is a dual, almost contradictory one. The writer of the eighth Psalm, deeply moved by the sight of the star-filled night sky, stressed this contrast, saying: "When I consider thy

[1] Professor of the sciences in Königsberg and St. Petersburg (1876).

heavens, the work of thy fingers, the moon and the stars, which thou hast ordained; what is man, that thou art mindful of him? and the son of man, that thou visitest him? For thou hast made him but little lower than God, and crownest him with glory and honour. Thou madest him to have dominion over the works of thy hands; thou hast put all things under his feet" (Psa. 8: 3–6). Here we have the contrast between impotence and greatness, between exaltation and lowliness.

Over against the universe man's body is just a speck of dust, a scarce discernible point, virtually nothing. At every moment he must reckon with the possibility of being swallowed up by the universe and of perishing in this great ocean of blind forces. Yet in his spirit he exalts himself proudly over the universe. He is impotent and yet king. He is but a speck, yet with his spirit he embraces the whole world. His thread of life can be cut at any moment, and yet he bears eternity in his heart. Pascal says, "Man is but a reed, weakest in nature, but a reed which thinks. It needs not that the whole Universe should arm to crush him. A vapour, a drop of water is enough to kill him. But were the Universe to crush him, man would still be more noble than that which has slain him, because he knows that he dies, and that the Universe has the better of him. The Universe knows nothing of this."[1]

Nevertheless all these instinctive powers and capacities are only the formal endowment of man to enable him, like a mirror, to reflect the nature of God. They only receive a real, material content, when man's actual condition coincides in practice, through their right use and blameless functioning in positive holiness, with his appointment. Only then does his mind radiate the wisdom, his emotions the love, and his will the power and holiness of his eternal Creator. Only when the soul is good and perfect does the formal endowment become a real possession.

Under no circumstance, however, could this have been imparted to man by creation. For it lies in the very conception of moral perfection that it must be the product of a free, personal decision of will and of personal activity. Therefore room had to be left for moral development, and consequently that which was imparted by creation could be nothing more than a predisposition that made such a development possible.

This of necessity involved that man, though not "holy" in the full sense of the word, was created at least pure and without sin. His eternal calling was to radiate the image of his Creator in holiness and without distortion by a real participation in the moral characteristics of God. Hence he had to begin his existence without spot or defect. "The image of God as eternal vocation and nature of necessity included the image of God in time." It must, however, not be forgotten that this created image of God was no more than a condition of pre-moral purity, which should *become* a *genuine* moral *holiness* only through a personal and free development.

---

[1] Blaise Pascal: *Pensées*—The Greatness and Littleness of Man.

This "original righteousness" (*justitia originalis* in dogmatic theology), given the first men in creation could therefore be only a *neutral* sinlessness. Only when God had given His commands and man had obeyed them, could this *mature* into a truly moral possession. If Adam and Eve had not eaten of the fruit of the tree of temptation, they would have acquired a knowledge of good and evil along the way God had intended, and they would have followed an unbroken path upwards to glory and holiness.

The tree of knowledge gained its name from the purpose for which God had appointed it. The popular idea that it was called the "tree of knowledge of good and evil" because through it man reached this knowledge (cf. Gen. 3: 22) is ruled out, because God so named the tree *before* man's fall (Gen. 2: 17). Hence it cannot have been named from an effect that occurred only *after* the fall. In fact man should have learned in the midst of temptation what the good *is* and what the evil *would be*, but through his sin he learned what the *evil* is and what the good *would have been*. The tree did not receive its name from that which it actually gave man but from that which it should have given him.

The same is true of the tree of life. Both names are to be explained in the same way. Both point to the blessing which God intended them to impart. The tree of life was linked to man's earthly and the tree of knowledge to his spiritual nature. The former was to impart its blessing, when its fruit was eaten, the latter when its fruit was refused.

The tree of life was so called because through it the life man already had as an initial and partial possession was to be transformed into the full possession of a never-ending life. The tree of knowledge was so called because through it the knowledge of good and evil, already (through God's command) given to man as an initial and partial possession, was to be increased to a real and full possession. Thus the serpent promised what God actually wanted to give, only in another way. In a distorted form it also kept its word. For after their fall the first men did in fact recognize good and evil; but "instead of perceiving the evil from the summit of the good, they recognized the good from the distant abyss of evil" (Delitzsch).

All this means we must distinguish between two forms of the image of God, one innate by creation, the other man's final goal. Their relation one to another is that of a plan and its fulfilment, of the means and the purpose; hence they in no sense coincide. In the New Testament the image of God is viewed mainly as the *realization* of man's appointment;[1] the Old Testament creation-narrative thinks rather of man's mental and spiritual *endowment*.[2] Both the Scholastic philosophers of the Middle Ages, and the earlier Protestant theologians have pointed this out.

The image of God as an endowment is found in the fact that man is a moral personality with self-consciousness and intelligence. Outwardly,

[1] Rom. 8: 29; I Cor. 15: 49; II Cor. 3: 18; Eph. 4: 24; Col. 3: 10.
[2] Gen. 9: 6; I Cor. 11: 7; Jas. 3: 9; Acts 17: 28.

physiologically and psychologically, this is revealed by his look directed upwards, his faculty of speech, and by his ability to reflect his inner feelings in his face, by blushing, laughing and crying. Inwardly and non-corporeally it is revealed by his immortality, and also by his self-consciousness, his mental powers and his reason, and above all by his moral capacity, viz. his ability to judge what is good and evil. It is further seen in his conscience, acting as the inner law-giver which *before* the act pronounces a "categorical imperative" and *after* it pronounces judgment upon it, and, finally, in his freedom of will, the capacity to choose whether he will or will not obey the Divine command.

All these are not something added at some time to human nature; they are the *essential basis and substance of his personality*. They enable him to live a personal, spiritual life, the "essence" of the concept of his being man. Without them he would cease to be man. Here we find the real difference between him and the animals; and therefore *this* image of God was not lost by the Fall.

Nevertheless man has fallen very far and very grievously. For even if the image of God as a formal endowment, i.e. as the moral substance of his personality, persisted, yet the image of God as a real spiritual possession and an actual state was lost. The "original righteousness" which, once God's command had been heard by men, had started the process of raising pre-moral purity to moral holiness, has disappeared. "The works of the mechanism remain, but they no longer drive it; the flower is still there, but colour and scent have vanished."

This all explains why Scripture on the one hand describes the image of God in man as something *lost* by the fall and *regainable* only by redemption,[1] and on the other hand still recognizes an image of God in *fallen* man.[1]

The goal of redemption is not only to bring man back to his lost paradise of former purity, but above all to make it possible for him to attain the glory and beauty of his appointed *goal*; the essence of sanctification is now to be found in the gradual transformation of man's character into the moral image of God, which from the first he had been intended to attain.

The Creator has given man three basic psychic powers, viz. will, intellect and emotions. Through these the Most High wills to glorify His own inward nature in His creation. The holiness of human free will should mirror His holy *freedom*. The joy of human emotions should reflect His *blessedness*, for He is the All-sufficient, the God of all glory. The thought and knowledge of human intellect should be an image of His *spirituality*, for God is "Spirit" (John 4: 24); He is the Lord of all spirits.

We must, however, go further. This trinity of inner powers should make man a spiritual and moral copy of the relationship in essence and activity between the Persons of the Godhead, Father, Son and Holy Spirit.

---

[1] See Footnotes [1] and [2] respectively on the previous page for references.

K

It is axiomatic in the concept of God that He moves purely "from" Himself, "to" Himself, and "in" Himself. The Father is the Lover, the Son the Beloved, the Holy Spirit the Spirit of love. The Father is God existing "from" Himself, the Son is God attaining "to" Himself, the Spirit is God moving "in" Himself.

God's proceeding from Himself is His freedom; for His actions arise solely "from" Himself and are controlled by no other cause. God's attaining to Himself is His blessedness; for His activity always returns "to" Him (I Cor. 15: 28). In Himself, the All-perfect, God eternally reaches His goal, and is thus the completely Self-sufficient, the absolutely Blessed. His movement in Himself is His spirituality.

When, however, these three characteristics, freedom, blessedness and spirituality, are glorified by man in his creatureliness in his will, emotions and intellect, the image of God, the mystery of the Divine Trinity, which rules over us, becomes within history the active basis of our own personality; far from its being a contradiction of our human nature the mystery of the Trinity in the Eternal God is found in us, its image in time and space. Thus man is not a copy of the Divine Trinity by virtue of his merely external trinity of body, soul and spirit, but rather in his moral and spiritual calling to the inner trinity of freedom, blessedness and spirituality.

III. Man's Eternal Appointment to Sonship

1. THE ORGANIC ELEMENT IN REDEMPTION. SONSHIP AS THE SOURCE OF LIFE

God's decree of salvation rises even higher than we have traced. When He willed to establish a spiritual relationship of love between Himself and man, it was not only to be a purely moral resemblance in character, a mere agreement in thought, emotions and will, but also above all a unity in life, an organic relationship of personalities. God wills not only, as with the angels, to place in man the moral certainties of His holy nature and so to glorify Himself in them, but he wills also to permit them to attain to fellowship with Himself, to become "partakers of the divine nature" (II Pet. 1: 4). He wills that His own eternal life should shine into them and unite them eternally with Himself, the Almighty Creator. This and nothing less than this the Bible intends us to understand, when it speaks again and again of the redeemed as sons of God.[1]

"God sent forth the Spirit of his Son into our hearts, crying, Abba, Father. So that thou art no longer a bondservant, but a *son*" (Gal. 4: 6, 7). "For as many as are led by the Spirit of God, these are *sons* of God" (Rom. 8: 14). "But as many as received him, to them gave he the right to become *children of God*, even to them that believe on his name: which were born . . . of God" (John 1: 12, 13). "Behold what manner of love the

---

[1]E.g. Rom. 8: 15, 21; Gal. 4: 5; Eph. 1: 5.

Father hath bestowed upon us, that we should be called children of God: and such we are" (I John 3: 1).[1]

This linking of the Creator with His creature, of the Uncreated with the created, in a word, the fact of the redeemed's being sons of God within the framework of creation, is completely beyond all that contemporary thought can comprehend. For all that, it is clearly taught in Scripture and it presents the highest unfolding of God's determination to glorify Himself in love. For even the Creator can give nothing higher than Himself, the All-Highest! And in nothing less can his own love reach full satisfaction. "For the greatest work of art can never be as precious to its creator as his own son who shares his outlook. No creation of his hand can embody and interpret the inmost and most sacred concepts of his personality as can his heir, with whom he can share the whole wealth of his artistic vision and ability. It is in the son that the image and likeness of the father can be reflected as in no other creation, and therefore it is for sonship that man sees himself created in the likeness of God" (J. Kroeker).

2. SONSHIP AS SIMILARITY OF NATURE

True sonship implies some degree of identity of character between father and son. Here the Oriental has a deeper insight into the blood-bond between father and son and the resultant, far-reaching harmony in nature and character between them than have many in the West. A clear understanding of such living links is fundamental also for our understanding of certain key statements of Scripture about the nature of true sonship. It has been rightly said, "A 'son' for the Oriental is always one who in his nature, in the essence of his being, is determined and formed by him from whom he springs" (Ralph Luther).

Therefore the Bible frequently uses the expression, "to be a son" simply in the sense of "to be similar, to bear the characteristics of one's father." Sometimes indeed the New Testament goes so far as to use the word "son" where a literal relationship of father and son did not and indeed could not exist.[2]

Thus Jesus speaks of the "sons of the bridechamber" (Matt. 9: 15), obviously not meaning literal sons. They were simply the friends of the bridegroom, who were present as guests at the marriage-feast, whose mood was one of festive joy, a joy felt by the bridegroom in a special measure, but shared in a similar way by his friends and companions at the wedding.

Likewise John the Baptist speaks of the "sons of the devil," again implying by it a certain similarity of nature. He meant men whose character and manner of life is satanic.

In answering the Sadducees Christ speaks of the "sons of this age"

[1] Cf. also John 3: 3, 4, 5; I Pet. 1: 23; 2: 2; I John 2: 29; 4: 7; 5: 1.
[2] [This is true also of the Old Testament. (H.L.E.)]

(Luke 20: 34), again implying a certain conformity of nature. He meant men whose ways of thought and attitude to life are conditioned by the nature and conditions of this present age. In the same context the Lord speaks also of the "sons of the resurrection," meaning the redeemed, who will one day bear the stamp and characteristics of the coming, trans-figured world, the world which will become manifest with the re-surrection and the beginning of the new life.

Behind this usage lies a clear understanding that truly to be a son means a conformity of being with the father from whom the son is descended. Once we grasp this, we realize that sonship must be inseparably linked with the true image of God. Son of God and image of God belong together. Hence already here on earth true sonship is an obligation to live out the nature, i.e. the love and holiness, of our heavenly Father in practice. Therefore the Lord says in the Sermon on the Mount, "Love your enemies, and pray for them that persecute you; *that ye may be* 'sons of your Father' which is in heaven" (Matt. 5: 44, 45). The "sons" should love *in order that* they may be "sons"!

This will be attained perfectly in eternity. Then we, glorified, will as "sons of God" bear the eternally transfigured image of our Father, then there will be the perfect union of God's life and God's nature, of inherent potentiality and character, of sonship and the image of God.

3. SONSHIP AS FELLOWSHIP IN LIFE

Here also the Oriental sees the inner relationships more clearly. The son is more closely united in his life to his father than in Western society. With us in the West the adult son gradually makes himself independent of his father. He then lives, so to speak, his life for himself. But in the East it was normal for the grown-up son to remain linked with his father (John 8: 35); it was the normal thing for him to work together with him.

This is how Jesus also pictured His relationship to His heavenly Father. Father and Son work together. The Son does only what the Father bids Him. In this deep sense sonship is therefore fellowship in life.

Therefore the perfecting in eternity of our standing as sons involves also living in the presence of God. Then we shall be as sons with our Father. We shall live in His presence united with Him eternally, and so fellowship with God will be eternally transfigured when our sonship is perfected.

Already here on earth fellowship with God is one of the privileges belonging to the royal nobility of the redeemed. The children of the great King have the right to enter the presence of their heavenly Father. They have the right to approach the throne of grace in prayer. Sonship and the life of prayer belong together. Whoever neglects his prayer life is in practice denying his standing as son. It is true that in our prayer life we feel ourselves humiliated by our dependence and need; at the same time it is just in prayer that we are lifted into the immediate presence of the great Lord of the world. Prayer is a piece of eternity within time. In prayer we experience the presence of the heavenly goal while we are yet pilgrims here on earth. To pray in faith is to experience in advance what we shall yet see. To be a son means to be a man of prayer. Those who down here on earth enter God's sanctuary will one day enter His heavenly palace. Priesthood and kingship, temple and throne are linked eternally. This thought directs our gaze towards the goal. Sonship and glory belong together. To be a son is to be an heir.

4. SONSHIP AS INHERITANCE AND SOVEREIGNTY

"The Spirit himself beareth witness with our spirit, that we are children of God: and if children, then heirs; heirs of God, and joint-heirs with Christ; if so be that we suffer with him, that we may be also glorified with him" (Rom. 8: 16, 17). Our inheritance is the eternal kingdom. We are to "inherit the kingdom of God" (I Cor. 6: 10; Eph. 5: 5). With the perfecting of sonship our Father in heaven gives His children and sons dominion and kingship. The sons are also to be kings. As sons of the King of Kings they are also to wear a crown of glory. Therefore they are to reign with Christ from eternity to eternity.

But in all this let us not forget the solemn "if so be." The attainment of this lofty goal is linked with the condition that we yield ourselves. Only then shall we attain to the full possession of the privileges of true sonship, to kingship and to the heavenly crown, "*if so be* that we suffer with him, that we may be also glorified with him" (Rom. 8: 17).

Our attaining the full goal of royal sonship is not an automatic and necessary result of conversion and regeneration. The level of nobility we reach in the future perfecting of our sonship depends on how faithful we, who have been called to sonship here on earth, have in fact been in our position of humiliation.

We grant, all is of grace. No one can compel God to bestow His salvation and His glory upon a sinner, however much he may strive and try to make himself noble. But it is equally true that God does not give His salvation to everyone! He links His free gift to the condition that a definite, inner attitude of heart be present in His creature. He gives His gift only where there is true surrender. He gives "free" grace, but not "unconditional" grace. Everything comes from God, but nothing comes by itself. You must play your own personal part.

The goal which grace holds before us is infinitely high, but we must make our calling and election sure (II Pet. 1: 10). The crown is only for the conqueror. Only where there is true commitment, will we reach the peak of perfection. The degree of our faithfulness determines the level of our future position of honour. With all our emphasis on free grace and with all our faith in the sole efficacy of God's power, we must nevertheless clearly recognize these facts, consider them seriously and act accordingly. "Be thou faithful unto death, and I will give thee the crown of life" (Rev. 2: 10). Then too we shall experience the truth of Paul's words, "Faithful is the saying: For if we died with him, we shall also live with him: if we shall deny him, he also shall deny us" (II Tim. 2: 11, 12).

5. CHRIST THE FIRSTBORN AND HIS BROTHERS

Nothing we have written alters the fact that the infinite distance between Christ, the eternal Son of God, and those born of the Father in Him, will remain for ever. He is the one Divine Son of the Most High (Mark 14: 61, 62); they are the many sons of the heavenly Father within His creation.[1] He is the "only begotten Son" (John 1: 14, 18; 3: 16), the "Heir of all things" (Heb. 1: 2), "God over all, blessed for ever" (Rom. 9: 5); they are those who have been pardoned and rescued from sin and misery.

Yet He is not ashamed to call them His "brethren," "for both he that sanctifieth and they that are sanctified are all of one" (Heb. 2: 11). And therefore He, the effulgence of the glory of the Father and the express image of His Person (Heb. 1: 3), is at the same time the "Firstborn among many brethren" (Rom. 8: 29). He is at the same time *over* them and yet *in* them. He is throned at the right hand of the Majesty on high (Heb. 8: 1), and yet nevertheless grants them the glory which the Father has given Him (John 17: 22).

IV. MAN'S ETERNAL APPOINTMENT TO KINGLY RULE

1. MAN'S KINGSHIP AND STANDING AS SON

In the light of the above, the heart of God's salvation is that we have been called "into the fellowship of his Son, Jesus Christ our Lord" (I Cor. 1: 9; Heb. 3: 14). Only thus can man become the crown of creation. Only this exalts him above all other creatures. Without this all his expectations of rule at the last over suns and worlds would be only a foolish dream of fantastic vanity, a meaningless and deceptive megalomania. For in physical strength and material size man is a mere nothing, even in comparison with the earth, which itself is scarcely even a speck of dust in the universe; in spiritual strength, in morality and intelligence, he ranks, at least at present, far beneath the angels of heaven, those mighty heroes, the executors of the Divine good pleasure (Psa. 103: 21; cf. Psa. 8: 3–6).

But what exalts him *above* all these creations is his calling to be united in an eternal fellowship of life and nature with Christ, the Son of the Highest. With Divine logic his eternal, kingly rule is built on his standing as a son, wrought in Christ. The words of Scripture are, "Know ye not that the saints shall judge the world?" (I Cor. 6: 2). "Know ye not that

[1] Hence the Lord never spoke of "*our* Father," embracing both Himself and His people, but only of "My Father and your Father," cf. John 20: 17.

we shall judge angels?" (I Cor. 6: 3). "Fear not, little flock, for it is the
Father's good pleasure to give you the kingdom" (Luke 12: 32). Therefore
it says further, "If we endure, we shall also reign with Him" (II Tim. 2: 12),
and, "He that overcometh, I will give to him to *sit down with Me in My
throne*, as I also overcame, and sat down with my Father in His throne"
(Rev. 3: 21).

2. THE ETERNAL GOAL

This is the living hope to which we have been born again through the
resurrection of Jesus Christ (I Pet. 1: 3). This is the "inheritance, incorrupt-
ible, and undefiled, and that fadeth not away," which through our faith
is reserved for us in heaven by the power of God (I Pet. 1: 4). Here below
we live, it is true, in weakness and imperfection. "It is not yet made
manifest what we shall be. We know that, if He shall be manifested, we
shall be like Him; for we shall see Him even as He is" (I John 3: 2). And
"when Christ, who is our life, shall be manifested, then shall ye also with
Him be manifested in glory" (Col. 3: 4). "Having therefore these promises, beloved, let us cleanse ourselves from all defilement of flesh and
spirit, perfecting holiness in the fear of God" (II Cor. 7: 1). For "everyone
that hath this hope set on Him purifieth himself, even as He is pure"
(I John 3: 3).

On January 18, 1701, in the castle church in Königsberg, in the fortress
of the former grand masters of the Teutonic Order, the first Prussian king
Frederick I was crowned. The day before, the Order of the Black Eagle
was instituted, to be the highest order in the Prussian state. The first
recipients were seventeen men who had served the king especially well.
Through the conferment of the order of the Black Eagle they automatically entered the hereditary nobility and received the rank of lieutenant-
general.

I visited the church where not only Frederick I but also Wilhelm I (the
later emperor Wilhelm I of Germany) was anointed as king. On the walls,
the choir-stalls and pillars I saw decorations seldom seen in a church. There
were hundreds of coats of arms of the knights of the Black Eagle. I myself
counted over seven hundred.

The meaning of this most unusual ornamentation in a Christian church
is obvious. It was to maintain the memory of this historical event. When
the ruler is honoured his servants also shall be honoured. *The coronation
place of the king should at the same time be the hall of fame for those that had
served him faithfully.*

Crowns and principalities pass away. Dynasties sink into the dust.
Human honour and earthly glory are alike transitory. But one thing
remains—the eternal kingdom of the Most High. The essence of this
kingdom is the Person of the King. The kingdom is concentrated in His
Person (Luke 17: 21). The kingdom is *Himself*!

But He does not retain His kingly glory for Himself alone. His people are to share His splendour. They shall reign with Him for ever and ever (Rev. 22: 5). "Father, that which Thou hast given Me, I will that, where I am, they also may be with Me; that they may behold My glory, which Thou hast given Me: for Thou lovedst Me before the foundation of the world. . . . The glory which Thou hast given Me I have given unto them" (John 17: 24, 22).

PART IV

THE PRACTICAL REALIZATION OF MAN'S KINGLY CALLING

CHAPTER XI

ITS DIVINE FOUNDATION: THE EXISTENCE OF GOD

MAN has been appointed to kingship. His vocation influences both his present and his future, on earth and in heaven, and also the development of the earth in time and eternity.

The individual, as a member of this totality of mankind, should also share in this calling; for God's salvation is not only for mankind but also for the individual. He is not only the God of humanity, but also the God of each separate soul.

All human dignity originates with God. From the supreme King of the universe is derived all kingship among men. God is the source of all authority. The existence of this living, personal God is therefore the presupposition for and the foundation of all human nobility; belief in Him, His existence and His revelation, is the necessary condition for all real implementation of this high calling. And just here faith stands on an eternal, unshakable rock-foundation.

I. The Universality of Belief in Higher Powers

There are no real exceptions to the universal testimony to man's belief in an invisible world. Already Cicero, the great Roman (106–43 B.C.), referred to this. Luther declared, "There has never been a people so impious that it did not establish and hold divine worship."

This factual universality of religious beliefs, earlier occasionally doubted, has been shown to be beyond question by modern ethnology and the science of religion. Peoples or tribes entirely without religion do not exist.

We grant that this is not a "proof" of God's existence in the sense of an incontestable, as it were mathematical, proposition. Nevertheless this fact has high value as a testimony. It shows clearly that the predisposition to religion is common to all men, that belief in a higher world is not a fundamental contradiction to human nature, and that belief in and worship of God are in harmony with the universal nature of man. This is the true element in the Argument from Universal Consent.

II. The Living Power and Certainty of True Faith in God

We should add to this the fact that a genuine faith in God proves to be a life-transforming power which frees captives, turns the slaves of sin into victors, and broken men into useful members of human society. It leads to overcoming psychic inhibitions, practical transforming of the inner and the outer man; it gives renewed life and true nobility of mind.

In so doing it demonstrates its reality. A stream must have a source; a light must proceed from a light-bearer; a force proves the existence of a centre of force. Mere imagination cannot produce a new man. Behind the *effects* of faith must stand the *reality* of faith.

This is an argument for the existence of God from the results of faith in Him. It testifies to the fact that true faith in God is an ennobling power, and that the reproach that faith is a retrograde tendency, making man useless for earthly and social life, rests on a total misunderstanding. It is just those who believe in God who become useful in life. Everyday work is for them service for God.

Such a living faith is continually on the winning side. For unbelief would gain nothing, even were it right; but it loses everything if it is wrong. Faith, however, would lose nothing, even were it wrong; but it gains everything, if it is right. This shows that true, living believers are always those most to be envied. Among those who have used this as an argument for the existence of God was the celebrated French mathematician and philosopher Blaise Pascal (1623–1662).

III. The Testimony of Nature to the Existence of a Creator

On other grounds too it is logical to believe in God. Everything that is must have an original cause. Just as there can be no watch without a watchmaker, no work of art without the mind and the hand of a creative artist, even so we must—if we argue back logically—reach an ultimate and first cause for the universe, which has caused everything but is itself caused by nothing. In view of the sublime power, subordination to law, beauty and purposefulness of nature, this first cause can be conceived of only as a creating Spirit of perfect wisdom and omnipotence, i.e. as a personal, living, creative Founder of the universe.

One cannot logically deny this conclusion. As one modern doctor expressed it, "My scientific conscience *forbids* me not to believe in God" (Dr. Horstmann).

"God is the cause of all things, and whoever thinks in terms of cause and effect thinks in the direction of God" (Dr. A. Neuberg). "Just because I reflected I remained a believer," was the testimony of Pasteur, the French chemist.

Even non-Christian philosophers who rejected the Biblical revelation saw themselves compelled to acknowledge the force of this argument for a general belief in God.

Voltaire said, "I do not know what I should think about the world. I cannot believe that this clock exists but not a clockmaker." And Diderot (1733–1784), one of the most influential writers of the revolutionary period of enlightenment in the eighteenth century, declared, "The wing of a butterfly or the eye of a moth suffice to confound all who deny the existence of God."

The English astronomer Newton had a ready answer for an atheist. In his laboratory stood a large, new globe of the heavens, on which the whole mechanism of the movements of the sun, planets and their moons could be demonstrated. One day an atheistic acquaintance came in and stood amazed in front of the globe; he asked, "Who made it?" Newton looked him full in the face and answered, "Nobody!" Newton intended him to understand that the wonder of the solar system, in which everything moves harmoniously according to eternal laws, could not have arisen by itself. Only a creative Spirit could have conceived and created it and kept it in motion until today.

"The invisible things of Him since the creation of the world are clearly seen, being perceived through the things that are made, even His everlasting power and divinity" (Rom. 1: 20). "Lift up your eyes and see: who hath created these?" (Isa. 40: 26, R.V.mg). "The heavens declare the glory of God; and the firmament sheweth his handiwork" (Psa. 19: 1).

Dr. Luthardt has said, "If a shipwrecked man on a desert island were to find a geometrical figure drawn in the sand, would he not conclude that some other man was there, and would not his heart overflow with a thrill of joy? But the world is more than a geometrical figure! So should not our heart and spirit be filled with joy and gratitude, because we see a higher, a divine intelligence, full of wisdom and goodness, ruling in it?" (p. 37).

Linnaeus, the Swedish botanist of outstanding importance in the history of the natural sciences, said, "I have considered the animals; they are dependent on the plant-world, which in turn is rooted in the earth; the earth circles the sun in its undeviating course, and the sun, turning on its own axis, is held in its path through space by the incomprehensible First Cause, the Architect, Upholder and Ruler of the universe. As I have listened attentively, I have seen this one, eternal, infinite, omniscient God going on His way and have been overcome with amazement."

This is the testimony of the Cosmological Argument, which is linked with the Teleological Argument. The first starts with the question "Whence?" and the second with the question "For what purpose?", as applied to the world. The former looks to the original cause, the latter to the goal of all existence. But in truth they belong together. The latter fills the empty concept and framework of the former with a concrete content.

In all this the Biblical concept of God surpasses the philosophical concept of God in the Greek thinkers. For this living first Cause of the world is no mere "thought thinking itself," no "unmoved mover" of the world (Aristotle), but the *active* God of Abraham, Isaac and Jacob, the Father of Jesus Christ, the God of history and redemption. He is "uncaused," but not "unmoved," not only "reposing," but above all acting, not only the background of all existence, but also the God who makes Himself known in the foreground of nature and the history of salvation. Human logic cannot "prove" His existence, but it can testify clearly to Him as a logical necessity. Here there is a gulf between the philosophical and Biblical concepts of God, which can only be bridged by the Divine self-revelation and human faith.

Thus the truth contained in the cosmological proof of God fits into the framework of the Biblical revelation as a "testimony" to God. It testifies that purely logical thought compels us to accept the existence of an eternal Cause of the world, a compulsion which the Bible affirms and, at the same time, infinitely surpasses.

God's reality is comprehensible to human thought, but goes inconceivably far beyond it. It does not contradict, but surpasses our reason. The path of clear logical thought leads towards God, but God's reality and His thoughts are, nevertheless, "higher than our thoughts" (Isa. 55: 8).

IV. The Error of Polytheism, Pantheism and Deism

It has been objected that this Cosmological Proof, linked with those mentioned earlier, does not completely refute heathen polytheism, and does not necessarily lead to Biblical monotheism. For it remains conceivable that at the beginning of the universe not only one, but several creative causes were at work, either together or successively.

A basic tendency of modern science is to reduce all events in nature, both organic and inorganic, to the same, uniform, basic laws, so that the whole universe is determined by a uniform plan. We need only remind ourselves of the physical principle of matter in motion—"solar systems," as it were—both in the world of stars and also in the world of the atom.[1] Similarly spectro-analysis has shown a surprising uniformity throughout the universe. For it has proved that the matter which the heavenly bodies are composed of consists of exactly the same elements as this earth, so that the universe is governed by the same principles, both physically and chemically. This amazing uniformity of the cosmos testifies to the thinking mind that only *one* planning Mind, as the sole Founder of the universe, called the whole of creation into existence. Thus the whole of natural world becomes a testimony against all heathen polytheism.

Professor Rendle Short wrote: "The most distant stars appear to be all

[1] Cf. p. 36.

of a piece, chemically and physically, with our own solar system. The animals and plants of past geological time, and the processes of nature, were very like what we study today. Everywhere everything shows the work of one Hand and one Mind. A conflict of creators would have wrecked the world and the universe long ago."[1]

We find much the same in *Space and Spirit* by Sir Edmund Whittaker, F.R.S., Professor of Mathematics in the University of Edinburgh: "The fact that the same mathematical laws are valid over the cosmos, that it is shown by science to be interrelated and consistent, leads to the inference that there is only a single mind involved in the whole creation. This mind is one over the entire universe."

It has also been objected that the Cosmological Proof, linked with the others already mentioned, deals only with space and time. It does not lead, therefore, beyond nature, and consequently does not reach the absolute, outside the framework of time and space. Therefore it is no answer to pantheism, which affirms that God and the universe are one.

Goethe was right in mocking the pantheistic idea of an impersonal deity, a world-spirit, but not a personal God: "The professor is a person, but God is not." It is also *a priori* impossible to accept an unconscious intelligence. This is a contradiction in terms. Similarly it is impossible to speak of unconscious ideas, for ideas demand a conscious, rational principle which produces them. That is why the psalmist asks, "He that planted the ear, shall he not hear? he that formed the eye, shall he not see?" (Psa. 94: 9).

Once again we may quote Rendle Short: "Nor will a merely impersonal God satisfy the indications. A Mind has been at work, with purposes to foresee and to bring to pass, working by laws and with materials that we can up to a point understand; it is a Mind that works along the same lines as our own minds, but on a vastly higher level. And mind is not something that floats about in space. It is not inherent in a block of granite. It is connected with a personality, with plans, executive ability, likes and dislikes. So it is not surprising that the Bible quotes God as saying, 'Let Us make man in Our image, after Our likeness.'" (II, p. 82).

Moreover, pantheism is, logically considered, only a polite form of atheism. For if one asserts that God and the world are the same, finally this comes to the same thing as saying, "There is only one world, but there is no God." "The statement of pantheism, 'God and the world are one,' is only a polite way of sending the Lord God about His business." (Schopenhauer).

Albert Einstein, the greatest mathematician and physicist of recent times, testified: "My religion consists of a humble admiration of the illimitable, superior Spirit who reveals Himself in the slight details we are able to perceive with our frail and feeble minds. That deeply emotional con-

[1] *Modern Discovery and the Bible*, p. 82.

viction of the presence of a superior reasoning power, which is revealed in the incomprehensible universe, forms my idea of God."[1]

Finally, it has been maintained that Deism is not refuted by this proof. Deism proclaims that there is indeed a personal, creative God, but that He does not intervene in the course of this world, governed by natural laws, by means of miracles and revelation.

We would quote Goethe again:

> What God were he that outside all doth linger
> And the wide world scarce touches with a finger!
> It Him becomes *within* His world to labour,
> Himself in Nature, it in Him to favour:
> So that what in Him lives and moves and is
> Shall never lack the strength His Spirit gives.

In fact, "we see the universe full of energy in motion, in the atom with its circling electrons, in the vibrating ether, in the ray of light, in the electro-magnetic wave, in the lines of force which traverse space; everywhere there are only forces. *It is as if the universe were breathing.* The same is true of the world of life, in the cell with its incessant segmentation, in albumen with its lines of force, in the mysterious developments in the germ; everywhere we find streamlined events, nature in constant motion" (Neuberg).

V. The "Spiritual" in Matter. The Conquest of Materialism

In the universe there is actually inconceivably little real matter. Here we are faced by three incomprehensible miracles in nature.

The first is the almost incredible *minuteness* of the basic constituents of matter.[2] Five million iron atoms placed side by side would cover less than a twenty-fifth of an inch. The second is the surprising *size*—in comparison with this minuteness—of the distances between the particles of the basic stuff of matter, both in the atomic world and in the world of stars. From this there follows the third, the *emptiness of space*, both in the minute world of the atom and also in the mighty world of the stars. This causes everything material to disappear almost into nothing and simply compels our thinking to seek reality in nature not in matter that occurs so seldom, but in other factors.

The German physicist O. W. Gail, whose books have appeared in almost all European languages, has illustrated these puzzling relationships by a series of most impressive comparisons. At the request of Professor

---

[1] Quoted by Short, II, p. 35.

[2] No human eye has ever seen an atom. No microscope can reach down into the realm of the atom, not even the celebrated electron microscope. Nevertheless the size and mass of individual atoms is known with amazing exactitude. From visible effects physics measures the invisible causes, and these calculations are more accurate than those made by a yard-stick or goldsmiths' or chemists' balances.

Hahn the physical data given were checked before publication by the physicist Dr. E. Bagge of the University of Munich. Thus Gail's comparisons are based on a rigidly scientific foundation, however easily understood and fantastic they may appear. It goes without saying that the measurements involved had to be enormously magnified to make these relationships "visible;" in the following Gail has worked with a magnification of one billion (1,000,000,000,000).

If a sheet of tissue paper were so enlarged as to be too thick to be inserted between the earth and the moon, i.e. more than 240,000 miles thick, then the nucleus of an atom would be as large as a pea! (Gail, pp. 24, 25).

On the same basis of magnification a single microbe could cover the whole of Africa, from the Nile delta to Cape Town, and a hair from a man's head would be over 4,000 times the diameter of the earth itself.[1] Man would be a giant in the universe, 1,000 times taller than the distance between the earth and the sun, i.e. 1,000 times 93 million miles. He would have reached the sun already only four-fifths of an inch from the soles of his feet! But at the same degree of magnification the nucleus of an atom (we repeat) would be the size of a pea.

Inconceivably smaller still are the electrons which rotate around the nucleus like "atomic planets" round their "atomic sun." If the atomic nucleus were as large as a pea they would be like pinheads.[2]

To these wonders of minuteness we must add that of the relatively great distances between them. If, for example, a whole atom had the same volume as St. Paul's Cathedral, then its nucleus would be a tiny ball a little more than one-fifth of an inch in diameter, and everything else in the "cathedral" would be completely empty space. What an inconceivably minute occurrence of matter![3]

As the diameter of an atomic nucleus is not much larger than the 100,000th part of the diameter of the whole atom, the "substantial" nucleus comprises only the 100,000 times 100,000 times 100,000th part of the volume of the whole atom, i.e. the 1,000,000,000,000,000th part. It is as though the globe of the earth with its diameter of about 8,000 miles consisted of just one or more spheres each 43 feet in diameter, circling round its surface, with a sphere of 430 feet diameter at its centre, but with the rest of its volume consisting only of empty space![4]

[1] The diameter of a hair from a man's head is about ·006 in., while that of the earth is approximately 7,960 miles.

[2] In the atom of uranium there are ninety-two such atomic planets, in that of iron fifty-six, of carbon twelve, and of hydrogen only one.

[3] In addition, probably only the neutron in the atomic nucleus is "substance." Everything else, i.e. not only the revolving electrons but also the protons *in* the nucleus itself—are quantities of energy, bound by definite space-time relationships.

[4] It has been asked how one can bring these facts into harmony with the solidity and hardness which is to be observable in most substances. Dr. Fritz Hitzbleck has

This emptiness in atomic space corresponds exactly to the emptiness in inter-stellar space. Between the atomic nuclei and the electrons in their microcosmic world there exists in relation to their size, the same tremendous expanses of "nothing" as in the macrocosmic world between the planets and the sun.

In the world of the stars, according to Professor Schwarzschild, the distribution of suns and planetary systems is as sparse as if, on an average, a single pinhead were to be found every 20 to 60 miles; the "empty" space between the stars and star clusters must be measured in light-years (1 light-year = approximately 6 million million miles). Thus the distribution of "matter" in the universe is everywhere fundamentally the same.

That we are not concerned here with fantasies or romantic hypotheses of modern physicists is proved by the fact that the most significant achievements of modern technical science have been built up upon these discoveries. Only because what we call opaque and solid is in fact more comparable with a loosely-woven spider's web with wide, empty meshes, and because in this particles move with inconceivable speed, is it possible for light-rays to penetrate window-glass, for X- and cathode-rays to pass through solid matter, for wireless-waves to transmit sound and pictures from continent to continent at such speed that we can perceive anywhere in the world what is spoken or played in New York, Shanghai, Sydney, Cape Town or London within a fraction of the same second. Only for this reason could atomic and hydrogen bombs be developed, as well as the fuel for inter-continental ballistic weapons and earth-satellites.[1]

answered this question in a popular and simplified form by using the following comparison: "To find an answer to this difficulty, all we have to do is to turn a bicycle upside-down and look at one of the wheels. As long as it is stationary we can easily put a finger between the spokes. If we now set the wheel in *slow* motion, it is still possible, because the spokes follow one another very slowly. But the *quicker* the wheel turns the sooner this becomes impossible. If we imagine the wheel turning with an exceptionally high speed, then the spokes give the impression of a *disc* which we could touch without running the risk of getting in between them. Similarly, since the eye can no longer follow the single spokes, the whole wheel appears to be a transparent disc. Through the tremendously fast rotation, the single spokes have, as it were, become a solid disc" (p. 35).

Thus the atom consists in reality almost completely of empty space; but it receives its form and "solidity" through the immense speed of the electrons which travel around the nucleus. The length of the radius of the revolutions of the electrons give the atom its "size." It is this extremely fast revolution of the basic particles which cause the visual impression of something material.

[1] "In the atom we stand at the foundation of all existence and sense the working of the fundamental law of the world, a law which we cannot comprehend, because it lies outside our dimensions and is identical with the act of creation. . . . Despite all this physicists have succeeded in working with the atom, in splitting it, in transforming it, and in liberating its energy. It is like a miracle: man cannot comprehend the processes in the atom; but he can influence and direct them. He can to a certain extent calculate the incomprehensible, and the result is confirmed by experiment" (Gail, p. 14).

All this proves conclusively that the essential in the world is not "matter" and "substance," but rather energy, motion, dynamics and the laws governing them. Thus the natural world has something "spiritual" in it. Indeed, "it appears as if in the last analysis only energy remains as the ruling principle and that all these little building-stones—atomic nuclei and electrons—are scarcely anything more than partly transitory, partly lasting manifestations of energy" (Neuberg, II, p. 360).

Thus the dynamic picture of the world given by modern science increasingly senses the presence of a "background" which determines everything, a background into which, however, we cannot look. We can only know its "effects," i.e. the "foreground." But it is the background which is decisive. This is, as the English physicist Eddington expressed it, "an unknown which does something, and we do not know what."

The surprising thing is that we can measure, register and statistically express these effects, and even partially describe the activity of this unknown mathematically and perceive some of its laws. This is the miracle of mathematics. Mathematics is the bridge, the only bridge, linking us with the world of the unimaginable in creation. Hence the universe points us towards a Power which has something in common with our own mind, viz. "a way of thinking which we, for the want of a better term, call mathematical." Or, as the same scientist and astronomer, Sir James Jeans, said elsewhere, "The universe appears to have been designed by a pure mathematician."[1]

The mathematician Sir Edmund Whittaker writes: "Our knowledge is vastly greater than it was . . . for we have attained the concept of a mathematical structure embracing the entire universe. The world is a system for which predictions can be made, a cosmos, not a chaos. The facts revealed by experience have a character of rationality: mathematics, which is a system of abstract thought, has the power of solving the concrete problems of physics."[2]

This, however, brings us to the idea of some form of "spirit" in the world of "matter." Spirit and matter are not so opposed that no bridge leads from the material world into the region of the spiritual and psychical. The Spirit too is no intruder into the material kingdom but its Creator, Master and Ruler. The spiritual is revealed as the decisive element in the universe, and "the universe itself begins to resemble more a great idea than a great machine" (Jeans).

These results of most recent research cast a surprising light on the old statement of the Bible, "By faith we understand that the world was created by the word of God, so that what is seen was made out of things which do not appear" (Heb. 11: 3, R.S.V.). These "things which do not appear" are obviously not the electrons, protons and neutrons themselves.

[1] *The Mysterious Universe.*
[2] *Space and Spirit*, p. 129.

L

If they were, the dualistic concept could suggest itself that God had found these invisible energies already present at the beginning of creation and had then used them, as it were, as His building material. But the Bible teaches quite unmistakably in other places, even if not expressly here, a creation out of nothing (especially Gen. 1 in its use of the Hebrew *bara*).

It is rather that by these "things which do not appear," which are at the basis of creation, God's creative *word* is meant. "God speaks, and His word has the capacity, beyond our understanding, to manifest itself in this visible reality as energy" (Rohrbach). The creation-narrative testifies ten times, "And God spake," and the Psalmist declares, "For he spake, and it was done; he commanded and it stood fast" (Psa. 33: 9).

There is no doubt that we should not ascribe the possession of modern scientific knowledge to the writers of the books of the Bible. Nor is the Bible a textbook of science. But God, who knows all things, has by inspiration from the first so fashioned His Word that it at times goes beyond the understanding even of the instruments of that inspiration (I Pet. 1: 11, 12) and, freed from all temporal interpretations and scientific theories, proves its correctness at all times and under all circumstances.

Because this is so, there is to some extent a growing approach of theology and science. "The antagonism between theology and physics has lost its sharpness" (Howe). However different they may be in their nature and their aims, yet both of them, atomic physics and Biblical faith, "trace the visible world, perceptible to our senses, back to an invisible reality, which has up to now remained closed to our organs of sense however perfect and accurate the aids they might use; this reality can be grasped only by our thoughts" (Titius, p. 620).

The decisive element throughout nature is what does not appear; true reality is to be found in the invisible. The immaterial is the background of all existence.

This invisible background, however, points faith towards the real, original cause of all, viz. the invisible God. All the invisible energies which move the universe are part of God's eternity.

When we consider these facts, we see the absurdity of Deism, for it maintains that God the Creator brought the world into existence, but then ceased to be active in it. Every purely materialistic view of the world in addition has had its foundations destroyed. The whole materialistic picture of the world of the nineteenth century has been turned inside out. Instead of energy being an attribute of matter the exact reverse is true; matter is a manifestation of energy.

"We cannot understand matter so long as we use the concepts of materialism. For the modern physicist the materialistic view of the world has ceased to be a real danger" (Gail). The proposition, "everything is matter," was enunciated at a time when not a single experiment involving atomic physics had as yet been performed.

In this connexion we may quote a statement by Lord Kelvin, in his time President of the Royal Society and Professor of Physics in Glasgow, of whom the Nobel Prize winner, Sir William Ramsay, Professor of Chemistry in Bristol and London, said that there was no honour bestowable by man great enough for him. Lord Kelvin said: "If you think strongly enough, you will be forced by science to believe in God, which is the foundation of all religion," and also, "I have many times in my published writings within the past fifty years expressed myself decidedly, on purely scientific grounds, against atheistic and materialistic doctrines."[1]

"Everyone who has really understood a little of contemporary physics is completely immune to the nonsense of materialism. The old, materialistic arguments, still propagated today among 'Freethinkers,' can affect him only as a bit of outmoded wisdom. He can only laugh at it and indeed he must; he will then radiate health to his whole surroundings. He need do no more than pass on to others what he himself has seen as a deeper truth. Truth is always best left to work by itself. One need do no more than let it shine out as brightly as possible" (Bavink, p. 79).

Some have objected that this all must lead to pantheism, which teaches the immanence of the Deity in the universe but denies the personality of God. The logic of this argument is, however, quite inadequate. For "if we believe in a personal God, then energy is for us a *part* of God's eternity." God Himself is *above* the universe as well as active *in* the universe. The idea of God does not in some way disappear in the universe. Both the immanence and transcendence of God, His presence in *and* above the world are true at the same time.[2] The whole process of the universe is upheld by God, but at the same time He is the Lord and King enthroned *over* the universe.

The conviction expressed by Paul in his Areopagus-address—"In Him (God) we live, and move, and have our being" (Acts 17: 28)—fully agrees with all these results and principles. Christ, the Son of God, supports and upholds all things by the word of his power (Heb. 1: 3). The whole universe is held together by Him; "In Him all things hold together" (Col. 1: 17, R.V.mg.).

All energy originates with God. If He were to cut off this supply of power from the universe, atomic disintegration and the destruction of the world would be the immediate consequence, and the universe would collapse.

Since God upholds His creation, Scripture removes "the source of everything visible to the hand of the omnipotent, invisible Creator, from which these immeasurable forces have flowed unceasingly already for millions of years. These are the forces which come from God and which

---

[1] Quoted by Short, II, p. 17.
[2] Only this mediating point of view of "Pan-*en*-theism," lying between pantheism and a one-sided Theism, corresponds to the scriptural view of God.

have not only called the immeasurable universe into existence but also keep both the minute electron and the giant stars in space in continual motion" (Hitzbleck, p. 69).

We see then how incomparably superior the Biblical picture of the world is to that of its contemporary, heathen environment. In the world-picture of antiquity and in its further development in the Middle Ages, both realities, that of the visible and of the invisible, were spatially separated from each other as different spheres.

The earth lay at the centre; over it was heaven with God's throne and the dwelling places of the angels and the blessed spirits. All influences of God's invisible world on the earth came through angels sent down through space from above or through forces acting in a similar way. Deep down below the earth was the world of the dead and of the lost spirits, the underworld. This gave a picture of a "three-storied world."

According to the Bible, however, both these realities, the visible and the invisible, although in no way identified, as in pantheism, are interwoven. This is an immediate result of the simultaneous transcendence (Psa. 93) and immanence of God (Psa. 139).

Even if the human instruments of inspiration shared the belief of their contemporaries in a picture of a "three-storied world"—and we see no compelling reason for flatly denying this—yet there is no verse in Holy Scripture that teaches that the earth is a disc in the centre with Hades or hell, as the case may be, as the dwelling-place of the dead and the lost, spatially *underneath* it, or that the heaven where God and the angels are is to be found *spatially above* the firmament, which is arched like a crystal bowl over the surface of the earth.

Whatever we may think of the writers, it is not their opinions but the exact words of the Bible that are decisive. For often the God-intended meaning of the words of Scripture goes beyond the understanding even of the inspired writers themselves (I Pet. 1: 10–12).[1]

The fact is that Holy Scripture conceives of both the above-mentioned realities completely realistically and does not divide them into two regions of space, separated by "astronomical distances," to use a modern expression.

The prophet Elisha's servant only needed his eyes "opened" for him to see the mountain of Dothan "full of horses and chariots of fire" (II Kings 6: 17). An angel "appeared" to Zacharias in the temple (Luke 1: 11). In the story of the proclamation and song of praise of the angels at the birth of Christ it simply says: "An angel of the Lord stood by them (the shepherds) . . . And suddenly there was with the angel a multitude of the heavenly host" (Luke 2: 9, 13). In all these expressions the Bible is extraordinarily sober and reserved.

[1] Cf. our remarks on "How the Writers of the Bible understood their Writings," p. 229.

Above all, it does not only speak of God's dwelling-place on high, "The Lord is exalted; for He dwelleth on high" (Isa. 33: 5), and "For thus saith the high and lofty One . . . : I dwell in the high and holy place" (Isa. 57: 15) —but also of His power which permeates the universe, and of His omnipresence in heaven and in all regions of the earth: "In Him we live, and move, and have our being" (Acts 17: 28); "Whither shall I go from thy spirit? Or whither shall I flee from thy presence? If I ascend up into heaven, thou art there: if I make my bed in Sheol, behold, thou art there. If I take the wings of the morning, and dwell in the uttermost parts of the sea; even there shall thy hand lead me, and thy right hand shall hold me" (Psa. 139: 7–10).

So both these realities belong together. "The Bible, i.e. the revelation which underlies it, sees these two, the visible and the invisible, not above or below or beside or around each other, but *in* each other, *the visible embedded in the invisible*, so that they interpenetrate each other. As men we continually live in both realities" (Prof. Dr. H. Rohrbach).

When therefore Scripture speaks of God as the "Most High" and of his heavenly world "on high," this cannot be meant purely literally and spatially. The invisible reality of God's world is so glorious and exalted, so eternal and infinite, that for us creatures of the dust, so long as we are not perfected, there can be no "description" but only an "idea" of the heavenly, and even this can be mediated to us only by the plentiful use of picture-language.

It is in this sense that we must understand the existence of the Eternal "above" us. It is a material illustration of the otherworldliness of the Divine. It is a symbolic representation within space of the sublimity of Him who is outside space. Therefore also the Bible symbolizes this "outside" by "above," spiritual superiority by a higher spatial position, that which is outside space and time by the higher in space, which is perceptible to the senses.[1]

His thoughts are "higher" than our thoughts (Isa. 55: 9). Jesus has received from His Father a Name which is "above" every name (Phil. 2: 9). "Thy righteousness also, O God, is very 'high' " (Psa. 71: 19). "Make mention that His name is exalted" (Isa. 12: 4).

Thus the whole nature of heaven and earth is permeated by the might and life-giving power of God. All that we see in the world outside of us, above us and around us becomes, as it were, an outstretched hand which points to Him, the Invisible and yet Ever-present One, to His existence and His activity, His wisdom and His power.

VI. THE MORAL ORDER OF THE WORLD AS A TESTIMONY TO GOD

Man is a moral being; this is the foundation of his nobility as man. He possesses the power of moral judgment, a conscience, and freedom of will.

[1] Cf. Sauer: *The Dawn of World Redemption*, p. 30.

The importance of this is that these qualities do not lie, as it were, loosely side by side in him, but are so bound up with the basic nature of his personality that man, at least when morally normal, is *happy* only when he is *good*. This means that his intuitive estimate of life is dependent on his moral behaviour, that *already by creation* it is not left purely to his discretion whether he will or will not do good; he carries the principle of rewards and punishment in his own breast, or, otherwise expressed, his moral capacity acts as a law-giver, as an inner commander, as rewarder and punisher, as a "categorical imperative." This inherent, inner linkage of morality and happiness, of duty fulfilled and life enjoyed proves *the existence of a moral order in the world* and, since a law is unthinkable without a law-giver, this again demonstrates the existence of a holy, perfect, law-giving God.[1] Thus the moral basis of our human nobility, due already to creation, becomes a testimony to the existence of the King of the world, the God who has created and ennobled us.

"Conscience is a majestic ruler. All bow before its authority. We may disregard its commands, but then we must hear its voice in rebuke. We can harden ourselves against this rebuke, but we cannot obliterate it. We can never reach the point where it is no longer there. Conscience does not depend on our will. We cannot control it. We cannot command it, but it commands us. We do not stand over it, but under it; it does not stand under us, but over us. It follows therefore that it does not take its origin from our will and thought. It has not been produced by our own mind, but by a moral Spirit outside of and above us. Conscience is the final and highest court of appeal. It is the highest and decisive law in all things. Thus it is the product of the highest Spirit, of the supreme Law-giver, of the absolute moral Will. The fact of conscience is a proof of the existence of God" (Prof. Dr. Luthardt).

It has been claimed that this moral proof for the existence of God has lost its force through the results of ethnological research, because men vary so much precisely in their moral standards. Indeed, what one people regards as moral and good is rejected by another as wicked and contemptible and vice versa.

This objection has force only if one breaks up the moral demand into definite, *single* commands. As soon, however, as one speaks of a moral demand *in general*, it cannot be denied that everywhere where men exist a moral law is felt to exist, i.e. that there is a consciousness that a "thou shalt" exists for man. The commands and sub-sections men think they can recognize may vary, but the fact of the demand is recognized everywhere.

That is why already Cicero said, "It was always the conviction of all truly wise men, that the moral law was not something devised by man or introduced by the nations, but something eternal, to which the whole

---

[1] This is the Moral Proof, especially developed by Kant; it is part of the wider Anthropological Proof.

world must conform. Its final foundation, therefore, rests in God, who commands and forbids. And this law is as old as the spirit of God Himself. Therefore the law upon which all duty is based is in reality and above all the spirit of the supreme Deity."

We may end this discussion with some words of Clerk Maxwell, one of the most eminent of English scholars, in his time a President of the Royal Society, Professor of Physics in London and Cambridge and, together with Lord Kelvin, the most important mathematical physicist England has produced. He said, "I have looked into most philosophical systems, and I have seen that none will work without a God."[1]

VII. The Limitations and Value of the Proofs of the Existence of God

It is clear that none of these proofs demonstrate the existence of God as does a proof in mathematics. This, however, neither could nor should be the case.

It could not be so, because God, the Infinite Being, is never intended to be an intellectual problem for the mole-like speculation of men, because the concept of God bursts all human categories of thought, and so the mere attempt of dust-born creatures to "prove" the existence of God would be nothing more than a childish self-overestimation, the boundless presumption of a small-minded megalomania.

And it should not be so, because otherwise the intelligent man could then get to know God more quickly than the less gifted, the scholar before the unschooled; because then the experiencing of God would be removed from the moral sphere to the realm of the intellect, and so God would be more easily found through the lectures of the professor of philosophy in the university than from the preaching of His witnesses in the Church.

There follows therefore from the infinity of God His intellectual undemonstrability, and from the universal validity of faith, that He can only be experienced through the moral will.

The Divine revelation must be such that everyone can acquire knowledge of it, irrespective of his level of education. For all without distinction have been created for the truth and have a deep need of it. So it must be available for all. Therefore the revelation of God must be so formulated that all can grasp its essential elements.

The classical philosophers often affirmed that their science was not for the masses, but only for the intellectual aristocracy. Christianity, however, is for all. For God "willeth that all men should be saved, and come to the knowledge of the truth" (I Tim. 2: 4). Christianity therefore has exalted the highest truth to a power which affects daily life; it has also raised the

[1] Quoted by Short, II, p. 18.

simplest man, who has truly surrendered to it, to an incomparably higher moral level than that on which stood the greatest men of antiquity.

Our relationship to truth, moreover, is not merely intellectual but principally moral. Even in things of this life I know only those things I have devoted myself to; I devote myself only to those things I have *decided* to devote myself to. Thus my will rules my thinking.

The same applies to the highest questions of all. Here too the will controls one's thinking. Here everything revolves around one's attitude to the world and to morals; we discover the obvious fact that the perception of the truth is a moral act. It lies in the will and not finally in the understanding. It is more a matter of conscience than of mind.

It is not our intellect which convinces our heart, but our heart which convinces our intellect. Or, to quote once again well-known words of the great French mathematician Pascal, "God has so willed that Divine truths should not enter the heart through the understanding, but that they should enter the understanding through the heart. For while one must know human things to love them, one must love Divine things to know them." The German philosopher Fichte also said, "Our system of thought is often only the story of our heart. All my convictions come out of my character, not out of my intellect, and to improve the heart leads to true wisdom." It is the will which decides to accept or reject. One must *want* to know the truth. "Faith in God is not a science, but a virtue" (Luthardt).

To deny God therefore is not only an error of the understanding, but a mistake of the heart. To dispute His existence is not only a contradiction of our reason—for God is necessary for reason—but also extreme inner poverty. For it makes the world cold, dead and empty and takes the soul and truth from everything.

But after the heart has found God, reason seeks Him as well. And so man, even simple man, attains to the highest, true wisdom. As the German scholar Professor Ch. E. Luthardt, whom we have quoted a number of times, said, "Whoever has accepted the truths of Christianity—and everyone can do that—knows more than Plato and is wiser than Socrates."

Thus all ways can lead us to the concept of God. Our whole life demands God as the truth and the goal of our existence. In all the relationships of this life we see traces pointing towards one higher than they. The highest accomplishments also of human life point beyond themselves to a Supreme Being. They want to serve us as steps, that we may climb up beyond them to God. God alone is our resting place. The concept of God is the true satisfaction for our thinking mind.

Thus the so-called proofs of the existence of God, as testimonies to His existence, have an enormous value. They show that it is permissible, indeed reasonable, and even logically necessary to believe in God, and that the whole of nature points to the Eternal, that belief in God and a feeling for reality do not contradict one another, but belong together. They prove

that we live either in a meaningfully ordered [*sic*!] meaninglessness or in
a purposefully constructed cathedral of creation; that we, even from a
purely intellectual standpoint, have the choice only between mere appearance and reality, between universal deception and true existence, and that
the ultimate motto for our existence must be either "vanity of vanities"
or the eternal nobility of man.

CHAPTER XII

TRUE HUMAN NOBILITY POSSIBLE THROUGH MIRACLE AND REVELATION

G OD is the foundation of all human nobility. Without the Eternal King there would be no noble and eternal values anywhere in the universe. That is why the testimonies to the existence of God are of such high and practical importance for our thinking and living.

There are two main obstacles to the factual realization of man's high appointment: his transitoriness and his sin, his mortality and his moral failure. The one is the existential, the other the practical, ethical denial of his high calling, and man is not in a position to overcome either. He is therefore dependent on a Divine intervention, on a revelation both in nature and history of a God who is almighty, holy and loving.

This brings us once again face to face with a most important problem. We must ask ourselves whether such a revelation is in principle possible. This links with the question, whether we are justified in believing in miracles. For both revelation and miracle belong inseparably together. Only on the basis of miracle is belief in revelation, in answered prayers and in the spiritual salvation of souls possible.

From the very outset it must be clearly stated, beyond possibility of misunderstanding, that this is not a theoretical, philosophical or theological problem, but the practical question of our own existence in time and eternity. On the answer to it depends our affirmation or denial of the eternal nobility of man. It is the decisive question and involves death or life.

Not merely the historical realities of the past but also the politics, economic life and morals of our present atomic age prove to everyone able and willing to see, that culture, civilization and progress have completely failed so far as the nobility of man is concerned, and that this can be brought in only by a Divine intervention, which will change the human heart by redemption, conversion and renewal. One does not need to be in any sense a Christian to see this; sound common sense and a sober, historical feeling for reality suffice. There is no need to wait for the world's death by cold or fire to be sure of this. If man does not experience an inner renewal he will one day—perhaps in the not all too distant future—destroy himself through the explosions of his atomic and hydrogen bombs. The basic problem of today is not the atomic bomb but the human heart.

So precisely today we stand before a decisive, unavoidable choice: either moral transformation or final destruction, either a renewal of mind or the annihilation of life. "The true problem lies in the hearts and thoughts of men. It is not a physical problem, but an ethical one . . . Science has progressed more quickly than conscience" (Einstein, 1948).

Up to now, despite all the ideals of philosophers and all the efforts of educationalists, there are no signs that man is on the road to a general, moral renewal. On the contrary, as his intelligence grows and his technical science progresses, the threatening danger of an ever approaching, suicidal catastrophe steadily *increases*, for man's heart remains the same.

Because of his moral impotence, demonstrable throughout millennia, man is dependent on a saving act of God, on a redemptive activity, which creates a completely new man by forgiving the faulty development of the past, by imparting new life, by granting power in answer to prayer and by creating the potentiality of and by guiding a new walk and manner of life. Only if such an intervention by God is possible, can man be freed from his fetters, and be transformed and raised to the full possession of the dignity bestowed on him by creation (Gen. 1: 26–28).

But even if man, who for millennia has demonstrated only his moral failure, should suddenly overcome all these troubles by a moral revolution, of the possibility of which, however, there are at present no traces, and should create a spiritual and cultural paradise on earth—a belief for which up to now there is not the slightest justification—even then, apart from the intervention of a higher power, everything would one day perish in the heat of the sun or fire or in darkness and ice, and death would be the final victor!

So we must agree that, if revelation and redemption, miracles and transformation of the world, i.e. any intervention of God in the course of nature and history, are impossible, and if everything must run its course fixedly according to the laws of nature known to us, then the only expectation valid for humanity and the individual alike, for earth and heaven, for planetary and galactic systems is dissolution and destruction, eternal night. Without the great miracle of the perfecting of the world, prophesied by the Bible, there can be only final annihilation and destruction; there can be no glorious future, no single value to last for ever, no eternal meaning for the universe, no realization of the high calling of man as king, no lasting, true nobility of man. Without this miracle everything will sink inevitably into endless meaningless. Either his *sin* or his *transitoriness* destroys the high calling of man.

Thus the problem of the relationship between the laws of nature and Divine revelation steps before our inner eye. We, twentieth-century Christians, must ask ourselves how far, despite our knowledge that creation is based on law, we can still believe in revelation and redemption, in personal deliverance and answered prayers, in our own eternal salvation and in the true nobility of man, in the return of Christ and a coming kingdom of God. Karl Heim has put it as follows: "At this point we stand before the final Either—Or, between the two possibilities which today alone remain.

"The one possibility is radical, hopeless *nihilism*, for which the whole, present course of the world is only an episode arising out of nothing and sinking again into nothing, leaving no traces behind.

"The second possibility is the universal *Easter-faith*, which the primitive Church carried into the world and which still lives based on its testimonies. According to this Easter-faith the present course of this world is not an episode but only the prelude of the new world-condition, which alone will give our personal life and the life of the nations its true, eternal meaning" (II, p. 170).

But how is this conceivable? Would not such an intervention by the Creator in the course of nature mean a breach of His own laws of nature? Would not a God who worked miracles come into conflict with the world-order which He Himself had appointed?

Still more, would not God intervening in the course of nature and history be God contradicting Himself? Would not the miracle-working God of *revelation* be in conflict with Himself as the God of *nature*, as the Creator, Regulator and Upholder of the world? But since this could never happen, do not the laws of nature therefore make salvation within history impossible?

When the possibility of revelation, answered prayer and miracles is doubted, we are concerned not with the *omnipotence* but with the inner *harmony* of God, His conformity with His own nature. That an almighty God *could* redeem, answer prayers and work miracles is self-evident to everyone who believes in the existence of a personal God, and would never be questioned by them. But here the question is whether God is *willing* to reveal Himself and to work miracles, and whether in fact He *does*.

(1) God is sovereign. He could repeatedly, if He desired, destroy the chain of cause and effect, even as we can tear a piece of fabric. If He really wished to do this and to tear His natural laws asunder by certain actions, no created being would have the right to find fault. The laws of nature did not exist before God, and God did not have to come to terms with them. The first and original is rather the immediate, undetermined activity of the Lord of the world Himself. God is the Creator, and not the prisoner of His own laws. He stands *over* the laws of nature, and they stand under Him. Therefore He can command and rule as He wills.

As to the question of what would be a self-contradiction in God, God Himself has to decide, and not we tiny, dust-born creatures, with our greatly limited powers of thought, bound by time and space. Besides all this, we are in no way able fully to comprehend the eternal. Indeed everything outside time and space always seems to our mind to be ir-reconcilably contrary to natural law (Kant, "antimony"). Therefore man must be silent and acknowledge the sovereignty of the Most High.

Besides all this we would do well to note that "belief in miracles," even in the twentieth century—precisely among those that doubt the Biblical revelation—is far from being "old-fashioned." This is amply proved by modern spiritism (or spiritualism), occultism, astrology, fortune-telling, magic and sorcery. The fact is that millions today are "far more inclined to believe in the miracles performed by Satan than in those worked by God. There are far more practitioners of spiritistic and magic arts than there are ministers of the Gospel, and people swarm to these servants of Satan" (Rohrbach, II, p. 29). Thus modern man has to a great extent his own special "belief" in revelation and miracles, only that this has of course been demonically distorted.

(2) No one, not even the greatest scientist, knows absolute, "iron" laws of nature in their final form and with universal validity. Indeed, it is just the scientist who knows how relative they are.

Laws of nature are summaries and formulations of observations of a series of similar natural events. Doubtless they are as such achievements of the investigating mind worthy of the highest admiration; they have at the same time an immense practical significance, for they enable us to predict with confidence the probable outcome of a natural process. But at any time new observations may be made which will make a change in their formulation necessary. Indeed, just one single, new observation is sufficient for this. Facts do not have to adjust themselves to the laws we have formulated, but we have to derive the laws of nature from the facts.

It should be obvious, that the more the observations the greater the probability of the rules derived from them. Therefore the more single observations on which they are based, the more the laws of nature may lay claim to validity. But this does nothing to alter the fact that they remain statements of probability, more or less "satisfyingly exact average values in statistical form" (Prof. A. Titius). A law of nature is therefore nothing more than the formulation of the average result of numerous events previously observed.

When all is said and done, therefore, all laws of nature can never become more than a statement of probability. The absolute remains unattainable to our thought. Therefore every serious, scientific thinker will only speak most cautiously and modestly of the validity of the laws of nature which we have formulated.

(3) The laws of nature are no independent, self-acting forces which govern the world and direct the course of nature. They are not the power, full of wisdom, which gives order and purpose to the universe. They are the general conceptions, human forms of thought, in which *we* compre-hend nature; they are simply the rules (so far as we can perceive them) *we*

believe express the course of natural events. They are *our* formulations, in which we summarize regularly observed phenomena, and when our knowledge increases, they must often be altered.

No law of nature can determine the course of coming events. Laws of nature by themselves "cause nothing at all." To assert the contrary "would be as foolish as to imagine that the statistics of railway accidents or marriages of past years by themselves 'cause' so and so many railway accidents or marriages to take place next year" (Bavink, p. 63).

It is therefore impossible to set the powers and laws of nature in the place of God. The power of nature by itself would be only a blindly acting force which would have some effect, but not an intelligence bringing a coherent whole into being.

That God's power can attain yet other results which leave us amazed, earth-born creatures as we are, is a foregone conclusion for everyone who believes in a living God. Such exceptional operations of the power of God we call miracles.

(4) The laws of nature do not exclude the possibility of spiritual control. This is amply proved every time a master plays a violin or piano. When he does so, everything obeys the laws of acoustics, *i.e.* "invariable laws of nature," strictly and exactly, and yet everything is under a conscious, spiritual control, forming and shaping the whole according to its own free will. Every time we switch the electric light on or off we clearly show the existence of a spiritual control over the powers of nature, which does not in the slightest violate or cancel the system of laws governing the natural world.

So also, only on a larger scale, the laws of nature and world rule are not mutually exclusive but belong together. God directs and governs the world *through* his regulations in nature. They are the mighty sceptre in the hand of the great King of the universe. But they are nothing more!

Atomic physics has some important comments to make at this point. We know today that invariably the first change which takes place in an atom, the first "quantum jump," is unpredictable. Without any perceptible cause the electron jumps from an outer into an inner path. The unpredictability of the first "quantum jump" is not due to shortcomings in physics, but is rooted in the nature of things.

When atomic nuclei are bombarded it has been shown that by no means every "bull's eye" causes reactions in a nucleus. If, for example, a definite number of *exactly similar* nuclei is bombarded by *exactly similar* projectiles shot with the *same* energy under *exactly the same* conditions it should be expected that the same cause would produce the same effect in all the nuclei. But this is far from being the case. The bombarded nucleus has to a certain extent a choice of different possibilities: it can allow the projectile to rebound without itself suffering any damage, it can absorb it, it can split itself or allow parts to be torn out of it, or it can fail to react at all. In every case it remains an unpredictable *free decision* of nature, as to which of these possibilities happens (Gail, pp. 40, 46). One and the same cause can give rise to different effects.

"We do not know why this is so. One thing, however, is certain: the causal principle, where cause and effect follow one another without exception, does not apply to the sub-microscopic world of the atomic nucleus. The individual nucleus shows a peculiar freedom of reaction; it can give different answers to a given interference. Atoms behave differently from bodies on a larger scale, so that instead of speaking only of 'causality,' a sort of freedom of 'freedom of choice in nature' has even been suggested. This discovery, that the otherwise strictly causal connexion in all that happens does not appear to be valid in the microphysics of atomic nuclei, electrons and light quanta, is one of the most startling discoveries of modern science. True, it does not overthrow the concept of causality of classical physics, but it gives it a new meaning. The causality of events in the larger world of the forces and masses around us is not a principle in itself but a phenomenon conditioned by the statistical laws of *probability*. It is to be regarded as the sum of the averages of a very large number of single events" (Gail, pp. 65, 66, 127, 128).

Doubtless no one is going to ascribe an independent ability to make decisions or even a "soul" to the basic constituents of matter, the atomic nuclei and electrons; but it can no longer be queried that free decisions are somehow brought about in the innermost part of material nature. Physics, though it is so sober and mathematical, has realized that it is impossible to explain all that happens in nature merely as functions of mechanisms.

It cannot be doubted that even from the purely scientific point of view *the way is continually open for the influence of the Spirit in the material world*. The rigid denial of belief in revelation, basing itself on the claim that science denies the possibility of a free intervention of the Spirit in nature, has been scientifically overcome. In doing this atomic physics has through science cleared the path for faith. It is any moment possible for the Spirit to intervene in matter without in any way violating the system of laws of nature. It is in this sense that the mathematician Professor Rohrbach has said, "Atomic science is a gift of God to His Church!"

Naturally none of this has "proved" faith rationally; nor does it need it. But science has given it free course. We must clearly grasp that there are two spheres of reality, one in the background and one in the foreground, and the former is the origin of the latter. The thinking mind has to choose: either this background world originates from nothing and has simply called itself into being, or the affirmation is true, "I believe in God, the Creator of heaven and earth."

The choice, then, is between nihilism and belief in a Creator. It is, however, a denial of reason to believe that a world that reveals laws of life and beauty in every smallest detail, that is charged with tremendous energies, and is controlled by the exactest mathematical laws has come into existence completely by itself without a planning and thinking mind behind it. Only "the fool hath said in his heart, There is no God" (Psa. 14: 1). Although belief in God exceeds in its details our powers of thought, it is nevertheless reasonable and worthy of the human spirit.

We cannot stop here. If the powers of nature are to work out their possibilities in a meaningful way, they clearly *demand* a spiritual direction. The harpstrings remain silent until the player voluntarily brings his spirit into play. The laws of accoustics remain a mere abstraction and cannot reveal themselves on the strings or produce a melody until a controlling mind is present who makes the strings sound according to these laws. Only when a spiritual controller intervenes, do the natural laws of accoustics operate. Only so can the plan be realized and the melody be heard. In this every single tone is brought about exactly according to the existing laws of causation, but for all that only when the will of the player produces it.

Further, all research and technical science would be impossible, if a spiritual direction of natural powers and repeated interventions by the mind in the course of nature were not possible. Indeed, the whole cultural development of mankind is nothing other than a continuous, active directing and ruling of nature's complex causal net. Only so has man subdued its powers; only so can culture and civilization arise and develop.

This means that, if reason and will could not freely intervene in the law-bound course of the world, man could not rule over nature, or exercise his earthly kingship, and the whole physical side of his high calling, which is an essential aspect of "man's nobility," would remain eternally unfulfilled.

This is even truer, when applied to the world rule of the King of kings. Causality and Divine will, the laws of nature and Divine direction belong together. Only through the existence and intervention of the Divine World-Ruler does the idea of a world-plan, present in His mind, come to its realization.

(5) We may go further and say that the whole interrelation of natural events in the world is not really a chain of cause and effect, in which everything is always only the result of *one* preceding cause, but rather a causal *net*. In every single event numerous causal chains meet, coming together from the most diverse sources, just as the single strands of a net intersect in the knots.

If we were for once seriously to examine the circumstances on which any single experience depends, we would be amazed to see what a multiplicity of circumstances have caused it, and all the factors that had to be set in motion to bring a possibly insignificant event about. If we pursue this into the distant past, we could be made dizzy by the ever-increasing, absolutely endless causal chains, which come to light.

Thus every single event, insignificant and simple as it may appear outwardly, is in fact exceedingly complicated, and the whole system of events throughout the universe is an almost undisentanglable maze of untold single, yet closely connected causal threads.

With this a belief in a higher direction once again comes into its own. This can arrange and connect the causal chains as a general does the routes of the single units of his army. It may also sometimes apply entirely unexpected, new laws and suspend other known laws, yet in everything and at all times it remains fully consistent and causal.

(6) Causal chains do not necessarily continue straightforwardly and endlessly, for they can at any time be broken off by outside intervention. This can happen through outward, physical forces or through the decision of a spiritual being. Such a "breach" of a causal chain is then in no sense a breach or ending of causality itself.

A flower unfolds, blossoms, fades and withers. This all takes place according to a definite causal chain. A man picks it, and at that moment the chain is broken and another one takes its place.

Who will then assert that a higher power than man's is not able to break those causal chains we can observe and to switch them over into other, higher causal chains, which in turn are still controlled by causal laws?

(7) Miracles are not contrary to the order of nature, which derives from God Himself. When He works a miracle God uses hidden powers, which go beyond the limits of the totality of our contemporary understanding. They are therefore the projection of a higher world-order into our lower one.

The powers of the visible world of God are only a *part* of His infinite fullness of power. Besides the lower nature of the earth and of space, whose laws we for the most part know, there is also a higher, transfigured nature, of whose powers, as regards their quality, size and extent, we have no idea. These powers stand continually at the disposal of God, the Almighty. He can switch them on or off as He wills.

A miracle is an expression of God's freedom; it does not result from the powers and presuppositions of natural life, but enters their context as something new from God. "When the activity of God is incalculable, we call it a miracle; when it is calculable we say He is working through human laws of nature." In a miracle none of these lower laws are contradicted or even annulled, but only conquered for the one special event by higher and stronger laws, and in principle they continue to exist. God only *withdraws* isolated processes from under the working of the laws known to us and places them under the law of a higher will and a stronger power.

Even here on earth we can see the existence of stronger and weaker powers in nature. The laws of nature and causal chains can cross and then one may be subordinated to the other. In such a case the weaker law is subordinated to the stronger, and is in thousands of cases superseded by the latter for a time, but without itself being "broken." For one with no

M

knowledge of these stronger laws this appears to be a "breach" of the order of nature known to him, e.g. the flying of planes heavier than air, despite the law of gravity, to one ignorant of modern technical science.

Thus the momentum of a stone or ball thrown into the air overcomes the force of gravity. The gravitational power of the earth is subordinated to the living power of animal or plant in the spring of the tiger on its prey and in the growth of the plant not only downwards but also, in its main development, upwards. That in all these cases the law of gravity itself is not broken or destroyed is proved by the continued existence of the bodily weight of the stone, ball, plant or animal.

This principle is seen at its clearest in the miracles of the Bible. Here a stronger and "higher" causality, belonging to the eternal world, intervenes and causes an effect which would not be produced by these weaker, "lower" causalities; afterwards, however, it fits into our normal system according to its laws. Even when performing miracles God does not act contrary to His own laws.

Never, therefore, does the sovereign activity of God's Divine freedom act merely arbitrarily. The actions of His eternal omnipotence are never a violent crushing of His own world order. A miracle is never a contradiction between the God of revelation and the God of creation. His activity of sustaining the world and of *redeeming* the world are never in opposition.

Miracles are in fact "deviations from a weaker or lower law, but they are included in a higher one." They are operations of the highest laws, unknown to us and belonging to the eternal nature, within the realm of earthly nature, which itself is only partially known to us. Already Augustine said, "Miracles do not contradict nature, but only nature as known to us."

In His miracles God acts like a ruler who normally causes his realm to be governed by ministers, but who in special cases withdraws certain matters from their administrative power and has them brought before Himself for decision, and then personally enforces them through royal commissioners. In doing this he does not dismiss the ministers, but he sets these special royal deputies beside, indeed above them, and his ministers have to subordinate themselves to their authority.

In the last analysis this higher causality coincides with the highest ethical purposes of existence. To serve these is the highest and finest calling of nature. Therefore, if a miracle furthers them, i.e. if it is ethically conditioned, then it does not oppose nature but is rather in the highest sense in conformity with it. If a miracle serves the ethical purposes of Divine love, of the redemption and perfecting of the world, then it does not tear the coherent system of nature apart, but rather fulfils it. It is a "sign of the Divine presence in history as well as in nature" (Titius, p. 842).

We may go further. Revelation and miracle are nothing less than the entry of the glorified state of nature into its present state, as yet not glorified and disturbed by sin. They are a foretaste in this age of the truly rational order of things. They are a victorious proclamation of the logically right, royal relationship of the spirit to the body in its unhindered rule.

The results and technical application of atomic physics throw a surprising light on this. Today the transmutation of elements is already possible, and men can at any time carry it out in atomic laboratories and plants. As success upon success quickly followed upon Rutherford's first achievement in 1919, the transmutation of atoms soon became almost an "everyday occurrence in the research institutes." The idea of the unchangeability of elements belongs to the past.

The basic constituents of matter are everywhere the same. Whether it is mercury, gold or sulphur, carbon or oxygen, we are ultimately only concerned with protons, neutrons and electrons. Which element it is depends only on their number.

If an atomic nucleus consists of seven protons and neutrons and is encircled by the same number of electrons, we call it nitrogen. If there are six, then it is carbon. If there are eighty, then it is mercury; if seventy-nine, then it is gold.

If the atomic nucleus gains or loses one or more protons or neutrons, then the element becomes another. So uranium becomes radium with its radiations, and radium becomes lead. Should we therefore succeed in shooting a proton out of the nucleus of a mercury atom, then the transmutation of mercury into gold has been accomplished, and the old dream of the medieval alchemists has been fulfilled. The physicist of today could, in fact, "make" gold. The "philosopher's stone," sought for in vain for centuries by the alchemists, which makes this miracle possible, is electricity at a tension of a few million volts.[1] ·

This leads us to ask, if men in their laboratories, by bombarding atomic nuclei and removing protons and neutrons from them are able to transmute elements into other elements, e.g. base metals into semi-precious or precious metals, why should God not be able to transform and transmute elements into others? If man can change mercury into gold, why should God not be able to change water into wine?

Admittedly man requires mighty power stations for this transmutation. But does not God, the Almighty, have infinitely greater sources of power at His disposal, than man's greatest power plants? Indeed, did He not from the very outset, as the Creator of matter, Himself call these atomic powers into being and unite them? Hence they are only a part of His power, and He can at any time freely determine their composition.

[1] Atomic physics makes no use of this possibility; for the expenditure of energy needed would be so costly that the process of transmutation would not pay. The yield of gold would be too minute in comparison with the amount of energy required.—For the physical data of this section see Gail, pp. 34, 37, 61.

The essence of all matter is energy. But it is God who has placed energy in creation through His word. Why should He then not at any time be able to recall a particle of energy, e.g. a proton? Professor Rohrbach says rightly: "Is it not absolutely self-evident that God can perform miracles? If God wills that the oil in the cruse of the widow of Zarephath should not stop flowing, then it costs Him only a word, and the elements that form the oil are present . . . The same is true of the feeding of the five thousand . . . The universe is not a closed system, but is open towards God. From there new energy can continually be added or taken away according to His word . . . Even as a scientist, indeed just as a scientist, I can believe that the Biblical miracles took place exactly just as they have been reported to us . . . When water was changed into wine at the marriage at Cana we may suppose that God in a single moment recalled the atomic particles which formed the water molecules and created the atomic particles which composed the wine" (II, pp. 15, 27, 28).

We have no wish to find a rationalistic explanation for the Biblical miracles. But these considerations do prove it is radically wrong to assert that a miraculous act of God would be a breach of His own natural order and that hence, to maintain the harmony of the Divine nature and the consistency of the Divine activity, the possibility of such an act must be *a priori* denied.

From whatever angle then one approaches the question, the same conclusion must be drawn. Rational, meaningful and logical is only the concept of a personal, living, active and almighty God, Creator and Ruler of the world, Prescriber and Controller of the laws of Nature; as Creator and Ruler He reigns supreme above the world and yet at the same time bears witness to Himself through miracles and revelation within it.

Already the creation of the universe was a miracle, for a miracle is there, when something comes into being, which does not or, at least, does not fully arise from the powers and laws already present and known to us. This is in the fullest sense applicable to the Creation. For until the beginning of the universe nothing, apart from God, existed. Therefore the mere fact of the creation of a world out of nothing is the first "miracle."

Thus we live between two great cosmic miracles, the "miracle" of creation and the "miracle" of world-perfecting. These two miracles form the framework for the whole, contemporary history of the universe. Between them lie the untold miracles of the revelation of salvation.

At the centre of this chain of miraculous acts of God stands Jesus Christ, Son of God and Son of Man. The person of Christ is *the* miracle, the absolute miracle, the original miracle in person. In Him the creative centre of transfigured nature entered the untransfigured order of nature. Through Him therefore the members of this untransfigured nature attain bodily and spiritually to the glory of transfigured nature and to the eternal, heavenly nobility of man.

CHAPTER XIII

THE PRACTICAL WAY TO TRUE HUMAN NOBILITY

How is the individual to attain a personal experience of God? How is he to become a partaker of this high calling? How does his seeking become finding, his hope assurance, his experience of faith a genuine, living proof of God? How does he come to full possession of this dignity, to the never-ending riches of a God-permeated, human kingship?

On one of my journeys I was in Athens. There I stayed with a friend, the leader of a flourishing Protestant church. By training he was a mathematician, and he had been a high official in the Greek Treasury. He came from an absolutely modern, non-Christian family. As a student of mathematics in the University of Athens he devoted himself, alongside his studies, to reading philosophy. He wanted to gain from them new and sharp weapons for the battle against the Christian faith he proposed to wage by writing.

One day, while reading a French book, he came across a quotation from Pascal, the world-famous French mathematician and physicist. Just because they were the words of a mathematician, and that of the first order, they gripped the young student of mathematics. It read: "In the moment you accept the existence of the one God, against your own will Christianity with all its principles takes possession of you."

"How is it possible," he asked himself, "that, if one admits the existence of God, one must even *against one's own will* give one's assent to the Christian religion with all its doctrines?" Over and over again these words went through his mind, "even against your own will."

They could mean only that there is an inescapable, logical link between the acknowledgement of the existence of a personal God and the acknowledgement of the basic doctrines of the Christian faith, a logic which simply compels the thinking mind to go with it, even when it really does not want to!

The next morning he went to the Greek National Library and obtained the complete works of Pascal, which he studied with the greatest care. From Pascal he came to the New Testament and from the New Testament to Jesus Christ. Today he is a powerful witness to the faith and a fruitful preacher of the Gospel in the Greek capital.

The next few pages will bear witness to the correctness of Pascal's statement. Belief in the one, eternal God permits, when logically thought out to its conclusion, of no other doctrine of faith and redemption than the Christian one. Here the thinking man stands before unavoidable conclusions and compulsions. Even if he does not really want to—"even against his own will"—the honest and logically thinking man must come from a general belief in God to an acknowledgement of the Biblical doctrine of salvation.

I. The Biblical Way of Salvation

If a personal God exists—and the world within and outside of man is full of pointers and testimonies to His eternal and real existence—then He must be the fullness of all perfection, the essence of everything noble, the supreme good or, to express it Biblically, the Living, Holy and All-Loving One. As Creator and Ruler He must be linked with all His works. He has a claim upon them and can call them to account, and only in as far as they are in communication with Him do they partake of true life.

1. THE NATURE OF SIN

This introduces us to the central problem. God is holy and we are unholy. God is pure and we are impure. God is free and we are loaded with a thousand fetters and chains.

Therefore there can be no true, inward, mental and spiritual link between God and us. The Holy One can have no fellowship with the unholy (I John 1: 5). Sin is a severing of oneself from God, the misuse of the freedom of will, the rebellion of creaturely, individual will against the will of God as expressed in the world order. It is the attempt of the creature to make his own personal ego the absolute ruler of himself, and the centre of the small world of his own personality (the microcosmos), as well as of the nature which surrounds him (the macrocosmos).

When man has done this, he has moved far from God. All that follows is inevitable. God is the Living One, the source of all life. To separate oneself from Him is to separate oneself from life, and brings death and destruction, death of spirit, soul and body. Thus death is not only the "punishment" of sin—"the wages of sin is death" (Rom. 6: 23)—but is inherent in its nature, so here again the iron logic of the Biblical proclamation becomes evident.

In this situation self-redemption cannot help. It would be to try to be good apart from the source of goodness. It is presuming to build a new man out of the achievements of the old. It is the impossibility of reaching the Infinite by finite means.[1]

If there is to be a redemption at all it must come from God. The Infinite must condescend to the finite, the Holy to the sinner. Only so can the abyss be bridged which separates God from man.

[1] For a fuller discussion of the impossibility of self-redemption, see p. 122.

2. THE NECESSITY OF RIGHTEOUS PUNISHMENT AND ATONEMENT

This redemption must be in harmony with the Divine nature. Sin must be dealt with judicially; God's *holiness* demands this. Were there no objective cancellation of guilt and sin, a resumption of fellowship and intercourse with the fallen sinner would mean fellowship between light and darkness, holiness and unholiness, which would be irreconcilable with the Divine perfection (I John 1: 5; Jas. 1: 17; II Cor. 6: 14).

This is also demanded by the Divine *honour*. His holiness must be maintained unimpaired not only in the nature of the Creator Himself but also in the consciousness of His moral creation. Therefore forgiveness of sin cannot be simply an "annulment" of guilt, an act of feeble good nature by a "loving God." If it were, the moral creation would lose its consciousness of the righteousness and majesty of God. It could no longer respect a God who was a weak father like Eli, a "universal heavenly Father" who was only a father and not a judge, only "love" and not holiness. Such a "God," it is true, need be feared no longer, and we could "love" Him in spite of all our sins, but only because He would no longer be God but merely an empty phantom, a product of fantastic, wishful thinking, an imaginary, self-made, unreal idol. Even in His salvation God's holiness must be maintained. The justification of the unholy can never be effected through a breach of justice by the Holy One. Therefore a judicial treatment of sin *must* take place.

With this judgment becomes a vindication of grace, expiation a defence of reconciliation, the execution of the sentence a theodicy of redemption, "to shew His righteousness . . . that He might Himself be just and the justifier of him that hath faith in Jesus" (Rom. 3: 25, 26; cf. Nahum 1: 3). Thus God must deal judicially with sin, not merely for the sake of the consistency of His Divine holiness, but also for His honour and authority in His creation.

Finally, it is demanded by *the good of man* himself. Reconciliation with God without actual expiation would lead man to moral indifference. God's declaration of forgiveness would be a mere formality. We could be sure of it whatever the circumstances! Man would banish sorrow for sin in advance, even before God had granted him salvation. We might almost say that he would forgive himself his sin before God forgave him. Indeed, if in his God-estrangement he thought the matter through logically, he would simply throw away his conscience. For why should he still trouble about this stern, inner monitor, if at the last it did not matter whether man is holy or unholy, whether he has done good or evil? "God will forgive me; that's His job!" (Voltaire).

This means man's liberty would degenerate into licentiousness, his love of sin into enthusiasm for sin, his unredeemed state into an unredeemable one. The link, inherent in man by creation, between morality and happiness would be basically destroyed. The essential, necessary moral law, the innate "categorical imperative" of duty, the ability to attain human nobility imparted by creation would be dissolved and destroyed, and man would cease in any sense to be a moral being. The sentimental idea of salvation without expiation, which is a shadow without reality, would be the murderer of man's soul and conscience.

If this were so, God's only way out would be to change the will of man from evil to good instantaneously and immediately. But the resulting "will" would be only a robot for producing pseudo-morality. The only result would be the abolition of moral freedom, the removal of the human will, and consequently the degradation of man into little more than a highly gifted, more complicatedly organized animal. From this aspect too man would cease to be in any way a moral being, and so there could no more be a question of true human nobility.

From whatever standpoint we approach the problem, we find an absolute confirmation of the statement that reconciliation is possible only through expiation, forgiveness only after sin has been judicially treated, a revelation of salvation only after a revelation of righteous judgment. If the sinner is not to be destroyed, this righteous judgment must fall on a substitute.

We must go on and recognize that it is in the nature of such a righteousness that the expiation must correspond to the guilt. Since by its very nature sin is "death," the expiation must also involve death. "Apart from the shedding of blood there is no remission" (Heb. 9: 22). Only so can true life be restored. Redemption must consist in death, this great enemy of man, becoming the *means of his salvation*, and in the inevitable consequence and punishment of sin becoming the way of escape from sin (cf. Eph. 2: 16). Only through death can "death" be put to death (Heb. 2: 14). The much hated "blood theology" of the Bible here demonstrates its inevitability and necessity. "Was the Messiah not bound to suffer thus before entering upon His glory?" (Luke 24: 26, 46, N.E.B.).

To accomplish this work of salvation God sent His Son. Christ appeared and willingly went to death. "He was obedient unto death, even the death of the cross" (Phil. 2: 8). Upon Him as our representative and surety God permitted the whole weight of His holy judgment against sin to take effect, so that everyone who believes in Him may receive free, eternal salvation.

3. WHY CAN ONLY A PERSON OF THE GODHEAD ACCOMPLISH THE WORK OF REDEMPTION?

Although no one can ever completely explain this mystery, we shall indicate three fundamental reasons for this.

The first is the *moral* one. It is the great power of sin, which can only be broken by a Deity. Albert Einstein, the well-known physicist, spoke truly, when he said in a lecture held in 1948: "It is easier to change the composition of plutonium (i.e. to bring about nuclear fission) than to drive the evil spirit out of a man."

The second ground is a *legal* one. None other than God Himself can provide the atoning sacrifice. Since sin is rebellion against God, i.e. a revolt against the Infinite Himself, it incurs infinite guilt and demands an infinite expiation. This can be done only by an infinite being, i.e. by God Himself.

The third, decisive ground is the *creative-dynamic* one. It is not only his life history that makes the sinner guilty but also his whole nature, not only the desires of his will but also all he is spiritually. Therefore he must become a "new man" (Eph. 4: 22–24; Col. 3: 9, 10), and be "born again" (John 3: 3, 5). It is not merely cancelling the old guilt, or guiding the will in a new direction, but bringing the spiritually dead to life (Eph. 2: 5, 6), being born "of God" (I John 3: 9; Titus 3: 5), i.e. a *creative renewal* of the whole man himself (II Cor. 5: 17). God alone has the power to create. Hence no creature, neither man nor angel, but only a Person of the Godhead could bring this work of a new creation to pass. Redemption had to be carried out by a Divine Redeemer.

This Person of the Godhead is the eternal Son. The only Begotten of the Father through His eternal generation, the Son is the effulgence of the Godhead directed inwards and upwards to Itself (John 1: 1). Therefore He is also, in relation to the creation, the effulgence of the Godhead directed outwards and downwards, i.e. the Mediator of the decree of salvation, the "Word" that God speaks (John 1: 1, 14), the sole revelation of the eternal God's thoughts of life and love. "No one cometh unto the Father, but by me" (John 14: 6).

4. SALVATION POSSESSED AND ENJOYED IN CHRIST

So long as a man has not experienced this Redeemer, he remains bound by his old existence. It is only his personal acceptance of the saving work at Golgotha that opens for him the way into the new life. "The knowledge of God without that of our wretchedness creates pride. The knowledge of our wretchedness without that of God creates despair. The knowledge of Jesus Christ is the middle way, because in Him we find both God and our wretchedness."[1]

In God's act of love in Christ Jesus we find deliverance from our misery. That is the knowledge taught us by revelation, to which our heart and conscience answer: "Yea and Amen!" In Christ, the Mediator of salvation, the Head of the new humanity, man really experiences the way to freedom from sin and to true human nobility.

Among the greatest scientists of all time were Copernicus, Kepler and Newton. Professor Max Planck, a Nobel Prize winner, said of them that

[1] Pascal: *Pensées*, Preface to the Second Part.

they are a standing proof how deepest piety and scientific research are completely compatible with one another.

On his tombstone in the cathedral of Frombork in Poland, earlier the East Prussian port of Frauenburg, one can read the Latin epitaph Copernicus wrote himself. It reads:

> I do not ask for grace like that of Paul's,
> Nor do I seek the favour Peter received,
> But that which on the cross's wood
> Thou gav'st the robber, I diligently pray for.[1]

When Kepler was asked during his last hours what was the ground of his hope, he replied in full confidence, "Only and solely the merit of our Saviour Jesus Christ. In Him, as I firmly and steadfastly want to testify, all refuge, all my comfort and salvation are found."

Newton, Kepler's pupil, declared at the end of his life, "In my life I have learnt two important things. First, that I am a great sinner, and secondly, that Jesus Christ is a still greater Saviour."

II. THE PERSONAL EXPERIENCE OF GOD

"God has set eternity in man's heart" (Eccles. 3: 11, R.V.mg.). "Our soul is by nature Christian" (Tertulian).[2] Therefore it cannot find a home except in God. Until it finds its way there, its three powers are in a state of inner disunity.

Man longs for salvation. He craves the highest good. He seeks it in all this world's goods and pleasures and finds it not. He strives for true happiness and yet feels wretched. He has high ideals but knows not how to fulfil them. For his longing stretches out beyond the limits of time and space into the infinite distances of eternity. He seeks God, but—where is God to be found?

This striving after God, however, conflicts with another force in us which seeks to draw us away from God. All of us bear hidden within us a secret, strong resistance against God. Our will desires both: God and the world, holiness and sin, the eternal and the transient, the kingdom of God and our own life.

Thus our will is divided, and this inner strife in our desires destroys every happiness. "It is in vain, O men, that you seek from yourselves the remedy for your miseries. All your light can only enable you to know that not in yourselves will you find truth or good. The Philosophers promised you these, but gave them not."[3]

On the other hand just this longing is a testimony to the greatness of

---

[1] "Non parem Pauli gratiam requiro,
   Veniam Petri neque posco,
   Sed quam in crucis ligno
   Dederas latroni, sedulus oro.
[2] *Anima naturaliter christiana.*   [3] Pascal: *Pensées*, Of the True Religion.

man, albeit a fallen greatness. "The greatness of man is great in that he knows he is miserable . . . For what man ever was unhappy at not being a king, save a discrowned king?"[1] So our desire makes us unhappy but is at the same time the token of our high calling.

Man, called to be a member of heaven's aristocracy, has through sin lost the practical possibility of exercising his dignity. Appointed to peace, man is inwardly torn asunder. Chosen to rule, he has become a slave. His inner nature is storm-tossed by the incongruity between "I want" and "I can." At the centre of his heart the three forces of his soul stand in conflict. In the unregenerate this is between will and intellect and expresses itself in emotions as wretchedness.

Man's ego was designed for God, and so his will seeks the infinite and the eternal. But it can be satisfied only by what it uses and enjoys, and this it must first know. Therefore man's will is dependent for its satisfaction on man's capacity for knowledge. But so long as he is separated from God his intellect can offer him only things temporal and finite.

Thus there arises a conflict between man's will and intellect. It is the tension between "I must have" and "I cannot give," between a basic need and a basic failure, between the infinite and the finite. It is the conflict between the consciousness of one's own personality and the consciousness of the world, between longing for God and love of the world. The feelings react to all this by a sense of wretchedness, by a consciousness of inner emptiness. So the sinner, by the iron law of sin, is of necessity torn asunder. "There is no peace, saith the Lord, unto the wicked" (Isa. 48: 22).

The conflict between self-consciousness and world-consciousness, between the infinite and the finite, can be overcome only through the consciousness of God. For God is the Eternal and as such illumines infinity; He is the Creator of the universe and as such the source of all that is finite. So both the infinite and the finite find in Him their centre and organic unity. Therefore too it is only in God that our soul can find true harmony. As Augustine testified. "Thou hast made us for Thyself, and our soul is restless until it finds its rest in Thee."

This way to God has been opened to us by Christ alone. Only he who has come to Him with his debt of sin and has received forgiveness at the foot of the cross finds peace of soul. Only he who has experienced repentance and faith, conversion and the new birth has attained to eternal salvation. Only he can confess triumphantly:

> No condemnation now I dread;
> Jesus, and all in Him, is mine!
> Alive in Him, my living Head,
> And clothed in righteousness divine,
> Bold I approach the eternal throne,
> And claim the crown, through Christ my own.
>
> —CHARLES WESLEY

[1] *Idem*, The Greatness and Littleness of Man.

This is the one real, true proof of the existence of God.[1] He who has experienced God in Christ has the proof of God's eternal existence within himself. The proof from experience is ultimately the real proof of God's existence. As Christ Himself said, "My teaching is not mine, but His that sent Me. If any man willeth to do His will, he shall know of the teaching, whether it be of God, or whether I speak from myself" (John 7: 16, 17). The method used by modern science is the physical or chemical experiment. In the same way the spiritual "experiment," i.e. personal experience, is the moral way to God.

In all this Jesus Christ is the great point of decision. I can pass Him by, if I wish, and so murder my own happiness. I can believe in Him, if I wish, and thereby tread the path of true life.

Unbelief is self-deception and will one day be revealed as a terrible disappointment. Or, as Sören Kirkegaard, the great Danish thinker (1813–1855), said in an impressive but drastic picture: "A fire broke out behind the scenes in a theatre. The buffoon came on the stage to tell the audience. They thought he was trying to be funny and broke out in applause. He repeated his warning. They only clapped the more. So I think the world will go to its destruction amid the general applause of the wiseacres, who think it no more than a joke."

Unbelief is destruction; faith is the grasping of life. God has placed the decision between death and life—*your* eternal death and *your* eternal life—in *your* hand (Rev. 22: 17; Eccles. 11: 9).

"I call heaven and earth to witness against you this day, that I have set before thee life and death, the blessing and the curse: therefore choose life, that thou mayest live" (Deut. 30: 19).

III. The Royal Nobility's Practical Expression of Salvation

If we are now the royal children of the Most High, then we are under obligation to walk royally. A nobleman must be noble. High position carries obligations. Christians must walk "worthily" of their high calling (Eph. 4: 1; Phil. 1: 27; Col. 2: 10; I Thess. 2: 12). "Princes must have princely thoughts." "He who is noble devises noble things, and by noble things he stands" (Isa. 32: 8 R.S.V.).

The essence of their royal nobility is the image of Jesus in them, the image of the royal Son from heaven. They have been called to sonship in the Son of the Most High. This is the basis of their royal wealth and their inner dignity. "He in them and they in Him"—that is the secret of the new life.

Being in the image of the Son they are at the same time images of the Father, for the Son is the very image of God (Col. 1: 15; Heb. 1: 3). He, therefore, who lives in His image, radiates the Father's nature. "Ye therefore shall be perfect, as your heavenly Father is perfect" (Matt. 5: 48,

[1] The "Psychological proof of God."

cf. I Pet. 1: 15, 16). This is both their dignity and their highest duty, their gift and their task, their noble position and their vocation. From this fact their nobility shines out on all sides and transfigures all their contacts in life.

Whom God has ennobled are freed from the fetters of sin (Rom. 6: 18; Gal. 5: 1). They have been taken out of the dungeon of slavery and placed in the palace of salvation. When attacked by evil, they have a victory-giving power from God. "Sin shall not have dominion over you" (Rom. 6: 14).

Whom God has ennobled are freed from the power of circumstances. They look away from all earthly limitations to the heavenly sources of power. That means that walking as the saved royal nobility involves living in a holy freedom from worry. Being children of the Most High, they believe through experience the words of Jesus, "Your heavenly Father knoweth that ye have need of all these things" (Matt. 6: 32).

Whom God has ennobled are freed from human judgment (I Cor. 4: 3; Gal. 1: 10). However much they may try to spare men's feelings for the sake of their Christian testimony (Eph. 5: 15; Rom. 14: 8; 15: 31b), they refuse all servitude to man (I Cor. 7: 23), all eyeservice (Col. 3: 22) and fear of man, all dependence on fashion and the spirit of the age, nor will they allow themselves to be tossed about by the fluctuations of philosophical and religious thought. A servant of the Lord knows himself to be "before men an eagle, before God a worm." So he unites humility with a sense of dignity, modesty with the consciousness of nobility, subordination with a kingly independence. Therefore he is not ashamed of his heavenly King and is a courageous witness before men (Rom. 1: 16; Mark 8: 38).

Whom God has ennobled are broad-minded. They see things from a kingly perspective and so are raised above the petty and trivial. As kings they can bear with one another, forgive, serve (Matt. 20: 26, 27; John 13: 3–5; Luke 12: 37b) and love (Jas. 2: 8). Love, the basis of their Heavenly Father's being (I John 4: 16), gives nobility to their character (Matt. 5: 44, 45). "A Christian is a free lord over all things and subject to none, and a Christian is a servant in all things and subject to all" (Luther). Thus even the everyday gains a royal stamp, and time is transfigured by eternity.

Whom God has ennobled rejoice in His earthly creation. They delight in nature as in a temple of their heavenly Father. They see His wisdom in the works of His omnipotence (Rom. 1: 20) and thankfully accept the created world from the hands of the great Creator. They treat their earthly possessions as kings. They control money, but money does not control them. So they use the transient for the affairs of eternity and make for themselves friends for heaven with the unrighteous mammon (Luke 16: 9). They are owners and yet only administrators (I Cor. 7: 30, 31; I Tim. 6: 7–9; cf. Acts 4: 32); they are the blessed who bless, they are the receivers who give. They show the wisdom of kings in all that which truly endures; for "the fashion of this world passeth away" (I Cor. 7: 31b).

Whom God has ennobled have living links with the achievements of the spirit of man. They welcome science and art, civilization and cultural progress, and assist in its furtherance and development. A king must not neglect his kingdom, but must rule in it right royally. The ennobling of the human king of the earth has also ennobled his earthly kingdom. Hence investigation and control of nature, inventions and discoveries, improvements and refinements, in short, everything that helps to make the earthly creation serviceable, all belong to man's royal calling.

Whom God has ennobled rule their physical life. The control of bodily desires, self-discipline in bearing and appearance, the care of the body for grace and decency, the making of its members serviceable as instruments of righteousness (Rom. 6: 13)—in short, the welcome of the bodily shown by honouring and sanctifying the body, is part of the nobility of man. But all this should be not only for its own sake but also because of the future redemption of our body and its coming spiritual state.

Whom God has ennobled show a worthy relationship to suffering creation. Though they cannot end the universal pain of nature, they do not increase it. Indeed, as "redeemers" of the earth they are at pains to diminish it.[1] Even in the irrational creation they recognize a waiting for redemption. Indeed, all that is earthly is waiting for the day when *they* will be revealed, for the completion of the history of man made in the image and likeness of God, for "the revealing of the sons of God" (Rom. 8: 19–23). So until then the human "redeemers" of creation must not make its chains any heavier.

Whom God has ennobled live in holy consciousness of their nobility. They know the honour that is theirs as personalities, as civilized beings and as men, but over and above this they have the royal honour of belonging to the family of the great Divine King, the Lord of Lords and Ruler of the universe. Therefore they know how to guard their dignity, to avoid everything mean and shallow, to deny everything empty and low, and in holy dignity and royal freedom to walk naturally, worthy of their high calling.

Whom God has ennobled live in anticipation of their coming glory. Despite their welcome of earthly things their goal is a heavenly one. While paying due attention to the earthly, they give priority to the heavenly. Their treasure is in heaven (Matt. 6: 20); their home is in eternal light (Phil. 3: 20; Col. 1: 12); their Saviour is throned at the right hand of God (Heb. 8: 1). Therefore they seek that which is above (Col. 3: 1). A royal mind is a heavenly mind.

Whom God has ennobled worship the Eternal. They know they owe

---

[1] Through love towards animals, by opposing all cruelty to them and by avoiding all thoughtlessness in the use of animals in work.

their crowns not to themselves but to their crowned and glorified Redeemer. Only through grace are they what they are (I Cor. 15: 10; 4: 7). Therefore they take the crowns which they have received from the King and lay them before His throne (Rev. 4: 10), saying, "Unto Him that sitteth upon the throne, and unto the Lamb, be the blessing, and the honour, and the glory, and the dominion for ever and ever" (Rev. 5: 13).

Are we Christians in this sense? These are not philosophical or theological problems to be answered as we will. Here your own, personal, eternal salvation is at stake. God wants to bring you into the full possession of His life in Christ, and therefore He offers you His salvation. Accept it and be saved. Become a Christian in reality, and then God will lead you into the riches of His redemption in Christ to a triumphant state of blessedness, to a new, royal life, to salvation for time and eternity, and to true, everlasting, glorified nobility.

PART V

ON THE ORIGIN OF THE EARTH

COMMENTS ON THE BIBLICAL CREATION-NARRATIVE

INTRODUCTION

THE earth is man's kingdom. It is the stage on which the reality or his nobility and high appointment must be unfolded. "The heaven . . . is the throne of God, and the earth . . . is the footstool of His feet" (Matt. 5: 34, 35). But even this small world we call Earth is a testimony to the glory of the great Creator. It is both the foundation and starting point of the *eternal* appointment of its earthly king to nobility. The earthly creation is the preliminary step to the heavenly. In this lies its honour and its hope.

How did man's earthly kingdom come into being? This question can scarcely be separated from that of the royal nobility of man. So the Bible begins with a creation-narrative, culminating in the command of the heavenly King to His representative, the earthly king, to "subdue" the earth and "have dominion" (Gen. 1: 28). Thus in the Bible also the calling of man to be king is linked with the account of the origin of his earthly kingdom. The Biblical creation-narrative has been written from the standpoint of the kingship of man. It describes the formation of the earth as the origin of the human kingdom.

This, however, raises a multitude of questions, Biblical and scientific, old and new; manifold, and often contradictory, are the answers which have been given to them.

In the chapters that follow we have tried to treat some of these major problems concisely, impartially and objectively. Naturally much—even important points—could scarcely be touched on. Through a comparison of the grounds for and against each view the reader may himself be enabled to form his own judgment and to take up his own position in these matters.

CHAPTER XIV

THE MAIN INTERPRETATIONS OF THE BIBLICAL CREATION-NARRATIVE

(1) Almost all the Church Fathers, the medieval Schoolmen and older Protestant theologians held that the days of the Mosaic account of creation were literal days of twenty-four hours. So far as Britain is concerned special mention should be made of the seventeenth-century Irish arch-bishop James Ussher, whose Old Testament chronology became most influential and is still to be found in most editions of the Authorized Version. His contemporary Dr. John Lightfoot, Professor of Hebrew and Vice-Chancellor of Cambridge University, believed he could make such an accurate calculation from the Old Testament, that he maintained that the week of creation was the week from October 18 to 24 in the year 4004 B.C., and that the creation of Adam took place on the Friday of that week, October 23, 4004, at 9.00 a.m. forty-fifth meridian time.[1]

In the nineteenth century—but without excesses such as Lightfoot's—this view was advocated by the English expositor G. H. Pember (*Earth's Earliest Ages*, 1876) and by *The Scofield Reference Bible*, which is widely used today throughout the English-speaking world. In Germany we can mention among others the theologians Baumgarten and Keil, according to whom the Biblical writer in every case meant twenty-four hour days by the word "day" in the Creation-narrative. The same position has been recently represented by the American Dr. H. Rimmer (*Modern Science and the Genesis Record*, 1937).

(2) Among conservative exegetes and scientists who accept the authority of the Bible, very many have advocated the Period theory. This involved demonstrating the agreement of the acts of creation during the "six days" with the sequence of the geological strata. But this theory can be traced right back to early Christian times. Dr. C. F. H. Henry was right in stating in *The Protestant Dilemma* (p. 66): "It is certainly not true that the age-theory of Genesis is a modern fundamentalist device to save these chapters from a reddened countenance in view of modern science, for

---

[1] Cf. Bernard Ramm, *The Christian View of Science and Scripture*, pp. 121, 122.—As an interesting counterpart to this error of a believer about the history and age of the earth the "geological" error of a well-known advocate of unbelief may be mentioned. "Voltaire thought the fish fossils discovered in the mountains were fish skeletons thrown there by the Crusaders on their way to Palestine" (Ramm, p. 122).

church history discloses champions of an age-theory long before the rise of modern science."

Soon after the beginnings of modern geology and palaeontology, from the nineteenth century on, it was particularly supported by leading scientists who accepted the authority of the Bible, e.g. the Frenchman Cuvier (1769–1832), one of the chief founders of these sciences and one of the greatest names in the history of science. Surprised by the amazing harmony between Genesis and geology which was now becoming clear, he wrote, "Moses has left us an account of the formation of the world the exactness of which is more and more wonderfully confirmed from day to day."

The view was upheld by James Dana and J. W. Dawson, the two most important nineteenth-century geologists of North America, the former in his *Manual of Geology* and the latter in his *The Origin of the World according to Revelation and Science* (1877).

Theologians of this period who held this theory include F. Godet (Professor in Neuchâtel, Switzerland), J. H. A. Ebrard (Professor in Marburg), O. Zöckler (Professor in Giessen and Greifswald) and Dean Keerl. These are only a few of the names that might be cited.

In the twentieth century this theory has been defended by writers[1] like Professor F. Bettex (III), Professor Dr. E. Hoppe, the botanist Professor E. Dennert (I), the astronomer Professor Johannes Riem (I), the palaeontologist Professor Freiherr von Huene, University of Tübingen, and the surgeon Professor A. Rendle Short (II).

(3) A mediating point of view was taken up already in the nineteenth century by Johannes Heinrich Kurz, Professor of Theology in Dorpat;[2] it is advocated today in England by P. J. Wiseman, and in America by Dr. B. Ramm. The six days are held to be literal days of twenty-four hours, but not the days of the Divine activity of creation itself. Rather they are "days of revelation," in which God revealed His works of creation to man, which, however, assuredly needed vast periods of time. During the six days of twenty-four hours God showed man what He had brought to pass in the course of the geological periods. He did this in their true sequence, so that in the order of days of revelation the essential chronological order of the works of creation may be recognized, not, of course, in all its details, but nevertheless in its general outline.

The Church Father Augustine (354–430) expressed a similar, but not identical view, when he suggested that the six days were six pictures, in which God allowed the angels to see His works.

(4) The "Ideal" Interpretation of the six days is related to this. It was advocated by the theologians Hermann Strack (Professor in Berlin) and J. P. Lange, the editor of the well-known, large-scale commentary bearing

---

[1] The works in which they have expressed their view are mentioned in the Bibliography; the Roman numeral is the guide, where more than one work is mentioned.

[2] See previous note.

his name.[1] Human measures of time have no validity when we are dealing with God, who is outside the limits of time. For Him "one day is . . . as a thousand years, and a thousand years as one day" (II Pet. 3: 8). Hence the six days of *Divine* creating, as "days of God," are not to be compared in any way with earthly days, whether of twenty-four hours or of longer periods of time. According to Strack the six days denote, "six main points to be distinguished in Creation, six phases or aspects of the creative activity of God, six main viewpoints, under which the creative and world-formative acts of God can be arranged."

(5) The Restitution Theory of creation was occasionally advocated earlier, but it became especially widely favoured in circles that accepted the authority of the Bible after the science of geology came into being at the beginning of the nineteenth century. According to this view the fall of Satan took place between the first and second verse of Genesis 1. The world, originally created beautiful and perfect by God, as a result of Divine judgment and the destructive power of the evil one became *tohu-wa-bohu* ("waste and void"). The subsequent work of the six days was therefore not the real, original "creation" of the world itself, but a work of restoration.

This so-called Restitution Theory is not a product of modern speculation. Traces of it are to be found in Christian literature as early as the time of Augustine (*c.* 400). In the seventh century it was advocated by the Anglo-Saxon poet Cædmon. About the year 1000 it was accepted by King Edgar of England. It was particularly emphasized by the mystic Jakob Böhme in the seventeenth century. Michael Hahn also was among those that held it.

Since the beginning of the nineteenth century it has spread very widely. Many conservative readers of the Bible, acquainted with the results of geological research, saw in it a way in which the Bible and science could be brought into harmony. They accepted the long periods of development demanded by geology, but inserted them between verses 1 and 2 of the Biblical account. In addition most of them considered the six "days" to be literal days of twenty-four hours. Some, particularly the scientists who held this interpretation, agreed that the *tohu-wa-bohu* of verse 2 was a consequence of the fall of Satan, but maintained the Period Theory for the work of restoration during the following six days.

We find the Restitution Theory advocated in 1814 by the Scottish scholar Dr. Thomas Chalmers and again in 1833 by the English professor of minerology Dr. William Buckland, in his *Geology and Minerology considered with reference to Natural Theology.*

Others who have held it have been the geologist Professor K. V. Raumer (1865), the natural scientist Professor G. H. von Schubert (1860) and, quite recently (1947), the geologist Freiherr von Huene, Professor of Palae-

[1] The English translation has recently been republished in America.

ontology in Tübingen and one of the best known students of saurians of the present day. Among philosophers who have held it may be mentioned Friedrich von Schlegel and J. H. von Fichte, formerly Professor of Philosophy at Bonn and Tübingen, the son of the well-known philosopher J. Gottlieb Fichte. Amongst theologians we may mention Professors Franz Delitzsch, Michael Baumgarten, J. H. Kurtz[1] and E. W. Hengstenberg. We may also add the names of Bishop Oetinger, Dean Keerl, Professor Bettex,[1] Jakob Kroeker[1] and the evangelist General von Viebahn (1914). Dr. Haarbeck wrote (p. 57), "The most probable view is that, before the world as we know it existed, our earthly system was Satan's kingdom of light before his fall and that, as a consequence of his fall, his kingdom was taken from him and recreated as a dwelling for man." The writings of G. H. Pember[1] and *The Scofield Reference Bible* are widely known. More recently we find the view in Dr. H. Rimmer's work *Modern Science and the Genesis Record*.

This diversity of opinion among expositors who accept the authority of the Bible proves that we must be careful and cautious in coming to a conclusion and above all avoid self-confident dogmatism; we must have tolerance and understanding for those that disagree with us. Above all they show that we must in all modesty be conscious of our own insufficiency, and remember the question which the Creator Himself put to His earthly creature Job about the creation: "Where wast thou when I laid the foundations of the earth?" (Job 38: 4–7).

"The secret things belong unto the Lord our God: but the things that are revealed belong unto us and to our children for ever" (Deut. 29: 29).

[1] See Bibliography.

CHAPTER XV

THE SEQUENCE OF THE WORKS OF CREATION

I. Some Basic Considerations

1. is a purely "religious" interpretation of the biblical creation-narrative justified?

WITH the partial approval of "higher critical" circles some have developed a "purely religious" interpretation of the Biblical creation-narrative. This regards as important only its spiritual, prophetic and theological message;[1] its outward, historical and stylistic dress on the other hand is conditioned by the time of its writing and shares in the scientific errors of the ancient cosmic concepts of the Fertile Crescent. It is granted that the account is surprisingly free from all the mythological, often fantastic embellishments found in the Babylonian and Egyptian cosmogonies of its heathen environment. It was a sign of the condescension and goodness of God that He made His eternal, spiritual truths known to men living on a not very advanced level of culture scientifically, in the concepts of their time and of their contemporaries. Under no circumstances, therefore, should we attach importance to the scientific correctness either of the whole structure or of the detailed statements of the Biblical account of creation. Nevertheless it retains its character as the message and revelation of God.

The suggestion of a possible clothing of Divine truth in the garb of human, temporal and historical, factual errors contradicts the absolute truthfulness of God. In the final analysis it reduces to the principle, "The end justifies the means," i.e. the holy and perfect end justifies means which are not really fully in harmony with its holy, perfect nature.

It is true that the main and real aim of the Biblical creation-narrative is of a thoroughly spiritual nature. All our efforts to understand it scientifically must never forget this. This applies also to the whole of Scripture. We must agree with Augustine when he said, "We do not read in the Gospels that the Lord said, 'I will send you the Spirit, who will teach you about the course of the sun and the moon.' They were to become Christians, not astronomers." Nevertheless it cannot be denied that the first chapter of the Bible conveys its spiritual teachings in the form of a *historical narrative*. Unmistakably it affirms a series of acts of God following one on

[1] Cf. p. 47 "The Spiritual Message of the Biblical Creation-Narrative."

another and hence the progressive character of the process of creation. Therefore, just as we must not overlook the spiritual content of the creation story, we should also not despise what it contains regarding the history of creation.

The statement, "The Bible is not a scientific text-book," must therefore not be understood as if it meant that the original text of the Bible itself contained scientific, factual errors. Not even the smallest disharmony can or ever will exist between the word of God and the work of God. Even if the word of God does not go into details about the process of creation, it will nevertheless always be consistent with the facts—so far as these are really shown to be facts.

The suggestion would be illogical and lacking in reason that it is of no consequence whether the history of nature and man given us in the Bible is correct; all that matters is the fact that God speaks. For how should God speak to us men, who live in the midst of nature and history, other than in history and through it? That means, how should He speak to us other than principally through historical events, particularly through the events connected with salvation, and through the prophecies and discourses of the Old Testament prophets, and of Jesus and His apostles, discourses which took place in history? If God speaks to us men only through history, bound as we are to history, what would happen to His speaking, if this "history" were not history, if these events had not taken place, if these discourses of Jesus, the prophets and the apostles, had in fact not been given?

We grant that not past history is in itself the main thing (apart from the decisive events in the work of redemption), but the spiritual message, which God speaks to us and to our day, and to the day of every hearer, in that history and through it. But unless it had taken place, God would not have spoken, and our faith would be without any reliable foundation.

2. POPULAR EXPRESSIONS IN THE BIBLICAL PICTURE OF NATURE

This argument cannot be controverted by the fact that in its statements about nature the Bible uses popular expressions. Even we do so today, and we are certainly not upholders of the Ptolemaic theory, when we talk of the "rising" and "setting" of the sun and say, "The sun 'stands' here," or, "The moon 'stands' there in the heavens." "Who today would think of saying," asks Professor Hoppe, "instead of 'The sun rises,' 'The earth has turned so far upon its axis that the rays of the sun which are deflected by refraction fall exactly on the spot where I am making this observation'? Throughout the Bible we quite rightly find the everyday language of appearance, i.e. of the impression made on our senses by objects. That is how we speak and write today, unless we are writing a text-book about cosmic physics" (pp. 321 f.).

It is significant, however, that the Bible does not contain a single assertion about nature or history which, in its *substance*, has proved to be false. It is therefore our right, indeed our duty, to consider the creation-narrative from the scientific point of view as well.

3. THE SEQUENCE OF THE WORKS OF CREATION SHOWS A BASIC HARMONY BETWEEN GENESIS AND GEOLOGY

Here we face a most striking and remarkable fact, which must be acknowledged, quite independently of the attitude that faith or unbelief may adopt with regard to it.

However we interpret the "days" of the creation-narrative (whether as days of twenty-four hours or as periods, as literal "days of revelation" or as "days of God" of a completely different nature),[1] and however we explain the creation-narrative as a whole (whether as an account of the original creation or of a "restoration" of the earth after the fall of Satan, and this in turn either in literal days or in periods), the fact remains that the sequence of the works of creation mentioned by it corresponds in essentials to the sequence of the strata of the earth and of the fossils they contain, as demonstrated by modern palaeontological research.

This fact cannot be shaken by the assertion, so often made today—not seldom in a particularly arrogant spirit and tone—that the establishment of such an agreement between geology and Genesis is a superfluous, outmoded and out-of-date form of apologetics. It is a simple fact, which can neither be denied nor argued away; it has been expressed by Professor Karl Heim as follows, "What the Biblical author describes is a *concise summary* of a total picture which, according to the findings of geology, came into being in the course of over one and a half thousand million years" (II, p. 48).

It should be evident that the agreements between the creation-narrative and geology to be found mentioned later in this chapter must not be accorded too great a value. On no account may they be automatically assumed to be the conscious knowledge of the inspired writer, as though he had "meant" these results of modern scientific research. We should make it a general rule not to read the discoveries or theories of modern science into the thought of ages long past. The inspiration responsible for the Bible has absolutely no interest in this.

On the other hand the meaning of the sacred texts intended by God goes at times far beyond the understanding even of its own, human writers. It is possible that this may be the case here also. For God, who brought the whole world into existence and who knows its course of development exactly, is the real author of the Bible, and also of the creation-narrative. The human writer is merely the instrument used by His inspiration.

[1] Cf. Chapter 14.

4. OUR STARTING-POINT; THE VALUE AND LIMITATIONS OF THE COMPARISON OF GENESIS AND GEOLOGY

If we are to recognize the harmony between the Bible and nature we must on no account start from the teachings of science, and from them derive an exegetical guide for our understanding of the "six days' work." Faith based on the Bible and exposition of Scripture must go the reverse way, i.e. from the Bible to a consideration of nature, from the exposition of the God-given account to a judgment on the parallel, basic concepts of man's teaching about the origin of the world. The exposition must never become dependent on the scientific views, often quite uncertain, reached at any particular time. Nor may our motive ever be at all costs to harmonize the Biblical story of creation with modern thinking.

We must not overlook that, when we come to the oldest phases of development of the solar system, there is no absolute agreement among scientists and astronomers. Even shortly after the middle of last century G. C. Lichtenberg, Professor of Physics in Göttingen, enumerated over fifty theories on the formation of the sun and the earth and declared sarcastically that nine-tenths of them belonged more to the history of the human mind than to the history of the earth. In contrast to this for almost a century the theories of Kant and Laplace had predominated, and indeed, reigned supreme. Kant developed his theory in his *Allgemeine Naturgeschichte und Theorie des Himmels* (1755) and Laplace his in his *Exposition du système du monde* (1796).[1]

For their time both these cosmological theories were scientific achievements of the first rank. They agreed with everything known in the eighteenth century about the solar system. But fresh observations have led to further knowledge, which does not agree with them, and so they are today considered to be superseded, and in scientific circles, in their original form, they have long since been abandoned. "They are ghosts that haunt popular books" (Dennert, III, p. 69).

[1] The two theories differ in essential points. What was common to them was the supposition that the solar system originated from a primitive gaseous mass stretching originally beyond the orbit of the outermost planets. Thus the sun and all the planets, together with their moons, had developed out of a common, original gas. On the question as to *how* the planets had been formed out of the gaseous mass, the two theories differed greatly.

Kant thought more of single points with a stronger force of attraction *within* this globe of gas, towards which the particles of matter then flowed; this produced collisions and gradually formed conglomerations of matter and then heavenly bodies. Laplace believed in a tremendous rotation of this sphere of gas, out of which as a result of the movement portions were thrown *out* and were formed into spheres.

Thus the two theories—apart from the primitive gaseous mass—have completely different concepts of the origin of the world. It is therefore an inexcusable error when, even in school books, the two are brought together under the name of the "Kant-Laplace theory," which has never existed. What is usually meant by this name is merely a simplified form of Laplace's theory.

But even in more recent theories the human mind has not passed beyond exploration and hypotheses. This is true especially of the problems of the actual formation of the sun and stars and of the "star-age" of the earth, i.e. of the concentration of the original, cosmic, nebular matter to form the heavenly bodies. Thus even today, in the twentieth century there does not exist a uniform cosmogony accepted by modern astronomy and astrophysics as a whole. W. M. Smart in *The Origin of the Earth* (1951) enumerates ten different modern theories on the origin of the solar system.

Thus from the scientific point of view also we must urge great caution before we claim to have established "absolute certainties." Even the fact that a new theory involves the displacing of a predecessor proves that there is no theory which satisfies all scientists, which does justice to all the discoveries of science and which has, therefore, found general acceptance.

We can speak, by and large, of reliable knowledge only when we come to the later periods of the earth's creation marked by fossiliferous strata, i.e. the stage of development which falls into the purview of geology, which can fix the order of the geological periods with accuracy. If we use the language of the Period Theory of Genesis 1, that means we have certain knowledge only of the third, fifth and sixth days of creation.

We must also avoid the idea that, if we can establish certain harmonies between the Bible and science, we have "proved" the truth or the Divine inspiration of Scripture.

Firstly, as has just been said, not a few scientific investigations are still proceeding without offering us any certainty of their outcome. Secondly, our own exposition of Scripture is far from being free from error in all its details and must on no account be equated *a priori* with Holy Scripture.

Above all we must say: The Bible is a lion, and a lion can defend itself! God's Book does not need to be protected by its human, believing readers. Its authority originates with its Divine author. With all due regard for true science and good apologetics, prophets do not need professors to protect them. Before the forum of truth God's witnesses do not need human advocates. The wisdom of God stands firm, even without human science (I Cor. 1: 19–31). Or, as the great French mathematician Blaise Pascal wrote in the hour of his conversion in 1654: "God of Abraham, God of Isaac, God of Jacob, not of the philosophers and the wise."

Even if there should be isolated cases where the Bible in its statements about history or science is accused of error by obviously well-founded, scientific statements, we should side with the words of Augustine, the greatest of the Church Fathers, who wrote in a letter to Jerome, the most learned of the Fathers: "If I come upon something here or there, which does not seem to agree with the truth, then I do not doubt for a moment that either there is a mistake in the copy, or that the translator has not exactly expressed the thoughts of the original, or that I have not understood the matter."

5. SCRIPTURE AND ITS INTERPRETATION. SCIENTIFIC FACTS AND THEORIES

As already stated, we must not *a priori* equate Scripture with our exposition of it. The so-called contradictions between faith in the Bible and science are in fact not a conflict between the Bible and assured scientific knowledge, but between *interpretations* of the Bible and scientific *theories*; they are often a collision between popular traditions and philosophical speculations, which have been simply accepted from others without being tested.

In every case it is necessary, when interpreting Scripture, to see exactly what it says and what it does not say, and not to allow ourselves to be bound or prejudiced by explanations handed down to us. Our task is to examine the Biblical texts without bias and not to read any more into them than they really say. Let us be wary of falling into the mistake of the Church in the time of Copernicus. The representatives of Christianity believed they had to hold fast to the Ptolemaic picture of the world, in the face of astronomy, because they thought that the Bible demanded it. And yet they were wrong. Today many find themselves similarly placed with regard to geology and palaeontology. We far too easily confuse the real truth of Scripture with our interpretation of it and so fall easily into the danger of thinking that Scripture is being attacked, when our own personal explanation of it is not endorsed.

Unresolved questions are not necessarily hindrances to faith for honest men earnestly seeking the truth. The scientific thinker who goes into the depths also knows the limits of his possibilities of knowledge. And, above all, faith can wait. One day we shall know even as we have been known (I Cor. 13: 12).

Nevertheless it may be a help to some doubters and seekers after truth if, by showing the agreements between the Bible and science, certain obstacles are cleared out of his way.

In the second half of this chapter we give a few of the most important parallels between Genesis 1 and science. It is our hope that the reader, through the knowledge of certain major facts, will find a starting point for further thought. Here he is given facts and the possibility of forming his own judgment.

II. The Sequence of the Works of Creation in Detail

1. THE FACT OF CREATION

God made heaven and earth (Gen. 1: 1; Col. 1: 16). "In the beginning was the Word, and the Word was with God, and the Word was God ... All things were made through Him; and without Him was not any thing made that hath been made" (John 1: 1, 3).

Its message of a single world-cause, and of a creation from nothing by the eternal God, makes the Biblical revelation and especially the Biblical creation-narrative stand infinitely high above all the pantheons and cosmogonies of its heathen environment, quite apart from the fact that most of them are marred by a jungle of wildly romantic, grotesquely fantastic mythological embellishments.

(a) Biblical creation and Babylonian myth

The best known of the creation myths from the ancient pagan Near East is the Babylonian. It was solemnly recited as part of the public, official liturgy every New Year's Day in Babylon, that fountain and centre of culture in the ancient world. This is how it represented the formation of the world.[1]

It explains the origin of the world as a battle between Marduk, the god of light, later the city-god of Babylon, and the dark monster Tiamat, ruler of chaos. Thus from the very outset it is set in the context of a basic dualism. Finally Marduk gained the victory over Tiamat. The monster was slain, and her corpse divided into pieces out of which the world was formed.

Thus, the most advanced cosmogonic myth produced by the ancient New East regards "creation" really as no more than a triumphant "fashioning," only as a "forming" of already existing material. To the idea of creation from nothing by a single, almighty God Babylonian thought was not able to rise. Here only revelation by God Himself can give true light.

"By faith we understand that the world was created by the word of God, so that what is seen was made out of things which do not appear" (Heb. 11: 3, R.S.V.). If we are to accept a beginning and a creation of the world, belief in a personal, living, almighty God is necessary. Even modern, purely scientific research is not able to penetrate to this first and final cause of the universe.

Faith, nevertheless, knows how to appreciate the indications given by nature and natural science. Even if the achievements of the human mind and the sign-language of nature cannot "prove" the truth of God, they can nevertheless *bear witness* to it.

We find that the scientific thought of our day opposes the atheistic, materialistic assertion of the uncreated, eternal existence of the universe and of matter. We shall mention two of its arguments.

(b) The primal gas and the beginning of the universe

In spite of many differences in detail all modern, cosmogonic theories begin by accepting the existence of a hot, glowing, gaseous mass at a temperature of many thousand degrees. This is said to have cooled in some way, contracted, and started to rotate; thus out of this original mass,

---

[1] [The essentials of this epic, *Enuma elish*, will be found in Winton Thomas: *Documents from Old Testament Times*, pp. 5–13; the complete text is given by Pritchard: *Ancient Near Eastern Texts*, pp. 60–72. (H.L.E.)]

through centrifugal force and conglomeration, the heavenly bodies were gradually formed.

But such a theory creates very significant chemical and physical problems. According to Dalton's law gases have no quality that would make them group in denser masses; on the contrary, their particles repel each other. They have no natural or optimum volume but continually expand to occupy a larger space. The original gas must therefore have been uniformly distributed throughout space. Further, at such high temperatures elements are in a state of "dissociation," so that no chemical combination can come into being. There are only atoms which do not unite to form molecules.

Also the law of gravity could not possibly have come into force, because the gas was distributed with perfect uniformity throughout universal space. Equally the original mass of gas could not have begun to move by itself, as it were from "inside." According to the law of inertia, a body continues in its existing state (rest or motion) until that state is changed by an *external* force. But how could such an impulse have come from "outside," seeing that the whole of space was filled with this glowing gaseous mass, so there could have been no "outside," nor for that matter any real "inside"?

A change in this condition could have come about only by cooling. But this again would not have been possible, because there was no colder "outside" into which the gas could have radiated its heat and brought about a loss of temperature, which would have led to a contraction of the gas. Thus to speak of a cooling of the primal gaseous mass, without first showing where this radiated heat could have gone, is to dodge a major difficulty.

We see then that, unless we accept a higher power which is not part of the gaseous mass, we cannot comprehend the origin of the universe. The astronomer Johannes Riem has put it as follows, "We have established that the pure fact alone of the existence of our cosmos is an unambiguous argument against materialism and an unambiguous proof of the creative power and omnipotence of the highest cosmic Intelligence. Otherwise we would still be in the midst of the old chaos" (I, p. 43).

If we were to try, as do many, to explain the origin of the nebular mass out of which our own solar system was formed by the collision of two *earlier* suns or solar systems, this would not advance our argument a single step. For then our task would be to explain the origin of these *earlier* suns. The whole problem would only have been pushed backwards, but in no way solved.

The existence of an ordered cosmos can be made understandable only by a belief in the existence and the creative activity of a higher, cosmic Power. Equally, at the same time, all this becomes an argument against the eternal existence of matter and for a beginning of the universe through a creation.

Thus we stand before an inescapable choice. Either we believe in God, as the Creator of heaven and earth, or we must abandon from the very outset all attempts at explaining and understanding these decisive questions about the foundations of the universe.

(c) The evidence of radio-activity against the eternal existence of the universe and matter

In the disintegration of radio-active substances modern science offers us further evidence that the universe had a beginning. At the same time it is also a measure by which we may determine the age of the earth's strata and of the earth itself. Professor Karl Heim writes, "We have within our solar system a fairly safe means of determining the age of heavenly bodies, *viz.* the disintegration of radium among radio-active substances, the rate of which is known. Experiments have been carried out on rocks, containing radio-active substances, on the amount of disintegration which has already taken place. From this we can calculate how long ago the rock in question was formed. We can speak of 'rock-clocks' in the geological strata, which have ticked uniformly throughout the millions of years of the earth's history, from which we later wanderers on this earth can see and read off what o'clock it is. From these 'clocks' we see that our earth is, according to the oldest geological strata, about one and a half thousand million years old; it is probably still older, but in any case it cannot be more than three times this figure" (II, pp. 32, 33).

Dr. Ramm gives the following simple description of the phenomena of radio-activity. "A material is radio-active, if it gives off small atomic particles, which fly away from the active substance at great velocity. Radium and uranium are the most commonly known of such substances. The atomic bomb and allied studies in atomic physics have made the public very conscious of radio-active phenomena. As uranium gives off high-speed particles it disintegrates till eventually it becomes lead. The speed of this process of disintegration is known and is the same no matter what temperatures or pressures the substance is subjected to. Pressures and temperatures have been applied in the laboratory to these substances of far greater intensities than are found in the crust of our planet, and the process is neither accelerated nor retarded" (pp. 122, 123). Hence physicists, by these "lead-methods," can tell by the degree of disintegration, i.e. by the proportion of uranium-lead in uranium ore, how old a sample of uranium is.[1]

Dr. Ramm uses the following comparisons to make clear to those who

[1] Dr. A. Neuberg writes (II, p. 82), "One gram of uranium disintegrates in 80 million years. Therefore when one gram of uranium-lead is present in 100 grams of uranium the rock will be about 80 million years old." All these figures, however, cannot as yet, despite the most careful experiments, be regarded as certain. Therefore the utmost reserve is necessary with regard to all detailed statements.

do not know the methods of radio-active measurements how the information is obtained.

He refers to a pendulum clock. The number of inches the weights have
fallen show how long the clock has been going since it was wound up.

By measuring how much petrol is left in the tank of a car, the tank
having been full at the start of the journey, we can gain an idea of how
many miles we have driven.

The height of the clock-weights and the amount of petrol left in the
tank give us a corresponding possibility of reasoning back to the point in
time at which the clock was wound up and the car journey was started.

Similarly, by determining the atomic weight and the proportion of
uranium present to the residue (uranium-lead or helium), we can calculate
how long the process of disintegration of a sample of uranium has lasted
and when it began. At the same time this makes it possible for us to
determine the approximate age of the geological strata in which the
uranium was found. By further measurement and calculation a date has
been reached for the beginning not merely of the earth but of the universe.
For our purpose it is not important whether this lies two or three thousands of millions of years back as believed by many physicists, or whether
these figures should be smaller or even larger. What matters is the fact
that modern research demands the concept of the beginning of the universe. This means that nature is not eternal but measurable in time, and so
must have begun at a given point in the past.

Certain astronomical facts should be added to these physical ones. It has
been established that the spiral nebulae of which the universe consists are
receding at immense speeds up to that of light, i.e. 186,000 miles per
second, so that the radius of the universe is growing steadily. The facts
may be found in the work of the English astronomer Sir James Jeans, *The
Expanding Universe*. Professor Karl Heim, a mathematician and scientist as
well as a theologian, has coined the expression "universe-bomb"[1] to cover
these amazing facts. This is to express the fact that, as the most careful
observations have established the fixed stars are moving away from us
into the remotest distances; this movement must have begun at some
point in time, perhaps three to four thousand million years ago. Thus both
sciences, physics and astronomy, testify quite independently of each other
to the fact that the universe has a "history," and that from the standpoint
of the most recent research we can no longer speak of an eternal existence
of the universe and matter.

"The daring dream of the philosophers that the universe is eternal has
today—even purely from the scientific point of view—become improbable" (Karl Heim). This means at the same time the expectation of an end
to the universe. It is like a clock, once wound-up, continually running
down and fated, if left to itself, one day to stop.

[1] *Weltgranate.*

We repeat that we are far from desiring to "prove" the statements of the Bible by scientific arguments. For all that, it may be of value not to overlook such a fundamental agreement between the trends of modern physics and geology and the fundamental statements of the Bible about a beginning (John 1: 1) and a creation (Gen. 1: 1). It may be that the numerical data of science require much confirmation or perhaps considerable rectification, but both sides—the Bible and science—are in full agreement in testifying to the fact of a beginning of the universe.

The following agreements between Biblical and scientific teaching about the origin of the world apply only to the Period interpretation of the creation-narrative.

2. THE ORIGINAL, FORMLESS STATE OF MATTER

The Biblical record tells us that "the earth was waste and void" (Heb. *tohu-wa-bohu*), i.e. shapeless and without content.[1] Scientific thought corresponds to this. Despite many differences in detail the acceptance of an unformed and shapeless mass of gas is the common starting-point of all modern cosmologies.

3. THE CREATION OF THE WORLD, OF LIGHT AND OF THE PLANTS BEFORE THE WORK OF THE FOURTH "DAY"

This order has frequently been the object of mockery but yet completely without cause.

The decisive question here, for those that follow the Period interpretation, is how the work of the fourth day is to be understood. Was it the actual creation of the stars themselves as heavenly bodies in space, or was it merely that they became visible as lights for the earth? Does the creation record give us a general outline of the history of the origin of the whole universe, or does it confine itself—apart from verse 1—to the history of this world? Is it cosmological or terrestrial?

Both explanations have been advocated by important expositors of the Bible. But in neither case is there of necessity a contradiction between the Bible and natural science. Only those can mock at the Biblical order who have not thought seriously and deeply enough about these problems.

Surely the question is legitimate, Were according to the Biblical account the stars really not created before the fourth day? Has not the writer said right at the beginning—and thus before the creation of light on the first day—"In the beginning God created the heaven and the earth?" And does not the book of Job show us the heavenly hosts of stars and angels already existing before the creation of the earth? After all they rejoiced to see it being made: "Whereupon were the foundations thereof fastened? Or who laid the corner stone thereof; when the morning stars sang together, and

[1] For the meaning of the Hebrew words *tohu* and *bohu* cf. p. 231.

all the sons of God shouted for joy?" (Job 38: 6, 7). In addition Genesif
1: 16 does not use the Hebrew word *bara*, which signifies a creation ous
of nothing, but *'asah*, which denotes a formation or preparation out ot
already existing material.[1] Surely it is merely speaking of what the stars
should be for the earth from the fourth day onwards, *viz.* lights to rule the
day and the night?

Once the earth's surface had solidified, i.e. after the completion of the
"star-age" of the earth, our globe must at first in the following geological
periods have been surrounded by a very dense atmosphere of water vapour.
The heat, constantly breaking through from the interior of the earth and
so causing its surface to remain at a high temperature, vapourized much
of the water on the earth and "surrounded it with a thick layer of mist,
something like that we meet in a laundry" (Prof. Rohrbach). So the stars
were already present, but were not clearly recognizable as such from the
earth. Then the work of the fourth day could simply have consisted in the
stars appearing as single lights in the firmament as a result of the thinning
and the clearing of the earth's atmosphere.

If this is so, there would be no question of the creation of the earth
before that of the sun. Then too the light of the first day would in reality
be that of the sun, only veiled by the thick covering of vapour and clouds.
At the same time it would create no difficulty that the origin of plant-life
is mentioned on the third day, i.e. before the work of the fourth day. For
the plants would have received the rays of light necessary for their life-
processes, but much reduced owing to the layer of clouds, just as happens
today in very cloudy weather.

This is the attitude of the note in the "Jubilee" edition of the German
Bible published in Stuttgart, when it says, "If we are told of the creation
of the stars first on the fourth day, it is not to describe the chronological
order of the creation of the universe; it was now that the stars first gained
their importance as lights for the earth, while their significance and position
in the universe is not mentioned at all."

Other notable expositors of Scripture, however, consider the text, taken
exactly, speaks of an activity of God with regard to the heavenly bodies
themselves, though it is true that it draws special attention to the relation
of the sun, moon and stars to the earth. God set lights in the firmament
of the heaven to be "for signs, and for seasons, and for days and years,"
"to rule over the day and over the night," "to give light upon the earth."
But it does not say that this was accomplished by any form of activity by
God in relation to the earth's atmosphere, but rather: "And God made . . .
the greater light (the sun) . . . and the lesser light (the moon) . . . and the
stars" (v. 16). Hence the work of the fourth day does not concern the

---

[1] *e.g.*, to build a ship (Gen. 8: 6), to erect a house (II Kings 12: 12), to make a coat
(Gen. 3: 21), to lay out a garden (Amos 9: 14). For a further discussion on the meaning
of these words, see p. 232.

atmosphere of the earth, but is to be understood astronomically and cosmically.

According to this view the first verse of the creation record, "In the beginning God created the heaven and the earth," is either a heading for the whole account or tells of the creation of the basic materials, of matter without form, or, expressed physically, of the "field of forces," out of which God, during the ensuing periods of the story of creation, caused the sun, moon, stars and the earth to emerge. In any case verse 1 does not speak of the creation of the heavenly bodies before that of the earth, for it mentions both heaven and earth simultaneously, "In the beginning God created the heaven and the earth."

So far as Job 38: 4–7 is concerned, while this passage should be given due weight, too far-reaching, cosmological conclusions must not be drawn from poetic language. In any case it speaks of the praise and worship of the Creator, which can surely only be predicated of living, conscious, spiritual beings. Therefore by the singing and shouting "morning-stars" and "sons of God" the angel-world must be meant, which praised the Creator at the foundation of the earth. But the angel world was created before the material universe came into being.

The word "day star" in Isaiah 14: 12, part of a highly poetical passage, is not used astronomically but metaphorically of a spiritual and personal being—in this case the King of Babylon, as is shown by the context "The oracle concerning Babylon, which Isaiah the son of Amoz did see" (Isa. 13: 1, R.V.mg.).[1] At the end of the book of Revelation the Lord calls Himself "the bright, the morning star." In Job 1: 6 and Job 2: 1 the angels are called "sons of God." Thus Job 38: 4–7 can scarcely be adduced as evidence that the heavenly bodies were created before the earth.

But even when the fourth day of creation is explained of the formation of the heavenly bodies themselves in space, the sequence of the preceding works of creation offers no serious difficulties.

(a) The presence of light before the formation of the sun

According to the cosmological theories of science the gaseous mass out of which the systems of suns and stars later developed had a very high temperature of many thousands of degrees Centigrade. Hence the whole of matter in the universe must, in its first stages, have been a single, glowing mass, a great, fiery "light." Consequently light existed, according to the teachings of modern astro-physics, for immensely long periods before the sun, moon and stars came into being.

"The simple man," writes a contemporary scientist, "sees in our sun the source of the light which floods our earthly world. By himself he cannot possibly come upon the idea that light in nature is not absolutely dependent upon the sun. In addition, there is the fact that in the orient there is no real

[1] [Cf. especially Isa. 14: 4. (H.L.E.)]

o

twilight. Full daylight bursts on us with the rising of the sun and ceases, just as suddenly, with sunset. Hence in these regions he could scarcely imagine any other principal source of light than direct sunlight. And yet in the Genesis account it is assumed that light is independent of the sun!"

Dr. Boardman was therefore not unjust when he asked in his book *Creative Week*, "Why will the Academy vote Moses a blunderer for declaring that light existed before the sun appeared, and yet vote Laplace a scientist for affirming precisely the same thing?"

The French physicist, Jean Baptiste Biot, saw himself driven by this astounding agreement to make the statement, "Either Moses was as profoundly instructed in the sciences as is our century, or he was inspired."[1]

(b) The formation of the earth before the creation of the sun

If we accept the explanation given by astronomy that the solar system was formed by the disintegration of a spiral nebula, we obtain the same order of events. For if the planets were thrown out of the fiery, primal gas as it rotated, then they must, because of their comparative smallness, have cooled and contracted in the cold of space (at a temperature of virtually absolute zero, $-273°$ C.) and have formed heavenly bodies much more quickly than the incomparably larger original mass. This latter, therefore, must have existed for a long time as an elliptically shaped, nebular formation before it could really have been called a "heavenly body" or "sun." And, in any case, only after it had thrown off all the planets could the remainder have been called the "sun."[2]

Thus already last century the geologist Professor F. A. Quenstedt of Tübingen said: "How true of Moses to say that the small earth must have formed itself into a ball long before the much larger sun!"

(c) The creation of plants before the formation of the sun

This involves the statement that plant life is not necessarily dependent on sunlight. This too has been the subject of much mockery by the sceptic, but again the Period theory has an answer. The living substance of plants, which includes chlorophyll, requires for its nourishment in addition to the carbon dioxide in the air, water and the necessary salts from the earth, also the action of certain rays of light. But it would be false to think that these must necessarily be *sun-rays*. Experiments have shown that a large section of the spectrum of sunlight is completely ineffective in a plant's process of assimilation. It needs practically only the light of the red, orange and yellow rays. Therefore the botanist Professor Dennert declares, "A light which contained only these rays would therefore suffice for this process. It follows that it is foolish and shortsighted to hold that the sun as such is

---

[1] Biot was Professor of Physics and Astronomy in Paris. He died in 1862.

[2] Cf. Prof. J. Riem of Hamburg Observatory (II, pp. 19, 46), Prof. C. E. Luthardt (pp. 71, 72), also C. Payne-Gaposchkin of Harvard, "The sun (as we know it) may indeed be younger than the earth, not older" (*Stars in the Making*, p. 107).

indispensable for plants. . . . It would rather have been possible that at the beginning a more general, light-giving, glowing mass of matter in space fulfilled the present rôle of the sun for plant-life." He adds, "In any case it is most remarkable that here once again the reporter does not give the much more obvious—because more intelligible to ordinary people—view that first the sun and then the plants came into being; he holds rather the reverse sequence, the possibility of which from the scientific point of view was first recognized towards the end of last century" (I, pp. 133 f.).

4. THE CREATION OF PLANTS BEFORE ANIMALS

The Period interpretation finds full geological confirmation for this. The lowest strata of rock exhibit, it is true, no fossilized plant remains. When these appear, they are from the first mixed with animal fossils. This could at first sight suggest a simultaneous origin. Yet a brief and simple consideration suffices to show that this cannot have been the case. For this there are two grounds.

Firstly, animals require oxygen for breathing, while they exhale carbon dioxide. Animals would have no possibility of life, if the atmosphere were too rich in carbon dioxide. Geology has shown that the earth's atmosphere at the beginning must have contained a very high percentage of carbon dioxide and was therefore unfit for animal life. Plants, on the other hand, breathe in carbon dioxide and breathe out oxygen, and could therefore have existed before the atmosphere had lost its abundance of carbon dioxide. So Professor Rendle Short writes: "Oxygen, both in the atmosphere or dissolved in water, is necessary for animal life, and it is normally only derived from the action of chlorophyll in plants." So there is "reason to believe that animal life was not possible until there was vegetation to supply oxygen to the atmosphere" (II, pp. 90, 94).

Secondly, plants are able to assimilate inorganic materials (minerals) and to change them into organic substances, into carbohydrates, i.e. sugar and starch. An animal on the other hand can live only from organic food, i.e. from that which is either living or has previously lived. Consequently the existence of animals presupposes the earlier existence of plants. Animals cannot come into being and live unless plants are already there. So the ancient Laurentian strata, which are today without fossils, must in their time have contained a purely plant world, the traces of which, however, have been obliterated for us; they could not be "fossilized" because the individual plants were too small and their tissues too soft. After this plant world in the Pre-Cambrian there follows immediately in the Cambrian the period of invertebrate animals.[1]

The Biblical record of the third day of creation does not mention only the first, small beginnings of plant life, but also its first, large, obvious forms, i.e. not only grass and plants, but also fruit-bearing trees (Gen. 1: 12).

[1] Cf. also Prof. Frhr. v. Huene (p. 30), Prof. Karl Heim (II, p. 46).

The same is true of its description of the fifth and sixth days of creation, dealing with aquatic animals (v. 21, "great sea monsters"), winged animals and land animals. Here too for both "days" there is a detailed enumeration of the works of creation for the time when the animal kingdom had already reached certain higher, easily recognizable forms, which then had appeared in their basic, full development, i.e. as fish with skeletons, reptiles and birds, and (on the sixth day) the mammals. This sequence also, as held by the Period theory, is fully confirmed by palaeontology.

The plant world existed before the animal world. This is doubly true; both when we consider their beginnings and also their attaining of the peak of their process of development. The first beginnings of the plant world existed, as proved by the nutritional process in plants and animals, before the first beginnings of the animal world (in the Pre-Cambrian or Cambrian). And so far as the first higher forms are concerned, the same sequence holds good.

That Scripture does not completely enumerate all these details but lays its emphasis only on the historical highlights, on the most important stages and on the most distinctive forms of life, is grounded in its very nature. For the Bible is not a textbook of geology and palaeontology, but, in its real aim and purpose, a document of spiritual revelation. It limits itself, therefore, in its statements about nature to the fundamental, necessary and most significant. Therefore its creation-narrative names only the respective stages of creation, when they are present in larger and more visible forms.[1] Everything else is regarded as only introduction and preparation and is therefore not the object of detailed Biblical teaching. This is the field and task of science. Indeed, wherever there is a development of life we can apply the general principle that God always first shows His organic creations, when they have reached a certain stage of development.

5. THE CREATION OF AQUATIC ANIMALS BEFORE LAND ANIMALS

For the Period theory this is also confirmed by palaeontology. In the oldest Palaeozoic, i.e. strata in the Cambrian, Ordovician, Silurian and Devonian, almost only aquatic animals are found. The Silurian shows virtually none, the Devonian very few remains of land animals.

Not before the Mesozoic, in the uppermost Triassic formations, do we find numerous animals exclusively inhabiting the land. The real development of this great division of animals, particularly of the mammals, does not take place until much later in the Tertiary. But because the creation-narrative does not mention the respective stages of creation until they are present in their larger and more visible forms, the creation of the land animals must be referred to after that of the fishes and birds. We find it in fact in the first part of the description of the sixth, the last day.

[1] Similarly Professor Rendle Short says: "Genesis deals only with the main divisions" (II, p. 94).

6. THE CREATION OF WINGED ANIMALS BEFORE LAND ANIMALS

Real "birds" appear, it is true, fairly late in the geological strata, even after the first mammals, namely in the Cretaceous and especially in the Tertiary periods. Nevertheless the first winged animals appear long before this, as far back as the Silurian, in the form of great, flying insects.[1] The Hebrew uses a word here (*'oph*) whose range of meaning goes far beyond the narrow idea of a bird. In Lev. 11: 20–23 and Deut. 14: 19 it is used for insects. Brown, Driver and Briggs: *Hebrew and English Lexicon* gives "flying creatures" as the basic meaning of *'oph*.[2] Professor Lange notes at this point in his Commentary, "We conceive of *'oph* as a general term for 'winged creatures,' which applies also to insects."

In fact, winged animals existed as early as the Carboniferous. Some of them were of astounding size, e.g. the flying Titanophasma Fayoli, up to twenty inches long. Indeed, the Carboniferous forests possessed the largest flying insect in the whole history of the earth, attaining a wing span of twenty-eight inches. Thus the creation of winged animals, according to the common testimony of Genesis and geology, actually took place before the creation of land animals and mammals.

7. MAN AS THE TERMINATION OF THE PROCESS

Geology agrees that man is the last to appear in creation. Since his appearance many species of animals have become extinct, whose bones have been found together with human remains. But no species has been brought to light which has been formed since the beginning of the development of the human race.

Thus the creation of man is a creative act of God based on the broadest foundation. The whole earthly creation "presents itself as an architectural structure, rising continually in steps. First come the plants, then the aquatic and winged animals, then the land animals, and on the highest step stands man." Man is thereby the last and highest member of the whole, and as such the goal of the whole earthly creation.

The general, material, vegetable and animal creation stretches from the beginning to Adam. From Adam the mental and spiritual building begins, which is at the same time a shadow of things to come, and reaches to Christ, the last Adam (I Cor. 15: 45–50). We grant that its development was shaken to its very foundations by sin. But in Christ, the last Adam, the eternal victory will nevertheless be won.

So the earthly creation is preparatory for the spiritual, and the spiritual creation is the goal and perfecting of the earthly. The spiritual building of

---

[1] Prof. Dr. E. Hoppe (p. 218).

[2] [The same is true of Koehler and Baumgartner: *Lexicon in Veteris Testamenti Libros*. (H.L.E.)]

the Church and the new creation of heaven and earth will infinitely surpass the material building of the whole creation up to now.

SUMMARY

If all this is taken together—and the above is only a very small selection from the colossal material at our disposal—then in the light of the most recent, twentieth-century research and according to the interpretation of the Period theory, the statement of Ampère, the great French mathematician, physicist and electrician (died 1836), is seen to be still correct today: "The sequence in which the organically formed beings appear is exactly the sequence of the six days of creation, as Genesis portrays it to us."

For faith this is a testimony to Divine inspiration. It sees in the whole, Biblical story of creation a God-given account about the origin of all things, which could only be, and was, made known to man by revelation.

Similarly Professor Rendle Short declares: "These considerations bring to light a perfectly amazing accordance between the creation-narrative and the discoveries of modern science. When we remember the wild guesses as to the ultimate nature and origin of the Earth that were current amongst other ancient people, the accuracy of Genesis stands out in solitary grandeur. Geology is a young science; the classification of the strata is not much older than a hundred years; we may be sure the author of the creation-narrative derived none of his information from fossil-hunting. Neither guesswork nor intuition taught him to arrange events in the correct order. This narrative bears the marks of a divine inspiration" (II, pp. 95, 96).

At the same time the account is objective and brief. Our eyes are kept fixed on essentials, and even these are summarized. No value is laid on scientific completeness, nor would this have been in place. Similarly, nothing is said about the manner and methods of the Divine creative activity. Therefore Genesis and geology, in their broad outlines, tell us the same story, but their mutual relationship is only very general.

The time-scales, also, of the Biblical and geological histories do not completely coincide. The geological record is not as extensive as the Biblical. Where life is concerned, the geological documents reach back only as far as the Pre-Cambrian. Biblically expressed, that means following the Period theory, that geology cannot take us further back than the third day of creation. Only at that point does it handle the same theme and parallel the creation-narrative. For the preceding, earliest developments—i.e. the formation of the world of fixed stars and the solar system, and for the "star-age" of the earth—only certain general conclusions can be drawn from physical and astronomical observations.

In addition the Biblical creation-narrative uses a simple, easily understood, popular form of expression, *viz.* the everyday language of the time, which we may call a prescientific form of expression. The use of modern scientific classifications and terminologies—which in any case are continually subject to change in the course of research—was excluded *a priori*. This would have been the most unsuitable form conceivable for an account intended for ordinary men over a period of more than three thousand years; it would also have been a sign of a great lack of pedagogic wisdom. But God is all-wise in all His methods and perfect in all His doings.

Thus the whole narrative is an expression of the Divine wisdom, greatness and simplicity, it is a God-given *summary* of the process of creation, which in its great, concise features permits us to look into God's mighty workshop. It is so brief that it has been compared with military communiqués in time of war, when everybody knows that behind the few, lapidary words there are many events, implied by them.

The Roman Catholic scholar Dr. Ludwig Zenitti said in 1946, "The Mosaic account does not reproduce the whole history of the development of the earth, which has come to light up to now, in all its details. But it gives, in the scientifically correct, temporal sequence, the most striking parts of it, which appear to be essential and which will always remain so, both for the simple man and also for the deeper thinker."[1]

Or, as Professor Karl Heim expresses it: "For the reader of the Bible the surprising thing is that the design of creation revealed to us by palaeontological research agrees in all essential characteristics with what Genesis says about the third, fifth and sixth days of creation."

From the standpoint of apologetics the astronomer Johannes Riem gives the following summary: "The cosmological views which are set down in the Mosaic creation-narrative can safely face the severest criticism."

Indeed, Dr. A. R. Riley triumphantly declares, "The first chapter of Genesis has weathered the storm. It comes out of the conflict with flying colours. Its every proposition is now verified by the best scientists of the twentieth century."

APPENDIX

THE "SECOND CREATION-NARRATIVE" (Gen. 2: 4–7)

The agreements we have pointed out in the sequence of the acts of creation between Genesis and geology is no way invalidated by the so-called "second creation-narrative," which is said to exhibit a different sequence from that of Gen. 1. This second account is not a "creation"-narrative at all, and makes no claim to be one. This is proved by the fact alone that the writer of Gen. 2: 4–7 does not say a single word about the origin of water and air, the formation of the sun, moon and stars or the creation of the animal world. Apart from man he mentions only

---

[1] In *Begegnung*, April, 1946, p. 29.

plants, herbs, mist and rain. The purpose of this whole passage is rather to act as a transition to the story of man. The author wants to come to the story of Paradise. He wants to tell how God planted this garden and made all necessary provision so that man might begin his course. His purpose is not to give a progressive account of creation, but a description of the beginnings of human history. And because man begins this history, he does not, as in Genesis 1, constitute the goal, but the starting-point of the narrative. Hence reference is made to the real creation story in chapter 1 only in what measure was necessary for the account of Paradise and the fall. Not the sequence of the Divine creative activity was to be made clear here, but the fact that everything was formed for the requirements of man. Or, as the Swiss theologian Professor F. Godet expresses it: "In chapter 1 man is described as the goal of the development of natural life; in chapter 2 as the principle of the development of history. Nature ascends to him; history starts from him."

CHAPTER XVI

DAYS OF TWENTY-FOUR HOURS OR PERIODS?

THE question as to whether the days of Genesis 1 were literal days of twenty-four hours or periods of time will be considered in two sections.

First we shall take the literal interpretation and, as we enumerate its main arguments, we shall mention some of the answers given by the Period theory. Then we shall give a few of the Period theory's points of view, which its advocates regard as their main arguments.

Here again we have tried to be neutral in our presentation of the case. By comparing the arguments on both sides—the weight of which will be estimated differently by the individual reader—the thoughtful reader is invited to form his own opinion.

I. The Six "Days" as Days of Twenty-four Hours

The advocates of the literal interpretation maintain:

(1) The Hebrew word *yom*, "day," can at times, it is true, signify a longer period (e.g. Isa. 61: 2; Joel 3: 18; cf. II Cor. 6: 2 etc.); but when it is used with a numeral in the Old Testament it always means a day of twenty-four hours (Gen. 7: 17, 24 etc.), and here in the creation-narrative it is right throughout connected with a numeral ("first," "second" . . . day).

The Period theory suggests that this argument is inadequate; for why should one not speak of the "first," "second" . . . "*period*"?

(2) The division of the days into an "evening" and "morning" is a proof that only days of twenty-four hours can be meant (cf. Dan. 8: 14).

The Period theory replies that since the word "day" is used so frequently in the Old Testament with the meaning of a "period," no reasonable objection can be raised to the use of the words "evening" and "morning" in this wider sense as well.

(3) If a day is taken to mean period, it is difficult to understand how we should interpret the "evening" periods.

Professor Franz Delitzsch replies that for the Period theory also the words "evening" and "morning" have a clear meaning. "With every commencement of the Divine creative activity it became morning; with every cessation of the Divine creative activity it became evening." Professor Lange writes similarly in his Commentary: "According to the analogy of the first day, the evening is the time of a specially chaotic, turbulent state of things, the morning the time of the corresponding new, beautiful festive formation of the world." Professor Rendle Short also writes with regard to the mention of "evening" and "morning," "It seems probable that it is a symbolical way of saying that there were periods of alternate activity and quiescence on the part of the Creator" (II, p. 99).

The Restitution theory objects that this interpretation is impossible, since the evenings precede the mornings in the creation-narrative. The answer is that in reality the days in Genesis 1 precede the morning. Otherwise it would not say, "And it *became* evening, and it *became* morning."[1] Evening and morning here cannot therefore be the beginnings of the two halves of the day, but rather their ends. This was already the case on the first day of creation, where we must understand: With the creation of light the first morning began, and then it "became" evening, and finally, when it had once again "become" morning, one day was complete. In other words here we do not have the reckoning of the Law and priesthood, by which the day began at sunset (cf. Psa. 55: 17; Neh. 13: 19; Lev. 23: 32; Dan. 8: 14), but a still earlier one, antedating the Law, *from morning to morning*. Just as the first day began with a morning through the command, "Let there be light," each succeeding day began with a morning and lasted through until the next morning, that is, until a new period of creation began. "The day began in the morning, then came the evening, and the morning which follows the evening is that which begins the second day and therefore terminates the first."[2]

(4) The appointment of the seventh day as the holy day (the Sabbath) would be meaningless, unless we conceive of the days as literal days.

It is precisely here that the Period theory emphasizes that the seventh day, which follows the work of the six days as God's "day of rest," must indubitably not be understood as a day of twenty-four hours, but as a day in God's sense. Moreover God's resting from His work of creation continues until the present. Since the creation of man no new kinds of living beings have been formed.

The significance of the seventh day as the day of rest is "surely this, that man was God's last and greatest creation, and no further completely new and different type of animal has since arisen on earth" (Short, II, p. 99).

It is further maintained that the statement in the Epistle to the Hebrews concerning the "sabbath rest" of God and the "sabbath rest" which remains for the people of God proves that this sabbath rest cannot imply a day of twenty-four hours (Heb. 4: 9, 10).

(5) In the law-giving on Sinai the Israelite week was fixed by reference to the week of creation. "Six days shalt thou labour . . .: but the seventh

---

[1] The correct literal translation of the Hebrew.

[2] E. F. Kevan on *Genesis* in *The New Bible Commentary*, p. 77. A number of first-class exegetes, going back to Augustine, can be quoted in favour of this view.

day is a sabbath unto the Lord thy God . . . for in six *days* the Lord made heaven and earth . . . and rested the seventh *day*" (Exod. 20: 9–11). Here the parallelism proves that, as in the case of the Israelite week, at least Moses and his Old Testament readers could have thought only of days of twenty-four hours during the week of creation.

The Period theory considers its own explanation completely adequate, *viz.* the human week of seven days had its origin in the Divine week of seven epochs of creation.

(6) The writer of the Biblical account sees God specially glorified by the fact that He in each case used only one literal day of twenty-four hours for such mighty works. So easily does the Almighty create!

In reply to this the Period theory notes that this conclusion has often been drawn in popular thought but that there is no suggestion in Scripture itself that God was specially glorified by the speed of His creative activity. Psalm 33: 9 testifies only that it was God's royal and almighty *word* through which the world was called into existence. This verse says nothing about the time involved. In addition, attention is drawn to the fact that no event in the Bible is dated from the creation itself.

In any case it would be foolish to say that a period interpretation of the six days' work was in conflict with the conception and the dignity of a personal Creator-God. For though God could have created the world in a state of perfection in an instant, it nevertheless diminishes neither His wisdom nor His power, if He resolved not to do this. On the contrary, a gradual, upward direction of the course of creation is just as worthy of the glory of an almighty Creator as a single act, completed in a moment.

Even a creation in six literal days would not have been an act of God, finished in a moment without involving some use of time, however incomparably shorter this would have been than that assumed by the Period theory. So the fact that Scripture speaks of a six days' work is of itself sufficient proof that God did in fact act progressively in the formation of the world. It was this last fact that caused the scientist J. Reinke (Professor of Botany in Kiel) to say that the Biblical doctrine of creation is "the most important advance in human knowledge, atheism a reversion to pre-Mosaic barbarism."

God has in any case obviously placed the principle of development in creation. Otherwise we should have to deny the development of the hen from the egg! All individual living things come into being by progressing from lower to higher forms, in order finally to reach a fixed, highest level. Similarly, with the whole world of life in its different forms, there can have been, under Divine control, through a series of ever advancing, Divine, creative acts, each marking a new initiative, an organic, purposeful progression from lower levels to higher ones, conforming to a general law.

(7) The Period theory finds the division of the work of creation into six day-periods hard to explain.

This objection should not be completely ignored. We give an attempted answer, suggested by Professor E. Hoppe, though not all defenders of the Period theory would agree with all its details. Though it leaves many questions unanswered, it is certainly worthy of attention. It fits in with both ways of explaining the Mosaic narrative, the cosmogonic as well as the purely terrestrial, *i.e.* whether the work of the fourth day is to be interpreted astronomically or whether it concerns only the atmosphere of the earth.

Professor Hoppe wrote: "The first period covers the whole development of the cosmos out of matter through vibrations in the light-ether. The second period covers the development of the earth from a ball of gas into a solid earth with an atmosphere. This again may be looked upon as a scientifically demarcated period. The third epoch then covers the whole Pre-Cambrian, Azoic period, as it is geologically called, which closes with the appearance of plant life. The fourth day's work covers the period in which, if we follow the nebular hypothesis, the sun, after the other planets had become detached from it, contracted to form a sphere of its present size. Once again this is a scientifically marked period. Finally the fifth and sixth days divide the geological formations, stretching from the Cambrian to the Pleistocene into two, the line of demarcation being approximately in the Mesozoic with the appearance of the first marsupials. Naturally these periods are not imagined as being of the same duration; they are only periods of time each with a definite content. If one interprets the matter so, the account is not scientific teaching, but yet so reasonable, that one can fully agree with it, not only today but surely also at any time" (pp. 215, 216).

Not all advocates of the Period theory would follow such an exact division. It shows, however, that it is possible also from a scientific viewpoint seriously to look for an explanation why the creation-story has been divided into six periods, and why the particular demarcation was given them.

Finally it should be noted that as a result of geological discovery the explanation of the days of creation as literal days of twenty-four hours can be maintained only if linked with the Restitution theory of the creation-narrative. The "flood theory," which tried to explain all these discoveries about the history of the earth as results of the flood is impossible (see below).

These geological developments, however, which only folly and ignorance seek to deny, must have taken place at some time, if not during the six days then before them, *i.e.* between verses 1 and 2 of Genesis 1. In that case the six days' work can have been only a "restoration" of the earth; thus the literal interpretation of the days of creation stands or falls with the acceptance of the Restitution theory. Arguments for and against this will be found in chapter 16.

II. The Impossibility of the Flood Theory

The attempt to interpret the geological facts as results of the flood is impossible. This is shown by three main considerations.

(1) From the point of view of geology and palaeontology it is impossible that a single flood lasting a few weeks or months could have produced all the deposits that have been discovered. The study of fossilized plants and animals as well as the examination of the rock strata themselves have proved beyond all doubt that the earth must have gone through many, immensely long periods of development, until the effects of the elements, of water, air and fire gave it its present shape. Only folly and ignorance can deny these researches *a priori*.

From among the almost innumerable proofs we shall mention only the following. In his book *The Christian View of Science and Scripture* Dr. Ramm writes (p. 127 f.), "It takes a hundred feet of loose vegetable matter to make one foot of coal . . . In the Yellowstone Park (U.S.A.) are two thousand feet of exposed strata which reveal eighteen successive forests wiped out by lava. The individual forests had to mature, and then be covered with lava. Before another forest could appear the lava would have to be weathered to form soil for trees to grow in. The amount of time involved is far more than the few thousand years flood geologists are able to allow."

(2) The flood theory is further refuted by the fact that fossilized human remains have never been found among the fossilized plants and animals. Therefore that catastrophe (or, these catastrophes) must have taken place long before the history of the human race began.

(3) Above all, if a single flood had inundated and swept everything away, the fossilized plant and animal remains would lie in complete confusion, which would have been only slightly mitigated by gravity. The fact is, however, that they always exhibit an exactly arranged, *steady gradation* in their organization, when compared with the order of the strata.

In the oldest period of animal life, in the Cambrian, the invertebrates occupy the foreground. In the next period, the Silurian, the vertebrates appear in their lowest forms, *viz.* the first fishes. Then, in the Devonian, the fishes become more numerous. In the Carboniferous which follows the first amphibious animals appear. In the Triassic we find the still more highly organized reptiles, which reach a tremendous development in the saurians of the Jurassic. In the following periods, especially in the Cainozoic, the two highest classes of vertebrates become prominent, *viz.* mammals and birds. Finally man appears as the ruler of the earth.

Does not all this obviously show a gradually ascending perfecting of organization within the successive strata? The lowest and oldest layers of the earth contain simple beings. The following ones contain, in an in-

creasing degree, ever more manifold and more complex forms. Thus the
nearer we approach the present the more manifold and perfect does the
living world become. Finally there appear the most complex creatures,
which are seen as the goal and result of the earlier periods. To explain this
whole, systematically constructed, upward progression in the geological
strata is completely beyond the capacity of the flood theory.

III. THE SIX "DAYS" AS PERIODS

The following arguments are generally regarded as the main grounds in
favour of the Period theory.

I. THE FREQUENT WIDER USE OF "DAY" IN THE BIBLE

We should ask ourselves whether we have in fact interpreted the Biblical
text correctly. It should be obvious that in many passages, both in the Old
and New Testament, the word "day" means a period. Thus in the Church-
age we live in the "day of salvation," which from the coming of Christ
until now has lasted nearly two thousand years (II Cor. 6: 2). The prophets
speak of the "Day of the Lord," meaning by this the whole of the last
times, often including the millenium (Joel 2: 1, 2; 3: 14; Ezek. 13: 5 etc.).[1]
Indeed the Second Epistle of Peter speaks of the "day of eternity" (II Pet.
3: 18, R.V.mg.).

2. DIVINE MEASURES OF TIME FOR DIVINE ACTIVITY

We should also ask ourselves whether the days of creation were not
"days of God." Should they not therefore be measured by Divine measures? For with God purely human measures of time are no longer valid.
For Him "one day is a thousand years and a thousand years as one day"
(II Pet. 3: 8; Psa. 90: 4).

3. "DAYS" ARE SPOKEN OF BEFORE THE FORMATION OF THE SUN

Many advocates of the Period theory have not hesitated to ask how one
can suggest that the Biblical writer—from a purely human and logical
point of view, quite apart from inspiration—was so inane as to speak of
literal days (from the first to the third day) for the time *before* the sun was
made to rule the day and the night for the earth on the fourth day. For
not until the sun had been created or its light had penetrated through the
earth's atmosphere, once this had become thinner and correspondingly
less opaque, could one speak of purely literal solar days of twenty-four
hours. Thus Professor Dennert writes, "To me it seems impossible to
accept that such a clear thinker, as the writer of Genesis obviously was,
would not have noticed that he could not speak of a day in our sense
before the sun was there, which, even in the thought of the ancients, rules
the day" (IV, p. 25). Similarly Professor H. L. Strack declares (p. 8), "This

---

[1] Cf. E. Sauer. *From Eternity to Eternity*, pp. 74–77.

shows that the interpretation as earthly days (of twenty-four hours) is not only not necessary, but also impossible." We also find Professor Otto Zöckler calling the conception of the days in Genesis 1 as days of twenty-four hours an "exegetical impossibility" (p. 526).

This argument can, however, be answered by pointing out that according to Job 38: 4–7 the world of suns and stars had already been created before the foundation of the earth, so that the light of the first day was already sunlight, and that the work of the fourth day did not consist in the actual creation of the heavenly bodies, but in their becoming visible on earth through the clearing and thinning of the earth's atmosphere. Then morning and evening, day and night, could have existed literally before the fourth day of creation. It was only that the heavenly bodies would not previously have been clearly recognizable on earth because of the layer of cloud that covered it.

4. THE HARMONY BETWEEN THE SEQUENCE IN GENESIS I AND THAT OF THE GEOLOGICAL STRATA

The Period theory sees in the striking harmony we have already sketched in chapter 14 a decisive argument in its favour. The geological records and the Biblical creation-narrative simply tell the same story and run parallel to one another. This finds a further confirmation in the fact, shown by geology, that the Tertiary passes over without any radical break to the earth as it now is, i.e. into the Quaternary, the Glacial and Post-glacial periods, and so into the time of the human race. All this taken as a whole shows the harmony between Genesis and geology and proves the correctness of the interpretation of the days as periods and argues against the literal interpretation of the days of creation as days of twenty-four hours. So we find Professor Rendle Short saying: "The astonishing coincidence of the scientific order and of the Biblical order of creation seems to indicate that the Biblical days correspond to periods of geological time" (II, p. 99).

5. THE BIBLE IS NEUTRAL IN SCIENTIFIC DETAIL

The words of the creation-narrative, "Let the earth put forth grass, herb . . . fruit tree . . . after its kind . . . God created the great sea-monsters . . . after their kinds . . ., every winged fowl after its kind . . ., the beast of the earth after its kind" (vv. 11, 21, 25), have offered the advocates of the literal interpretation of the days proof for the fixity of species and a counter-proof against the Period theory. This has been answered by the following argument. The words "let the earth bring forth" apparently leave the question of *how* these living creatures were formed completely open. They rather give expression solely to the fact that all living creatures have come into being by the power of the Divine word. And so the Biblical account leaves the scientist completely free to study just how they came into existence, provided he acknowledges the Creator. It is completely compatible with the statements of the Bible to say that, when God created the various forms of life, He placed in them the ability to develop continuously and by the transformation of simpler forms to ascend to ever higher ones, but "each after its kind." To draw scientific conclusions about fixity of species from this expression is surely very rash. The same expression is used in Lev. 11: 14, 15, 19, 22, 29, where it quite obviously means simply "in all their varieties." Among other things the Israelites were not to eat the following birds: the eagle, the gier eagle . . . the falcon "after its kind," i.e. in all their varieties. Concerning a possible fixity of species—there are 790,000 now extant,[1] to say nothing of the unnumbered, extinct ones—absolutely nothing is said in this expression, neither affirming or denying it. The text is completely neutral.

We do not hesitate to reject the theory of evolution in the form put forward by its founder, Charles Darwin (1809–1882); this suggests that the whole course of nature has been governed without a goal by "chance," and that the individual species have all arisen by natural selection during the struggle for existence. What really matters is that we should believe in a *Divine direction and control* of the whole history of nature.

Beyond doubt there is a "struggle for existence" in nature, in which the weaker perishes and the stronger survives. There is also an adjustment of species to the environments they find themselves in. Similarly there may be a certain inheritance of acquired characters, so that in one sense one can speak of a *partial* development and of a transition from lower to higher forms of life. It is incontestable and attested by the fossils of the geological strata that plant and animal life in general have risen to continually new and higher forms.

It should be equally evident that the struggle for existence does not exist in nature to the extent and with the significance that Darwin gave it. It is mainly a *negative* principle of "weeding out," in which part, indeed much of the weaker perishes, but not all, so that the stronger win the victory and go ahead. But it is in no sense the great, positive factor in nature, continually producing new forms. Nor is it the sovereign, decisive principle in the whole of natural life. Not a few of the weak and even weakest forms found in the oldest Cambrian formations have not been exterminated, but are still living almost unchanged today. On the other hand, excellently adapted, strong, giant forms, e.g. the saurians of the Jurassic and Triassic, despite their superiority and strength, have not survived but have become extinct.

Since many highly developed bodily organs were already present in the earliest stages of life, they cannot, therefore, be regarded as the outcome of any form of inheritance, development or "evolution." "It is very

[1] [Some would place this number considerably higher. It is impossible to establish the number of species exactly. See estimate on p. 63. (H.L.E.)]

remarkable that the earliest vertebrates known, the Ostracoderms of the Ordovician and the fish of the Silurian, had eyes, which as far as we can judge from their fossil remains were like those of living fish, and in all essentials like those of mammals. There is nothing to show that these eyes were evolved from something simpler; they burst upon the scene for the first time already perfect. Some of the oldest fossils in the world, such as Olenellus, a trilobite from the Lower Cambrian, had faceted eyes like those of modern insects or crustaceans. In some trilobites one can even count the facets" (Short, II, p. 70, 71).[1]

It should be noted further that in all the above mentioned inheritances, developments and transitions from lower to higher forms within the boundaries of the respective families, which make transitions from lower to higher forms possible, we are concerned with forces which operate within one and the same family, genus or order.

There is a conspicuous lack of fossil material to explain how new classes and orders came into being. In spite of the greatest efforts and the most careful studies by evolutionary scientists, it has been impossible up till now to prove the existence of the "missing links."

Normally, in the geological strata the main species and genera appear suddenly in their basic forms without any recognizable links, direct, gradual or complete, with previously existing forms, i.e. there is not the least indication of their origin and pedigree. The fossil evidence in geology thus points to a number of fresh starts, i.e. each time a new order or family, equipped with new organs, suddenly appears.

Very many scientists try to explain this by mutations, which can in fact be observed in nature today. But it must not be overlooked that—though such a mutation can be the starting-point for higher forms of life—in most cases it leads to degeneration; an upward development by mutation is exceptional.

[1] The extreme conclusions about the inheritance of acquired characters which many advocates of the theory of evolution have been willing to accept may be shown by an example from Darwin. Darwin did not, as did later Haeckel, teach the descent of man from the apes, but from some unspecified animal. In this connexion he discussed the question how the tails of these pre-men and of the anthropoid apes gradually disappeared. He suggested that their ancestors had had long tails. As they often sat on them they became rough and callous and so were rubbed away. Since it is claimed that mutilations are sometimes inherited, he considered it not improbable that the tail had gradually shrunk. Darwin's actual words are: "As far as we can judge, the tail in the case of man and the anthropoid apes disappeared, because its lower part over a long period of time was damaged by rubbing, while its upper part, which lies embedded in the skin, shrank to suit the upright or half-upright position" (*The Origin of Man*). Our comment is that plenty of faith is needed by the person who is going to believe this. [In fact the possibility of inheriting acquired characters is regarded with the utmost suspicion by all biologists, except the neo-Lamarkians, for whom it is an article of faith—cf. *Chambers's Encyclopaedia* (1950), Article: Acquired Characters. (H.L.E.)]

He who believes in the living God and accepts the Period interpretation, finds this explanation of at least equal value, and probably preferable, *viz.* that at such turning-points in natural history God has repeatedly caused fresh starts, i.e. He has made a new beginning of living forms which had not previously existed, *through special, individual, Divine creative acts.*

The Biblical creation-narrative itself does not give us any details that would help us to solve these questions. It is clear that science cannot speak of a certain proof that all forms of life have evolved in an unbroken chain from a common original cell. This may be the natural philosophical faith of many scientists, but it is not an unequivocally demonstrated, indubitable scientific result. Even if it were, according to the view of many advocates of the Period theory, it would not even then necessarily be in irreconcilable contradiction to the Biblical creation-narrative, as this is completely silent concerning such questions of detail, but reports only the fact that everything was created by God through His word, but makes no statement about "how" God did this.

In any case, however, the fundamental lack of sense in Darwinism is revealed by its assertion that everything was and is still controlled by chance. As though a watch had ever come into existence without having been designed by the intelligence of a watch-maker, a cathedral by the purposeless throwing together of stones, a symphony, like the Ninth of Beethoven, by the accidental coincidence of ink-blots!

Sir Arthur Keith, one of the most prominent of recent British anatomists, was universally regarded as an agnostic, i.e. one who holds that no final answer to the problems of epistemology and ontology is possible, once went so far as to declare, "I would as easily believe the doctrine of the Trinity as one which maintains that living, developing protoplasm, by mere throws of chance, brought the human eye into existence."[1]

Finally, it should be noted that Darwin himself, despite his theory—in contrast to very many of his followers—was not an atheist but a Deist. This is proved by statements like: "Even at the time of my greatest wavering I was never an atheist in the sense that I denied the existence of a God." "The question of whether a Creator of the world exists has been answered in the affirmative by the greatest minds that have lived." "I accept that probably all organic beings that have ever lived upon this earth have been descended from some original form, which first received its life breathed in by the Creator." This is Deism, i.e. a belief in a Creator-God, who does not intervene in nature and who does not reveal Himself.

6. THE CHRONOLOGY OF GEOLOGY

The millions of years of geology must be accepted with the greatest reserve. Von Huene estimates 1,900 million years for the pre-Cambrian strata without fossils (the Azoic). So far as the age of the earth is concerned

[1] Quoted by Short, II, pp. 69, 70.

the estimates vary between three and five thousand million years.

The calculations might well be correct, if one could prove the uniformity of development at every period. The difficulty and inadequacy in all these calculations come from the obvious reason that conclusions have to be drawn for very long periods from observations made over a very short time. This applies also to the data gained from the disintegration of uranium into uranium-lead, although these calculations can claim a greater reliability than earlier methods.

Professor Rendle Short has put it well, "We are not much impressed by estimates drawn from the thickness of stalagmite or river-gravel that may overlie human remains, because these estimates can only be based on the rate of deposit at the present day, whereas in the past the rate was probably much greater. In the post-glacial period rivers were enormous, and gravels would accumulate a hundred times as fast as they do now. In some petrifying wells, calcareous deposits grow at an extraordinary rate, and this may have happened in some caves in the past."[1]

In spite of all these reservations, however, the old belief that the earth is about 6,000 years old is completely untenable. To form only a thin layer of one inch of coal we would need a beech-forest a hundred years old. In places, according to Professor Bettex, the Coal Measures are over forty feet in thickness. More than that, a number of seams of coal often lie one on top of another. In addition the period of the Coal Measures is only one of the numerous geological periods. How immensely long then must have been the complete process of formation of the whole surface of the earth. This remains in any case true, even if we cannot be sure of the details with exactness.

7. THE AGE OF THE EARTH AND THE HISTORY OF SALVATION

Finally, the following objections have been raised. How could there have been such long periods of creation, seeing that the present condition of the earth has lasted only a few thousand years? If it were so, the whole, revealed history of salvation in the Bible would appear very small and disproportionately short in comparison. Modern geologists are in essential agreement in estimating the age of the earth at not less than about 2,850 million years, which includes the "star-age" of the earth. If we, following the palaeontologist Professor von Huene, compare this period of time with the twenty-four hours of a day, then it can easily be calculated that the whole "long" stretch of world history we know in some detail, i.e. from 400 B.C. to the present day, bears the same relationship to the whole history of the earth as the thirteenth part of a second to a twenty-four hour day. This means that, if we could go back to 400 B.C., we should be standing a thirteenth of a second before midnight. It is true that the geological data are to be accepted only with the greatest reserve, but in any

[1] Prof. A. Rendle Short, *The Bible and Modern Research*, pp. 54, 55.

case we are concerned here with vast spaces of time, compared with which the long history of mankind and of salvation is only a minute fraction.

Upholders of the Period theory answer this more or less as follows. We grant that the time between the creation of man and the perfecting of the world is brief, lasting only a few millennia. But it should be remembered that this, too, is only a beginning, a time of development. It is a period in which certain restraints which have entered creation through sin have to be overcome. It may therefore be called the completion of the period of creation. The real, permanent condition does not begin until the new creation and transfiguration of heaven and earth, which will then last for eternity. In the face of eternity, however, the limited millions of years of creation and redemption will shrivel up into insignificance. One must keep eternity in view. It is only in this way that one can find the right measuring-rod to interpret these relationships.[1]

APPENDIX

How the Writers of the Bible understood their Writings

We do not question the *possibility* that the sacred writers themselves regarded the days of creation as literal days of twenty-four hours. We are far from attributing to them scientific knowledge beyond the limits of their time and culture. But here we are not concerned with the world-picture held by the sacred writers, and not even with their personal interpretation of the text, but with the sacred text itself. More than once the God-intended meaning of the inspired word went far beyond the understanding of the inspired writer. However much the human personality with its abilities, experience and conscious, intellectual effort (cf. Luke 1: 1-3) was brought into service—this is where the organic inspiration of the Bible differs from a magical, spiritistic dictation—the Spirit of God, nevertheless, did at times give the instruments of his inspiration words which, at least partially, in their final and deepest meaning remained hidden from them. Thus they prophesied much of future events without knowing when they would be fulfilled, and as they were "searching what time or what manner of time the Spirit of Christ which was in them did point unto" it was even "revealed" unto them in a special way that they did not need to know these things; for they did this service "not unto themselves," but for the generations of a coming age (I Pet. 1: 10-12). We also are repeatedly surprised to see how the New Testament reveals a much deeper meaning in certain Old Testament passages than was to be expected from the wording and context of the text in question. Everything is both historically conditioned and yet permeated by eternity, both human and Divine, both temporal and super-temporal.[2]

The Bible is not a text-book of science and consequently has but little interest in shaping and moulding the scientific world-picture of its readers, or even of its own writers. It is the Book of God for our *soul* and its purpose is to tell us what we need to know for the salvation of our *soul*. Therefore it may well be that the

[1] Cf. Prof. Dr. F. W. Schulz, (p. 167).
[2] Compare Matt. 2: 15 with Hos. 11: 1 or Matt. 2: 17, 18 with Jer. 31: 15.

sacred writers shared the conceptions of their time and in this sense will not have fully understood the sacred text. But the text itself was given by God and was so moulded by the Spirit of God that it did not itself share in the errors of the time.

"How could the writer possibly have arrived at the correct order," asks Professor Rendle Short, "if he was not gifted with a divine revelation? Where else in ancient literature, or in non-Christian literature written before the birth of geology as a science, is such a successful delineation of the order of creation to be found?" (II, p. 100).

Professor Karl Heim gives much the same explanation of the Biblical account of creation. "Probably the author of this simple story of creation thought of normal days. But the wonderful thing in this account, which when we read it always suggests the thought that *an invisible hand was guiding the pen of the narrator*, is the fact that in the Biblical description of the six days' work the great stages in the development of creation are described *in the same sequence* in which, according to palaeontology, they took place in the course of the tremendous space of fifteen hundred million years. . . . At a time when our present biological knowledge was lacking and our astronomical measures of time were unknown, the Biblical story of the six days of creation, with a prophetic, backward look, unveiled the design of creation in its whole, architectural greatness, as in a great vision, with such clarity from its foundation up to the crowning conclusion in the creation of man, that the palaeontological research of today can have the task only of building the monumental structure in detail, the plan of which in its basic features here appears before our eyes, which the rich material of modern discovery enables to complete in all its details" (II, pp. 48, 95).

CHAPTER XVII

THE RESTITUTION THEORY

I. The Six Days' Work as a Restoration of the Earth

"In the beginning God created the heaven and the earth." Through the creative word of the perfect, living, all-loving and all-blessed God a perfect world, full of life and light, full of joy and bliss, was called into existence. "But the incomprehensible happened. A mighty prince of light . . . became dark. His kingdom and sphere became night, and out of this night resounded the first 'No,' hurled into the face of God from whom all true affirmation comes. True, countless angels and the mighty host of heaven remained in the boundless sea of the Divine 'Yes'; yet Satan, now become the great dragon, led the legions of heavenly spirits, who were subject to him, astray, and turned the earth, once so light, into a dark chaos waste and void." So writes the well-known apologist Professor F. Bettex (II, p. 6).

Typical of the views of General von Viehbahn, a well-known German evangelist, are the following quotations from shorter writings. "The earth was waste, empty and dark. This was the result of Satan's rebellion. God's first step in His battle against Satan was, 'Let there be light!' . . . However it may be, a great catastrophe, which lay between the first and second verses of the Bible, had changed the first creation into chaos. The earth, which had emerged without a blemish out of the hand of God, became, as the result of Satan's rebellion, a desert. . . . A new creation was necessary before man, created in the image of God, was appointed to be ruler upon the earth. After this had taken place 'God saw everything that He had made, and, behold, it was very good.'"

Dr. von Huene, Professor of Palaeontology in the University of Tübingen, adopts the same position, saying "when God created heaven and earth in the beginning, everything took place without disturbance in harmony and holiness, and God committed this earth to Satan to administer. Through Satan's rebellion he, and also his whole kingdom, came under God's judgment. Satan wanted to be like God. Envy and pride were his sins . . . in the gap between verses 1 and 2 of Genesis 1 belongs the fall of Satan with all the powers that followed him" (pp. 60, 62).

These are the basic ideas of the Restitution theory of the creation-narrative. The Roman Catholic scholar Ämilian Schöpfer (formerly Professor in the Collegium Romanum in Rome) has objected to it saying that it has no support "either in the text of the creation-narrative or anywhere else in revelation." Richard Krämer attacks it as "pious trifling," as a "chaos of sensational assertions" which played a rôle already in the Gnostic and Manichean systems and which always revive in circles "in which mysteriousness makes an impression" (pp. 33, 34).

The injustice of the latter judgment may be seen merely by looking at the names of the advocates of the theory. In addition the problem is far too great and the defenders of this interpretation too significant for one, even if he does not hold it oneself, simply to dispose of this view with such a disdainful dictum.[1] Even if its supporters differ from one another to some extent in details, their common testimony in the question as a whole is still of noteworthy significance.

In our discussion we shall first of all mention the most important arguments in favour of the theory, and these will be followed by the chief objections. Once again, by a careful comparison of arguments and objections, the reader is invited to form his own judgment.

1. THE CREATION OF THE WORLD AND THE REVELATION OF GOD IN NATURE

The advocates of the Restitution theory ask the following questions. Is not all unconditioned creation always a revelation? Must not therefore the creation of the world, in its innermost nature, have been from the first a setting forth of the glory of the Creator-God? Is it not completely unthinkable that a dark, waste and empty world should ever have proceeded immediately from the creative hand of the God of light, order and fullness of life? A God who does not think chaotically will surely not create anything chaotic. Hence a chaos cannot have existed before the cosmos by Divine direction.

2. THE LINGUISTIC COMBINATION "TOHU-WA-BOHU"

The Restitution theory emphasizes that this combination of words occurs only in two other Old Testament passages, and in both of them it means a destruction which is the result of a divine judgment. Thus Isaiah, after a description of the terrible consequence of the fall of Edom in the day of vengeance, says, "And He (God) shall stretch over it the line of *tohu* (confusion) and the plummet of *bohu* (chaos, R.S.V.)" (Isa. 34: 11). We are to understand this as meaning that God will use the same care in making the destruction of Edom complete as the architect does in using measuring-line and plumb-line to build a house. The second passage is still more decisive. There Jeremiah describes the desolation of Judah and Jerusalem after their fall, and compares it, according to the explanation of the Restitution theory, with the pre-Adamic destruction. He says, "I beheld the earth, and lo, it was *tohu-wa-bohu* (waste and void): and the heavens,

---

[1] The reader is referred to the list of significant representatives of the Restitution theory amongst scientists, theologians and philosophers past and present on page 195.

and they had no light. . . . I beheld, and, lo, there was no man, and all the birds of the heavens were fled. I beheld, and, lo, the fruitful field was a wilderness, and all the cities thereof were broken down at the presence of the Lord, and before His fierce anger" (Jer. 4: 23-26). These are the only two passages in Scripture in which—apart from Genesis 1: 2—the combination *tohu-wa-bohu* is found, and in both cases it has the passive meaning of being made desolate and empty. In this the Restitution theory sees strong grounds for justifying the acceptance of the same passive meaning as playing at least a rôle in the third passage.

Elsewhere Isaiah speaks of the destruction of the last days and says, "The city of *tohu* is broken down" (Isa. 24: 10), an expression which should be translated as "the desolated city" (R.V. the city of confusion, R.V.mg. the city of wasteness.)

3. THE STATEMENT OF ISAIAH 45: 18

In addition the Bible says, "For thus saith the Lord that created the heavens; . . . that formed the earth, and made it; He established it, He created it not a waste (*tohu*), He formed it to be inhabited."

4. THE EARTH BECAME, NOT WAS "TOHU-WA-BOHU"

Advocates of the Restitution theory point out that the Hebrew verb *hayah* often has the meaning "to become," e.g. Psa. 118: 22, "The stone which the builders rejected is become the head of the corner." The first half of the next verse could be translated, "This has come into being (lit. become) from the Lord," cf. R.V.mg.

5. THE USE OF THE VERBS "CREATE" AND "MAKE" IN GENESIS I

The Restitution theory points out that, apart from verse 1, the Hebrew verb *bara*, "create," is found only twice in the creation-narrative, at the "creation" of animal (v. 21) and human (v. 26, 27) life. Otherwise the account always uses the word "make" (*'asah*), which means to form and shape out of already existing material (cf. footnote on p. 208). This is held also to be a proof that the first chapter of the Bible is not concerned with the first, original creation, but with the new shaping of the earth after its destruction.

6. THE ANGELIC REJOICING AT THE CREATION

It has been asked how it would have been conceivable, that the hosts of heaven would have rejoiced at the foundation of the earthly world and would have shouted for joy, full of worship and admiration for God's creative glory, if this creation had at the first been formless and empty, desolate and chaotic. After all it is God Himself who bears witness to these songs of angelic joy at the very laying of the foundation stone, at the very beginning of the earthly creation, when He puts the question to man in the book of Job, "Where wast thou when I laid the foundations of the earth. . . . Who determined the measures thereof . . .? Or who stretched the line upon it? . . . Or who laid the corner stone thereof; when the morning stars sang together, and all the sons of God (*i.e.* the angels) shouted for joy?" (Job 38: 4–7).

7. THE CREATION OF HEAVEN AND EARTH IS NOT INCLUDED IN THE SIX DAYS

From the standpoint of the Restitution theory, and from it alone—so it is claimed—it is clear why the Biblical account, which is surely not influenced by chance or accident, does not include the creation of heaven and earth among the works of the six days, but places it before them, although it is the foundation of all that follows and is hence really the most important thing of all. If, on the other hand, the second verse stood "in as close a connexion with the first as is usually assumed, i.e. if it described the condition in which God created earth and heaven at the first, then this first work would of necessity have to be reckoned among the six days of creation. No adequate reason can be given why it alone should form an exception. On the other hand our standpoint explains this easily and satisfactorily," says Dean Keerl, one of the chief defenders of the Restitution theory.

The Period theory claims that this argument has no great weight. For the first verse "In the beginning God created the heaven and the earth" is merely the heading of the whole, or a statement about the creation of the basic materials, whereas the purpose of the Biblical account of the six days is to show what God did with the earth, or how He developed the whole cosmos.

II. OBJECTIONS AND QUESTIONS

I. THE GENERAL IMPRESSION CREATED BY THE BIBLICAL ACCOUNT

The main objection raised against the Restitution view is that there is nothing in the creation-narrative that suggests a demonic, hostile power, and the consequences it had for the world of nature. It gives every un-biassed reader rather the impression that its purpose is simply to describe the unbroken development of the work of creation, and nothing more. That the earth as created by God "became" waste and void is not stated, but only that, in its original condition, it "was" waste and void, i.e. without form or content, when the six days' work began with the creation of light.

2. THE BREVITY OF GENESIS I: I

Many readers of the Bible find it most improbable that the original creation, called into existence as the foundation of all that followed, and culminating in a world of the most wonderful beauty, should be mentioned only in a single, very short sentence (verse 1) and then dismissed from the account, while so many verses, viz. thirty-two, should then be devoted to a work which was only a reconstruction of this original creation, and therefore in no sense the essential thing (ch. 1: 2 to 2: 3).

3. THE SILENCE OF THE BIBLE

Many expositors find it hard to accept the suggestion that the Bible could be silent about such a primeval catastrophe and such a long interval of time between verses 1 and 2 of the Genesis account. Some have tried to answer this objection by referring to the law of "prophetic perspective," by which two widely separated events, like two mountain peaks, may be seen together, without mention of the long interval—as it were, the "valley" between the mountains—between them, e.g. the first and second Advent of Jesus without mention of the centuries-long period of the Church. Similarly, it is claimed, in this case also the original creation of the earth and its later restoration are seen together, without any mention being made of the long geological periods in between. It is highly questionable, however, whether these two examples can be regarded as in any way parallel. For while, according to numerous prophecies in the New Testament, a second Advent of Jesus is unequivocally taught, there is no passage in Holy Scripture which indubitably teaches a restoration of the earth after an original destruction. So we may question the adequacy of this whole comparison. We should surely first know with certainty from other statements of the Bible that such a second "peak" exists here, before we speak of an intervening period and apply the law of prophetic perspective to Genesis 1: 1, 2.

4. THE BASIC MEANING OF "TOHU" AND "BOHU"

Those who query the correctness of the Restitution theory stress that although these words occasionally have a passive meaning in the sense of being made waste or empty, their basic meaning in most passages is simply "formlessness," "desert" and "emptiness," e.g. Job 26: 7, "He stretcheth out the north over empty space (*tohu*);" Isa. 59: 4, "They trust in vanity (emptiness, *tohu*) and speak lies;" Isa. 40: 17, "All the nations are as nothing (*tohu*) before Him."

It is very risky to base such an important interpretation of Scripture on an exceptional and rare use of words, whose normal meaning is quite different. It is surely more advisable to interpret the words *tohu* and *bohu* in their general and usual sense of "formlessness," "emptiness," i.e. as a simple description of the original form of the earth at the beginning of creation, as the characterization of the lack of content and form of the mass before the beginning of the Divine, creative impulses. It would then be much more natural to see in verse 1 the creation of primeval matter and in the work of the six days its shaping, under the direction of the Divine, creative will, into an earthly cosmos, in which man could finally appear and fulfil his task.

Dr. B. Ramm says, "A marble block and a crumbled statue are both formless. The former is in a state which awaits a form and from that formlessness emerges the image. When God made the earth He made it like a marble block out of which He would bring the beautiful world" (p. 140). The initial state of the universe was the undeveloped, material basis, so created by God, which contained in itself all the capacities and possibilities for light and life. Or, as Professor Lange has expressed it, "The first word (*tohu*) denotes the lack of form, the second word (*bohu*) the lack of content. The earth was at first unfinished in its order and empty of life."

5. THE BASIC MEANING OF THE HEBREW "HAYAH"

Advocates of the Period theory question the meaning given to the Hebrew word *hayah* in Genesis 1: 2. They agree that it can occasionally have the meaning "became," i.e. here, "The earth 'became' waste and void."[1] But this rarely occurs as in the already quoted words from Psalm 118: 22, see p. 232. Its real meaning is simply "was." "The earth 'was' waste and void." They consider it scarcely convincing when a rare use of a word is cited to establish such an important doctrine, which is not clearly taught anywhere else in the Bible, whereas the same word has the other simple meaning of "was" in thousands of passages of Scripture. Rules may not be based on exceptions.

6. THE USE OF THE VERBS CREATE, AND "MAKE" IN GENESIS I

Supporters of the Period theory have the following objections to make to the clear distinction made by the Restitution theory between "create" and "make."

They grant that the word *bara*, to "create," always refers to a *Divine* activity; but this is not always an immediate and finished production out of nothing. It is not seldom something produced by God by a development within history and hence very similar to *'asah*, to "make."

Thus God "created" the people of Israel (Isa. 43: 1, 15), which took place in the course of history (before and after Abraham and the Patriarchs until the Law-giving on Mount Sinai). Similarly the children of Ammon were "created" in their land (Ezek. 21: 30). Similarly God "created" the individual Israelites (Isa. 43: 7, Mal. 2: 10), again not an immediate creation out of nothing but the outcome of a process in history (from the time of Adam through Noah and Abraham until the birth of the person concerned); similarly He created individuals in general (Isa. 54: 16; Eccles. 12: 1).

On the other hand the word "make" (*'asah*), which has a more general

---

[1] [Consistently with Hebrew idiom we can at the best render, "Now the earth had become waste and void;" it is striking that amidst the often misplaced ingenuity of rabbinic exegesis this is never suggested. (H.L.E.)]

significance (cf. note on p. 208), is also used of the Divine activity in the creation of the world, in a similar sense to *bara*. Thus God "made" heaven and earth (Gen. 2: 2; Exod. 20: 11). He "made" the sun and the moon (Gen. 1: 16), as also the animals (Gen. 3: 1). He also "made" man (Gen. 1: 26; 6: 6). Indeed the noun '*oseh*,[1] derived from this verb, means Creator (Job 35: 10; 4: 17; Isa. 17: 7; 27: 11), the regular English translation "Maker" having this implication.

In one and the same sentence (Gen. 5: 1) the two words "create" and "make" are used side by side for the same act, viz. the creation of man. "In the day that God 'created' man, in the likeness of God 'made' He him." We find the same in Genesis 1: 26, 27, "Let us 'make' man . . . And God 'created' man."

The use of these two verbs is therefore—incidentally the same is the case both in English and German—not so strictly differentiated as the Restitution theory presupposes. This may be checked by reference to any Hebrew dictionary. Hence this difference must not be overemphasized. The Restitution theory draws far too extensive conclusions from such a narrow basis.

The words to "shape" and to "form" also fit without difficulty into the Period theory. For it is just this theory which speaks, after the "creation" of the basic materials of heaven and earth (verse 1), of their "shaping" and "forming" in the work of creation.

Hence, it is claimed that the argument of the Restitution theory based on the difference between these two words is therefore neither unequivocal nor clear nor in any way an outstanding proof of this theory.

7. THE MEANING OF ISAIAH 45: 18

The advocates of the Period theory do not consider that the reference to Isaiah 45: 18 has much value. "Thus saith the Lord that created the heavens . . . that formed the earth and made it . . . He created it not a waste (*tohu*). He formed it to be inhabited." Quite obviously, they say, this passage is not speaking of the initial state but of the goal of the creation of the earth. This is proved by the parallelism of the immediate context, "He formed it to be inhabited." This "to be" refers to the goal. Therefore the first sentence must not be understood in the sense of "He did not create it *as* a waste," but "He did not create it *to be* a waste."

This does not in any way deny that the initial state of the earth was one of formlessness—a *tohu* and *bohu* in an active sense. It rather suggests a developing process of creation which advances from a lower to a higher stage. Hence it is claimed that the argument of the Restitution theory based on this verse in Isaiah disregards the real context of this statement.

---

[1] [Strictly speaking the active participle. (H.L.E.)]

8. THE FALL OF SATAN AND THE "GAP"

It has further been objected that even if the geological strata could be inserted between verses 1 and 2 of the Mosaic record—for which however there is no valid, scientific or Biblical ground—there is still no passage in the whole of the Bible which connects the fall of Satan and this conjectural intervening period between the first two verses of Scripture.

9. THE CREATION OF SUN AND MOON

Are we expected to believe, if the Restitution theory is correct, that the sun, the moon and the stars were first destroyed, so that they too had to be recreated?

There are three particular objections of great importance which advocates of the Period theory bring against the Restitution theory.

10. THE ASCENDING ORDER OF LIFE IN THE GEOLOGICAL STRATA

If the Restitution theory is to be believed, the final state of the earth, after the end of the prehistoric geological periods, was its sinking after a destruction of all plant and animal life, into a watery grave which covered everything, i.e. the lowest point that the natural history of the earth has reached. The geological strata, however, demonstrate exactly the contrary, *viz.* a systematic and, we may say, planned advance of plants and animals to ever higher degrees of development, until the time immediately preceding the culminating point of the history of the earth, the appearance of man. In the geological strata, progressing from the bottom to the top, that is, from the oldest to the most recent layers, we find first the invertebrates, then fishes, amphibia, reptiles and vertebrates (mammals and birds), until man finally appears as king of the earth.[1] The Restitution theory is, according to the judgment of advocates of the Period theory, unable to explain this orderly progression in the appearance of the fossils and their incontestibly proven geological connexion with the world of life as it is today.

11. THE CONTRADICTION BETWEEN THE RESTITUTION THEORY AND GEOLOGY

The Restitution theory normally accepts the interpretation of the six "days" as days of twenty-four hours and also the Old Testament chronology much as it was calculated by the Irish archbishop Ussher.[2] It follows that at the end of the geological periods, shortly before Adam and Eve, *i.e.* about 4300 B.C., the whole earth must have been completely covered by water. Then, in the course of a single day of twenty-four hours, *viz.*

[1] Cf. our remarks on p. 213. See also the Geological Table on p. 250.
[2] Cf. p. 193, Interpretations of the Biblical creation-narrative, section 1.

the second day of the work of "restoration," it emerged out of this flood with a distribution of land and sea much as it is today.

But according to the facts of geology there has not been such a general flooding of the whole earth, immediately before the beginning of the history of the human race or even a few hundreds or thousands of years before it. The earth was far from being completely covered by water about 4300 B.C., as this interpretation of "waters" in Genesis 1: 2b supposes.

Therefore instead of reconciling, as it supposes, geology and Biblical exposition, the Restitution theory, in this form, is claimed by supporters of the Period theory to be in sharpest contradiction to geology and is unequivocally refuted by its findings.

12. THE CONTINUITY OF LIFE FROM THE GEOLOGICAL STRATA TO THE PRESENT TIME

There is an extraordinary identity or similarity between many present forms of life and the corresponding ones in the Tertiary and even the Cretaceous and Jurassic periods. Many of our present plants and animals can be traced back to the distant and, in some cases to the most distant geological periods.

Very many of our present mammals, reptiles and amphibia may be found in identical or allied forms among fossils from the time during or before the great Ice Age. This is true of 60 per cent of the 400 species of land-mammals, and of 75 per cent of the forty species of sea-mammals. The existence of the nautilus has been proved in the ancient rocks of the Palaeozoic.

Ninety per cent of the species of molluscs found in the later Tertiary formations (e.g. Miocene) still exist today. Fossils of sharks and other fish resembling our present ones are to be found as early as the Cretaceous and the Jurassic periods. In the much older Coal Measures (Carboniferous), spiders and scorpions existed similar to present forms. Indeed, many kinds of fish and mussels (e.g. Lingula, tongue-shells) have existed practically unchanged right from the Cambrian down to the present day, i.e. from the oldest strata of the earth which contain fossils.[1]

Much the same is true of plants. Of the 147 species of plants which existed before the Ice Age about 100 still grow in Europe today, e.g. violets, buttercups and blackberries. The plants found in the uppermost layers of the Pliocene include more than 130 species of flowering plants, almost all of which are to be found in England today. Equally there are species of poplar, acacia and willow growing today, some in Europe, some

---

[1] [Note especially the striking case of the coelacanth, specimens of which have recently been taken off the east coast of Africa. It has remained virtually unchanged since the Devonian, and until 1938 was considered to have been extinct at least 50 million years. (H.L.E.)]

in tropical countries, which existed at the end of the Tertiary period. The walnut, oak, plane and maple go back as far as the Cretaceous. Indeed, "at the end of the Cretaceous the plant world had taken on the appearance it still has today" (Dr. Brude). Some ferns, the same as those of today, are found even among the fossils of the much older Coal Measures.[1]

All this proves that no such radical breach took place between the geological periods and our present age, as assumed by the Restitution theory, and that the old geological periods are linked without interruption with the new ones. Thus, according to the view of the Period theory, the Restitution theory is refuted by the geological fact that no state of chaos existed between the human and the Tertiary periods. Rather the whole course, from the very beginning, is a single, great, coherent system of nature.

If in opposition to this—so the Period theory emphasizes in opposition to the Restitution theory—we were to locate the geological periods in or before the *tohu wa-bohu*, i.e. in the time before the six days' work, we could not avoid drawing the most improbable conclusion that the species of plants and animals in the Tertiary, which are identical with those of the present day, were *first destroyed and then created again*. Or we should have to believe that God, at the time of the creation of man at the beginning of Paradise, by a special miracle, first banished death from this animal world and transformed the animals, particularly the carnivores, physiologically in their instincts, in their natural food and consequently in their whole bodily structure, and then after the fall changed these same species of animals back into their original Tertiary state. To accept this, the Period theory emphasizes, is far more difficult than to link the present plant and animal life with the fossils. Nor does the Bible say a word about it. Thus it should be apparent that the Restitution theory creates more scientific difficulties than it attempts to solve.[2]

We see then that for the Period theory the history of the primeval earth is seen as a *single*, coherent process of development in which, however, two main states are to be distinguished. First there is the original state at the very beginning, when there was no disturbance by powers opposed to God; this was how it had proceeded from the creative hand of God and should have continued to develop. Then there is the later state with opposition to God's will, disturbances and Divine judgments, into which it fell as a result of the fall of the spiritual powers which stood in a special relation to it. The six days' work would then, covering an incomprehensible long period of time, and leading to the present form of the earth,

---

[1] Cf. Prof. A. Rendle Short (I, pp. 15, 39; II, p. 54); J. L. Campbell (pp. 258, 259).

[2] Thus Prof. A. Rendle Short declares (I, p. 39) "It seems very improbable that those Miocene, Pliocene and Pleistocene animals and plants which are identical with modern species should have been annihilated, and then re-created." Similarly P. J. Wiseman in *Creation Revealed in Six Days*, p. 26.

belong principally to the second state and would in the main coincide with the geological periods.

During these it would appear that, by Divine permission, the chaos-producing powers of the evil one opposed the Divine acts of creation. This would explain why hybrid forms, terror-working animals, bloodshed, sickness and death were so prevalent among the living beings of that primeval world. We find von Huene expressing this thought: "Something new came in addition, darkness, the night, which had an important rôle in the composition of the days of creation that followed. . . . The kingdom of darkness, of the prince of this world, shared in determining the work of creation after a start which was quite different. In the six days' work light *and* darkness (at least, so it would seem—Author) have their share" (pp. 59, 64).

No one can say anything about the condition of God's creation before the entry of evil. In any case, the Period theory declares, there are no adequate grounds in Scripture for speaking of a once completed "light-earth" (F. Bettex), an original "kingdom of light" (Th. Haarbeck), or of a "first original creation" or "first earth" (J. Kroeker). All that had been reached up to then was only an *initial stage* in the primeval development, and the details of this initial stage are known to no man.

So much only is certain, the original disturbance caused by the fall of Satan must have taken place very early in the course of this one, great, coherent development of creation, and in any case before creation had advanced far enough to involve life, for as the fossils prove, this was from the very beginning, from the earliest times subject to transitoriness, i.e. death. This would mean that although the fall of Satan did not necessarily take place between the first and second verses of Genesis 1, it must nevertheless have occurred sometime and somehow between verse 1 and verse 11, which speaks of the creation of the plants. The exact point in time no one can know.

Despite these satanic disturbances and the necessary judgments bound up with them, God will have continued, in ways which science may investigate, the work of creation by a gradual and systematic upwards development of living things and will in this way have caused plant and animal life to rise to its present level. This took place, under Divine direction, partly by heredity, branching, and various links in descent, partly by God's repeated, creative interventions. It is claimed that the existence of these is proved by the failure to find "missing links" between the principal families of living creatures, despite the most careful geological investigations. Finally man, without being in any way descended from the animal world in general, appeared on the scene to begin his course from the garden of Eden, which had been specially prepared for him.

So far as the carnivores of the Tertiary are concerned, many advocates of the Period theory believe that they remained in their hitherto wild state on the earth outside Paradise, even while man was in it. Paradise itself was a special area, and as such a place of peace, fullness of life, beauty and perfection. But in this respect it was different from the rest of the earthly creation, for if the whole earth had been a place of life and absolute perfection, a garden of Paradise would not have been necessary. The fact then that a Paradise was created at all proves that the earth was not in itself a suitable, worthy dwelling-place for man, who was appointed by God as the new king of the earthly creation. This means that the fact that a garden was planted in Eden is a proof of the imperfection of the earthly world outside Paradise.

So far as the plant world before and after the fall of man is concerned, the Divine curse declares that the ground should bring forth "thorns and thistles," but it says no more. It is purely arbitrary to go any further. The Bible itself says simply that the thorns and thistles, already present on the remainder of the earth, should penetrate into the ground which man cultivates and make his work very much more difficult. Professor Karl Heim has written: "The Old Testament tells, it is true, of the satanic temptation through which the first men fell into sin, and of their being driven out of Paradise. But it knows nothing of a transformation of the whole face of the world brought about by the fall of man" (I, p. 157).

Against this it is pointed out that the Bible says at the end of the sixth day (and this will cover the period in Paradise as well), "God saw every thing that he had made, and, behold, it was very good" (Gen. 1: 31).

The answer of the Period theory is, that the Bible sees the good out-weighing the evil in nature. It is of the present age and state of the earth with so much beauty and fullness of life in nature, but also with so many powers of destruction—disharmony and ruin in plant and animal life, beasts of prey in the air, field and wood—that the Bible says, looking away from all the negative things that have been brought in by sin and con-centrating on the real, positive essence and the original nature of creation, "O Lord, how manifold are thy works! In wisdom hast thou made them all: the earth is full of thy riches" (Psa. 104: 24). "O Lord, our Lord, how excellent is thy name in all the earth!" (Psa. 8: 1, 9). "The heavens declare the glory of God; and the firmament sheweth his handiwork" (Psa. 19: 1).

Such statements concern the glory of God in creation in general, and do not exclude the other side. Otherwise Scripture could not say of the world today, "Let the Lord rejoice in his works" (Psa. 104: 31); but the same psalmist in the same psalm is also conscious of the other side, "The young lions roar after their prey" (v. 21).

We should note that Psalm 148 not only exhorts heaven and earth, sun, moon and stars to praise God, but also says, "Praise the Lord from the earth, ye sea-monsters, and all deeps . . . beasts and cattle, creeping things and flying fowls: . . . let them praise the name of the Lord" (v. 7–13). Paul

Q

also bears witness to the revelation of God in nature, despite all its present discord, which he knew as well as we do: "For the invisible things of him since the creation of the world are clearly seen, being perceived through the things that are made, even his everlasting power and divinity" (Rom. I: 20).

This was the framework of nature in which man had originally received as his task from God, beginning at Paradise, to extend his rule and to carry and spread the life and blessing of Paradise over the whole earth. Had he carried out this his kingly vocation, the final result would have been a final liberation and redemption of all life in the world, as will in fact one day be the case, when the visible kingdom of God is established on earth (Isa. II: 6–8; Hos. 2: 18).

But the first result of man's fall was that he did not accomplish his vocation. Thus destruction remained in the animal world because of man. The ground also, cultivated by man, remained under the curse because of him. If, therefore, the creation still groans today, because it is subject to the bondage of vanity, then it is because of man. That means that the redemption of the creation cannot take place before the history of the redemption of man is completed; then it will be by sharing in the "liberty of the glory of the children of God" (Rom. 8: 21).

The advantage of this interpretation as a whole, so the advocates of the Period theory claim, is that it does more justice to the general impression created by the Biblical creation-narrative than does the Restitution theory. It is also in harmony with all the linguistic and exegetical details in the text and never goes beyond what may be found in Scripture. It has further the advantage that it is more obvious from the point of view of science. It harmonizes with the presence of death in the earliest geological periods as also with the link between the forms of life in primeval times and the plant and animal world of today, as the fossils clearly testify.

EPILOGUE

My wife and I are visiting the Brussels Exhibition in the autumn of 1958. In front of us lies the building which is its centre, the Atomium. It is one of the most daring, magnificent, strange and impressive constructions ever erected by human hands.

At the base, a giant sphere. High above it, over 300 feet up in the air, once again a giant sphere. Between them, a central sphere. Six tremendous, hollow spheres of uniform size, each with a diameter equal to the height of a six-storied warehouse, float, so to speak, in the air, joined only to the central mast and its three spheres by metal tubes. Each of these tubes is ten feet wide and weighs 300 cwt. Escalators pass through them, one of them being 115 feet long, the longest in Europe. All the spheres are made of light metal. The silvery, aluminium surface of the nine spheres, as smooth as a mirror, sparkles in the radiant sunlight. Over all the golden sun shines from a cloudless, blue sky.

Still more impressive is the idea behind this huge, unique metal construction. It represents a crystalline metal molecule, magnified 165 thousand million times. The nine giant spheres are, as it were, the nine atoms of this molecule. The empty space between them gives an impressive idea of the great, empty space between the atoms and makes the visitor immediately conscious that what was formerly looked on as solid matter is in fact almost empty space.

When the lights are turned on in the evening, hundreds of tiny lights sparkle upon these silvery "atomic spheres." They are to remind us of the electrons, which rotate around the nucleus of the individual atoms.

The Atomium is both a symbolization of the concept of the atom, and an embodiment of the tremendous power of atomic energy. It is meant to be a symbol of the atomic age. It not only bears witness to the outstanding achievements of modern technical science and architecture, but is also an emblem of atomic physics and its revolutionary influences on the life of twentieth-century man as a whole. Therefore it is both the centre and climax of this huge, world-embracing exhibition, at which peoples from all five continents have exhibited in their pavilions their special and outstanding achievements.

Just as the Crystal Palace in London was for decades a symbol of the Great Exhibition of 1851, for which it was built; just as the Eiffel Tower in Paris, erected for the Exhibition there in 1889, still towers 965 feet into the air; so also the Atomium, once the Brussels Exhibition has ended, is to remain for coming generations a symbol of the dawning atomic age.

We went from sphere to sphere on the escalators through the metal tubes. We looked at the great exhibitions in them on "the application of atomic physics to peaceful uses for the good of mankind." "The Atom—the Future Hope of the World" was the English we had read immediately on entering this miraculous building.

In the lowest sphere we saw life-size pictures of prominent, contemporary scientists, e.g. of Albert Einstein, the greatest mathematician and physicist of the twentieth century, of Otto Hahn, President of the Max Plank Society, who in 1939 was the first man to split the nucleus of the uranium atom, of Madame Curie, formerly Professor of Physics and Mathematics at the Sorbonne in Paris, the discoverer of radium.

With astounding speed our lift carried us upwards; in twenty seconds it covered the 320 feet to the highest "atomic sphere." It is the fastest lift in Europe. We found ourselves high up in the gallery of the great observation room and looked out of the great perspex window. The colourful picture of the Exhibition with its numerous pavilions from so many peoples and races and with its many thousands of visitors lay far beneath us. In the distance we saw the "seven-hilled city" of Greater Brussels with its suburbs and its immeasurable sea of houses. A mighty panorama indeed!

But one thing specially arrested our attention. It was a building close below us, just opposite us, in the immediate vicinity of the Atomium. It was a building of a type we had never seen in all our journeys in many lands. It was not really a "house," but simply a single, towering, thick wall, shaped like a giant open book, almost as high as a four-storied building.

On the front of the pavilion attached to this giant book we read in French, *La Bible—le Livre de Dieu pour tous les Hommes* (The Bible—God's Book for all Men). We were specially impressed by a text which, among others, appeared on a moving band along the upper edge and in the middle of this mighty "Bible," and was constantly repeated. Just as we were looking out of the uppermost sphere of the Atomium it appeared, and it alone, ceaselessly repeated in French, English, German, Spanish, Italian and Flemish.

In the evening the words were illuminated, and shone their message into the distance and down to the thousands who were passing by, like the great illuminated signs in the heart of our great cities. That is why this "Bible" was called the "Luminous Bible"—"Thy word is a lamp unto my feet, and light unto my path" (Psa. 119: 105).

The text we saw from the top of the Atomium in unbroken succession, in the different languages, was a word of the apostle Paul. No other text appeared the whole time we were up there. Over and over again, in the different languages, it was the word the great apostle to the Gentiles had spoken in another centre of human knowledge and art, on the Areopagus in Athens: "The times of ignorance therefore God overlooked; but now he commandeth men that they should all everywhere repent: inasmuch as he hath appointed a day, in which he will judge the world in righteousness" (Acts 17: 30, 31).

Everything all around us spoke of the greatness and mighty achievements of the human mind. We ourselves read these words of the great apostle of Christ from the uppermost sphere of the Atomium, and hence from the highest heights of the chief symbol of the science of our days.

God confronts man's knowledge, whenever he separates himself from Him, with the condemnation of "ignorance." God opposes all self-exaltation of man, in so far as he is guilty of it, with the command to humble himself. God proclaims to man, whenever he believes in his own "progress," the coming judgment.

There is no doubt that science and faith are not fundamentally and mutually exclusive. There have always been scholars of the first rank who have humbled themselves in reverence before God, who have indeed believed with their whole heart in the message of the Holy Scriptures.

In the course of this book we too have often expressed our respect for true science. It belongs to man's rule over the earth and is a part of his exercise of kingship and nobility. But far too often man has lived without thought of God's claim to dominion; he has denied His existence and has tried in his own strength without God to exalt himself. Therefore God's word calls him to return and repent.

The Atomium and the Bible, human knowledge and God's wisdom, human greatness and God's demand that we should bow before Him, who is infinitely greater; how deeply both impressed us.

In all this, however, God is merciful. He is patient with mankind. He has "overlooked" the times of ignorance. He gives man another chance. He "calls him to faith," as Paul bore witness in this passage, which we also read from the Atomium on this "Giant Bible." This is the message which moved us so strongly in those moments.

Then we left the Atomium. We found a spot from which we could see both together, as it were in a single picture, the Atomium and the Bible House. Both were in the centre of the Exhibition. There immediately in front of us was the Atomium itself, and, very close on our right, the great side wall of the lower rooms of the Bible exhibition. It was a large wall, sky-blue in colour. In the brightness of the sunshine we saw on this great, blue background, in dozens of languages, the most glorious word in the New Testament message of salvation, "For God so loved the world, that he gave his only begotten Son, that whosoever believeth in him should not perish, but have eternal life" (John 3: 16).

There they both stood, side by side in the same field of vision before our eyes: the Atomium as the symbol of the highest achievements of the human mind, and that most glorious word of Scripture, shining to us from its sky-blue background in the chief languages of the civilized world, given under the inspiration of the Divine Spirit. Never shall we forget that combination. The one showed, and rightly so, what man can attain; the other proclaimed something infinitely greater, what God, the eternal Saviour and Redeemer, can accomplish.

In the Bible pavilion itself Bibles, New Testaments and portions of Scripture lay ready in over 300 languages. Through all this the "Luminous Bible" and the Bible House were to be a witness for Christ. He alone and His work stood in the centre of the whole. Therefore no propaganda for any man or church was to be found there. Everything pointed to the one Person, Jesus Christ, and the salvation He has brought. By its outward, fundamental simplicity this pavilion differed from all others in the extensive exhibition grounds. Here we were not concerned with human achievement and human strength, but with the saving power of God and His summons to mankind, which, despite all its imagined, indeed, its actual greatness, is nevertheless lost without Him. Therefore no other name should be named and exalted here except only the name of the Redeemer of the world. "In none other is there salvation: for neither is there any other name under heaven, that is given among men, wherein we must be saved" (Acts 4: 12).

We have now reached the end of our study, and a long journey lies behind us.

We started by asking ourselves whether we could speak of the nobility of man. We put the question as men who accepted the Bible but who were at the same time men of the twentieth century. We asked it in faith in the greatness of God's revelation and in consciousness of the limitations and smallness of man, which have today become particularly clear in the morality of the atomic age, in the vastness of space as revealed by modern astronomy and in the findings of contemporary atomic physics.

From the very outset we expected to receive a definite answer from God's word. For from God, as the King of the universe, comes all kingship among His creatures, and therefore also all man's nobility. So He alone is able to give the most far-reaching answer to every question asked by the human heart, an answer which embraces heaven and earth, time and eternity.

From there we traversed a wide area. We saw God's glory in nature, and man as the goal and crown of His earthly creation. We next recognized the great, fundamental law of freedom in the kingdom of God's spiritual creation, and we sensed something of the first misuse of this freedom in the rise of powers opposed to God and the devastating consequences for wide areas of God's created kingdom.

In the midst of this mighty conflict between light and darkness the position of man in God's plan for the world took on a special significance for us. We saw in him not only the royal representative of God on earth, called in this his kingdom to joy in nature, to investigation of nature and to control over nature, and to cultural progress, but also the instrument in God's hand for the liberation and transfiguration of nature. Indeed, it is just from his dwelling-place, the planet called earth, so small in the vastness of the universe and yet so important, that the triumph of the Divine revelation is to spread abroad throughout the universe, until finally there shall be not only a new earth but also a new heaven. Therefore man, conscious of his nobility, should walk worthily of his high calling.

Jesus Christ, the Son of God and the Son of Man, is the creative Centre of the whole.

On our journey through time and space we also cast a glance into eternity. Some rays of light from the heavenly world illuminated for us man's call for eternity, his appointment to worship, to be the image of God, to sonship and to eternal dominion.

We then asked the question, "How can all this be realized in practice?" We gave a threefold answer. The existence of God is the presupposition for all human nobility. God's government of the world, *i.e.* His kingly rule over nature and history through revelation and miracle, makes association with this God and His eternity possible. Although this world is governed by the laws of nature, this bridge to heaven remains open. God's plan of salvation opens for us the way by which in practice we attain true nobility.

Finally we asked how there originated the stage on which these fundamental events of our salvation took place and which is at the same time the earthly kingdom of man. This, however, brought us face to face with the mystery of how the great God created. We found ourselves surrounded by many riddles, despite all the information given us in the Divine revelation and all the research work of the human mind. However much He may condescend to His creatures, God remains, in His glory as Creator, enthroned in solitary majesty high above all that He has created.

All this should lead us to humility, gratitude and worship. The earthly king lays down his crown, which he has received from the Creator, before the throne of the heavenly King. He, when he has been forgiven, has been given the honour of upholding the honour of his God.

BIBLIOGRAPHY

* Signifies a translation from the German.

Bavink, Prof. B., *Die Naturwissenschaft auf dem Wege zur Religion*, Frankfurt a. M., 1934.

Bettex, Prof. F., *Das Lied der Schöpfung*, Striegau, 1919.

Bettex, Prof. F., *Himmlische Realitäten*, Striegau, 1921.

Bettex, Prof. F., *Naturstudium und Christentum*, Striegau, 1919.

Bettex, Prof. F., *Natur und Gesetz*, Striegau, 1923.

Campbell, Dr. J. L., *The Bible under Fire*, London, 1928.

Deissmann, Dr. A., *Light from the Ancient East*, London, 1927.

Dennert, Prof. E., *Bibel und Naturwissenschaft, Gedanken und Bekenntnisse eines Naturforschers*, Halle, 1911.

Dennert, Prof. E., *Die Wahrheit über Ernst Haeckel*, Halle, 1909.

Dennert, Prof. E., *Ist Gott tot?* Halle, 1911.

Dennert, Prof. E., *Es werde*, Halle, 1907.

Franzero, G. M., *The Life and Times of Nero*, London, 1954.

Gail, O. W., *Der Griff nach dem Atom*, Munich, 1947.

Haarbeck, Dr. Th., *Kurzgefasste Biblische Glaubenslehre*, Elberfeld, 1930.

Heim, Prof. Karl, *Jesus der Herr*, Berlin, 1935.

Heim, Prof. Karl, *Weltschöpfung und Weltende*, Hamburg, 1952.

Heim, Prof. Karl, *Der christliche Gottesglaube und die Naturwissenschaft*, Hamburg, 1953.

Heim, Prof. Karl, *Die Wandlung im naturwissenschaftlichen Weltbild*, Hamburg, 1953.

Hitzbleck, Dr. E., *Und dies Leben hat doch einen Sinn*, Wuppertal, 1951.

Hoppe, Prof. E., *Glauben und Wissen. Antworten auf Weltanschauungsfragen*, Gütersloh, 1915.

Howe, Prof. G., *Der Mensch und die Physik*, Wuppertal, 1958.

Huene, Prof. Freiherr von, *Weg und Werk Gottes in Natur und Bibel. Biblische Erörterungen eines Paläontologen*, Marburg, 1937.

Keerl, Dekan Ph. F., *Die Einheit der biblischen Urgeschichte*, Basel, 1863.

Köberle, Prof. A., *Christentum und modernes Naturerleben*, Gütersloh, 1932.

Krämer, R., *Die biblische Urgeschichte*, Wernigerode, 1931.

Kroeker, J., *Die erste Schöpfung, ihr Fall und ihre Wiederherstellung*, Giessen, 1926.

Kurtz, Prof. I. H., *Bibel und Astronomie*, 1857.

Luthardt, Prof. C. E., *Apologie des Christentums*, Leipzig, 1896.

Müller, Dr. P., *Schöpfung Wunder Unsichtbare Welt*, Metzingen, 1958.

Neuberg, Dr. A., *Das Weltbild der Biologie*, Göttingen, 1942.

Neuberg, Dr. A., *Das Neue Weltbild der Physik*, Göttingen, 1940.

Pember, G. H., *Earth's Earliest Ages*.

Ramm, Dr. B., *The Christian View of Science and Scripture*, London, 1955.

Riem, Prof. J., *Weltwerden*, Hamburg, 1925.

Riem, Prof. J., *Natur und Bibel*, 1911.

Rohrbach, Prof. H., *Der naturwissenschaftlich Gebildete und der christliche Glaube* (*Biblische Universitätsschriften*), Wuppertal, 1955.

Rohrbach, Prof. H., *Biblische Wunder und moderne Naturwissenschaft* (*Biblische Universitätsschriften*), Wuppertal, 1957.

Rohrbach, Prof. H., *Grenzen naturwissenschaftlicher Erkenntnis* (*Biblische Universitätsschriften*), Wuppertal, 1956.

Sauer, E., *The Dawn of World Redemption*, London, 1951.

Sauer, E., *From Eternity to Eternity*, London, 1954.

Schultz, Prof. F. W., *Die Schöpfungsgeschichte nach Naturwissenschaft und Bibel*, Gotha, 1865.

Short, Prof. A. Rendle, *Modern Discovery and the Bible*, London, 1952.

Titius, Prof. A., *Natur und Gott*, 1931.

Uhlhorn, Dr. G., *Der Kampf des Christentums mit dem Heidentum*, Stuttgart, 1924.

Whittaker, Prof. Sir Edmund, *Space and Spirit*, 1946.

Wiseman, P. J., *Creation Revealed in Six Days*, London, 1949.

Zöckler, O., *Beweis des Glaubens*, Vol. IV.

GEOLOGICAL TABLE

Group	Formation	Flora	Fauna		Principal Epochs of Human and Animal World
CAINOZOIC	Quaternary Post-glacial Glacial Pleistocene	Foliate trees: oak, willow, poplar, acacia, maple. Conifers, flowering plants.	Mammoth, rhinoceros, reindeer, cave-bear, deer, megatherium.	Earliest remains of man	Age of man
	Tertiary Pliocene Miocene Oligocene Eocene	Foliate trees: oak, willow, poplar, acacia, linden. Conifers: fir, pine. Palms. Flowering plants.	Species, genera, families of mammals. Mastodon, dinotherium, megatherium, mammoth. Giraffes, dogs, horses, birds.	Numerous Land animals	Age of Mammals
MESOZOIC	Cretaceous	Foliate trees: oak, willow, beech, maple. Higher conifers—palms. First flowering plants.	Extinction of saurians. Mammals. Vertebrate fish. Insects more numerous. Birds.	Reptiles	Age of Reptiles
	Jurassic	Conifers (Araucaria)	First birds (Archaeopteryx) Butterflies. Sea reptiles. Great age of saurians.		
	Triassic	Beginning of conifers (Araucaria).	Reptiles begin to flourish. Saurians. First mammals. Marsupials. Extinction of Loricata.		

Era	Period	Plant life	Animal life		Age
PALAEOZOIC OR PRIMARY	Permian	First conifers, ferns.	Prime of loricata. Palaeoniscus.	Amphibia	Age of amphibia
	Carboniferous	Great age of the tall shave-grasses, fern-trees, Lepidodendra, Sigillaria.	Great amphibia (Loricata). Insects. First reptiles. Extinction of Ostracion.		
	Devonian	First land-plants, trees. Beginnings of ferns, Sigillaria, conifers.	Fish more numerous. Crabs. Corals. First Loricata.	Almost exclusively water animals	Age of fishes
	Silurian	Algae. Seaweeds.	Lower vertebrates (first cartilaginous fish). Crabs. Corals. First insects. Palaeoblattina. Prime of Trilobites and Brachiopods.		
	Ordovician Cambrian	Algae. Seaweeds.	All the principal invertebrate orders, but no vertebrates. Earliest Trilobites. Brachiopods.		Age of invertebrates
EOZOIC (PRE-CAMBRIAN)		Doubtful algae.	First traces of organisms. Radiolaria, invertebrates.		

INDEX